Visual
Pattern Recognition

Visual
Pattern Recognition

P. C. Dodwell
Queen's University at Kingston, Ontario

HOLT, RINEHART AND WINSTON, INC.
New York   Chicago   San Francisco   Atlanta
Dallas   Montreal   Toronto   London   Sydney

Copyright © 1970 by Holt, Rinehart and Winston, Inc.

Library of Congress Catalog Card Number: 72-113055

SBN: 03-081425-1

Printed in the United States of America

0   1   2   3   22   9   8   7   6   5   4   3   2   1

Preface

In the preface to his excellent *Cognitive Psychology,* Neisser describes how he set out to write a dispassionate review of cognitive psychology but produced instead a monograph that was neither as neutral nor as eclectic as he had anticipated. I cannot claim to have started without a definite theoretical position to expound, but it is true to say that the form of this book is not quite the form originally planned. In fact, my intention was to show how structural models for processes of visual pattern recognition can further our understanding of those processes and to review relevant material in the literature. Particularly I wanted to show how the contributions of other disciplines bear directly on the psychology of pattern recognition. In a sense the book is largely an attempt to integrate these different approaches, the recent findings in neurophysiology being especially important in this regard. As writing progressed, it became increasingly clear that the structural modeling approach led to a more coherent theoretical picture of the visual system as pattern recognizor than I had realized. The material in the first half of the final chapter, for example, emerged in a more clearly articulated form and with a wider range of application than I had anticipated when I began the first chapter.

The general approach of the book is neuropsychological: It leans heavily on recent ideas about information-processing and looks to the biological structure of the system as the basis for its psychological functioning. The two themes that run through the book have been matters of major concern throughout the history of the scientific study of perception. The first one is the question of stimulus analysis or, as it used to be termed, "stimulus equivalence." Some decades ago a great controversy raged about the question of whether stimulus equivalence was compatible with the notion of the central nervous system as a fully connected network of elements with specific signalling functions. The *Gestalt* alternative of a "dynamic" field-type theory has few enough adherents today; particularly since the advent of digital computers for modeling pattern recognition, it has become obvious enough that pattern analysis and recognition can be handled in a variety of ways. Stimulus equivalence (for instance, recognition of a particular shape under various translations or rotations) turns out to be no particular problem. And yet the acceptance of computer analogies may have been too facile, and they do not absolve us from the responsibility of finding out how the brain really works. I shall have much to say about the *form* of computing network which the psychological and neuro-physiological evidence suggests and about how stimulus equivalence is attained.

The second major theme is perceptual learning. Statements in terms of the bare alternatives of heredity and environment are obviously inadequate, as is the statement that both are important and neither should be neglected. What we need to do is look into the manifold and subtle ways that "built-in" features of the visual system interact with external input to mold the total organism and its behavior. A good deal of enlightening evidence on these topics has been found in recent years, and its relevance to understanding visual perception is great. Once again it turns out that the evidence on perceptual learning fits neatly into the structural modeling approach, and the latter in turn suggests how the main problems about perceptual learning can be resolved.

The book is divided into two parts or—as I should like to say if the analogy is not too exotic—it is like a symphony in two movements. The major themes are stated in the first three chapters and are developed in a variety of ways thereafter. Chapter 6 is a bridge between the two parts, the first of which deals basically with pattern recognition in animals and the second with human pattern recognition. The division is made with good reason, I believe, though the continuity of thematic development should also be clear. To stretch the analogy a little further, the last chapter is like a coda which restates the main themes in appropriate metamorphosis. At the same time, each chapter is reasonably self-contained, so that it is possible to begin the discussion of binocular vision (Chapter 7), for example, without necessarily having read all that precedes it.

It will be clear from what follows that I have profited much from the ideas and research of many people, but I should like particularly to acknowledge an intellectual debt to Tony Deutsch, who first interested me in the problem of pattern recognition and started me thinking along the lines here developed. A number of friends and colleagues have been good enough to read the manuscript in whole or in part and have made valuable suggestions for its improvement. I should like especially to thank Dick Herrnstein and Doug Mewhort for reviewing the entire manuscript, and Phil Bryden, David Hubel, and David Murray for their comments on various chapters. Their advice and encouragement was appreciated. For the remaining deficiencies of the book I naturally take sole responsibility.

One feels a certain amount of anxiety about the fact that the field treated in this book is developing rapidly. With particular regard to Chapter 9, I am aware that new findings will render my exposition out of date in a relatively short time. More serious, perhaps, is the fact that a number of theoretical essays have appeared since my writing was undertaken and have come to my notice too late to influence in any important way the explanations and judgments I have propounded. Two examples are a paper of Sutherland's (1968) which tackles many of the same sorts of problems that are dealt with here and a book by Lovejoy (1968) on the attentional theory of discrimination learning. Had I the benefit of seeing these works at the time of writing, no doubt some modifications would have been made. In a sense one can never be certain that a presentation is complete, and to this extent some dissatisfaction with the product is probably inevitable. However, that feeling is itself a token of the fact that the field is a vigorous one, growing both in terms of volume of research and of theoretical developments, and that, of course, is a most satisfactory state of affairs.

The writing of the book was made possible through generous financial support from a variety of sources, which I acknowledge with sincere gratitude. The major part of the book was written while I was on sabbatical leave from Queen's University and holding a Fellowship from the C. D. Howe Memorial Foundation. The hospitality of Birkbeck College and of the Goldsmith's Library of the University of London during that time was much appreciated. The last chapter and final revisions were undertaken with the support of a Guggenheim Fellowship and while I was a Fellow at the Center for Advanced Study in the Behavioral Sciences at Stanford. Without the freedom from academic routine which these various bodies afforded me, I doubt that this project would have been completed within a reasonable time span.

Most of the original typing of the manuscript was done by Jean Walker, who deserves my special thanks, and I am also grateful to Jill Dent, Monica Freedman, Priscilla Jones, and Agnes Page for their help at various stages of preparation of the book.

I am also obliged to a number of publishers and authors who gave permission to reproduce figures, and I have acknowledged their contributions in the appropriate places.

July 1970   P. C. Dodwell

Contents

Visual
Pattern Recognition

CHAPTER 1
Pattern Recognition in the General Context of Theoretical Psychology

The aim of theoretical psychology is to explain the nature of behavior, taking that word in a wide sense; yet many psychologists—and philosophers—disagree on what needs to be explained and on the sorts of explanation that are appropriate and adequate. We have a multitude of theories, models, hypotheses, and hunches which serve to guide research, particularly in the well-developed areas of scientific psychology such as learning and perception; yet it is fairly uncommon to find in these areas a coordinated attack on questions of general theoretical import—questions concerning the kinds of explanation which should be sought and both the power and limitations of the theoretical bases for such explanations.

The aim of this book is to trace developments in the study of pattern recognition, to show how these are amenable to a particular type of theoretical treatment, and to examine the question of how far such methods can lead to progress in the understanding of perception. One hopes that the exercise, although undertaken on a relatively narrow front, may prove to have some relevance to the more general questions of valid scientific explanation in psychology.

The study of pattern recognition is receiving increasing attention and can be approached from a number of points of view; those of neurophysiology, systems engineering, and behavioral analysis are the most obvious. The ability of living organisms to recognize and distinguish different patterns must be among their fundamental properties. At a very basic level the transmission of genetic information involves the recognition of patterns—in this case, sequences of molecules. The survival of plants and lower fauna depends on specific physiological responses to external conditions, albeit of a rather rigid and unmodifiable kind. Higher up the evolutionary scale, movement, and especially self-initiated movement, introduces complications which have to do with the recognition of stable patterns within the rich flux of external stimulation. Here the possible mechanisms for achieving stability become a primary concern. Although the sort of pattern recognition of which an organism is capable depends very largely on its phylogenetic level, the property is common to all. The ability to synthesize proteins, respond reflexly to a stimulus, get across the road, choose a mate, or decide among complex problem-solving strategies all depend on it.

It might be argued that the concept of pattern implicit in the previous paragraph is too broad to be useful, that "pattern" is being equated with "any stimulus." For the purposes of this volume, it is necessary to describe what is meant by the term "pattern," although I do not believe it is sensible to attempt a comprehensive or watertight definition. By a visual pattern I shall mean a collection of contours or edges, which in turn are defined as regions of sharp change in the level of a physical property of light (usually intensity) impinging on the retina. I shall distinguish between "patterns" and "pattern elements," a distinction which is best left to emerge from the different usages the two terms will be given in the following chapters. Most of the discussion is concerned with mammalian visual systems, and there is good reason for this restriction. At least at the lowest level of the discrimination of simple patterns there is good evidence for a fair amount of communality within the mammalian order. When we consider man, however, we find that the range and subtlety of his behavior requires us to consider theoretical models which range far beyond the processes of neurophysiology which are the biological basis from which we start. But if we wish to explain pattern recognition, it is sensible to start with a seemingly simple and basic question: How does one recognize the difference between, say, a square and a circle? The attempt to answer this without falling back on a naïve and circular explanation turns out to be far from easy.

SOME ATTEMPTS AT SPECIFYING MODELS FOR PATTERN RECOGNITION

How does an organism *abstract* the attribute of shape? A square can be recognized as such in different sizes and orientations and in different parts of the visual field. The old doctrine of *local sign,* in which each unit of a receptor surface such as the retina carries with it a specific "tag," or quality, seems to be inadequate to handle the problem, since the recognition of a square is obviously independent of the particular groups of retinal cells excited. It was precisely against such a view that the Gestalt psychologists' polemics were aimed (for example, Köhler, 1929). However, the Gestalt position, particularly as expounded in Köhler's theory of isomorphism, is equally untenable for a number of reasons.[1] The first and most obvious reason is that the postulated physiological properties on which it is based are implausible, in view of what is now known about the structure and function of the mammalian brain. Moreover, Köhler's identification of pattern recognition with the generation of specific macroscopic patterns of electrical activity at the visual cortex has been proven wrong. Lashley, Chow, and Semmes (1951) and Sperry, Miner, and Myers (1955) showed conclusively that procedures which would radically disrupt macroscopic electrical conduction in the visual cortex have very little effect on pattern recognition ability. It can be argued that the theory of isomorphism does not necessarily fall through failure to verify its proposed physiological basis. This is entirely correct, but the more telling criticism of the theory is that it fails to do the job it is intended to do, namely, explaining stimulus equivalence. Stimulus equivalence means just that quality of abstraction referred to at the beginning of this section; to explain stimulus equivalence means to explain the capacity to recognize common characteristics of stimulus patterns which, considered simply as physical inputs to the system, may vary in a number of different ways.

The theory of isomorphism states that the pattern of retinal excitation is in topological correspondence with the pattern of cortical activity which it induces; the correspondence is not quite topographical, since the cortical pattern is distorted by certain innate forces of constraint which act directly on it (supposed by Köhler to be electrical field forces). The resulting pattern is held to be isomorphic with what is perceived; indeed the cortical pattern was generally thought to be the sole determinant of perception. Thus, the retina mirrors the external physical pattern of stimulation, and the brain mirrors, albeit in a distorted fashion, the events on the retina. But nothing is said about how these patterns are *recognized,* in particular about how two patterns are recognized as being the same even when they occur in different places in the visual field, at different times, or both. To say that *A* is perceived whenever pattern *a* occurs in some area of the brain is to postulate a sort of naïve psychophysiological parallelism, but it does not explain *how a* is always recognized as the identical

---

[1] For the history of the concept of isomorphism and its conceptual antecedents see Boring (1942, Ch. 2).

pattern whose external referent is the physical pattern or object A. It amounts, essentially, to the statement that one perceives states of one's own brain, since the recognition of spatially and/or temporally separated brain states (patterns of excitation) as equivalent implies an "observer" (homunculus) who recognizes (perceives) the patterns. But such a "perceptual act" again implies recognition of equivalent states in a brain, which implies a second-order "observer" for these second-order brain states, and so on to an infinite regress (Ryle, 1949). The theory of isomorphism thus pushes the problem of recognition out of the brain, as it were, without solving it. The same point may be made by pointing to the circularity in the explanation: "A is recognized whenever brain state a occurs." The circularity is present because a can be identified only in terms of A, and vice versa, and "equivalent patterns a_1 and a_2" can only be explained, ostensively, by pointing to external patterns A_1 and A_2. But what makes A_1 and A_2 "equivalent"? We can hardly say it is their common perceptual characteristics, because this is just what needs explanation. Yet what other path is open to a theory which does not specify clearly any properties of the "internal" representation of a pattern? For the theory of isomorphism it seems to make little difference whether we talk of two patterns as being equivalent in the brain, in the physical world, or on the retina. We are equally far from an *explanation* of their equivalence in all three cases, until some definite hypothesis about recognition is made which does not depend merely on the fact that one can *see* that two patterns are in some sense equivalent. Failure to deal with this problem is the great logical weakness of the theory of isomorphism.

Discussing the theory of isomorphism in this way may seem like flogging abandoned. The point I wish to make is that, in a real sense, it was a dead horse, since as a model for stimulus equivalence it has long been abandoned for the wrong reason, namely because its proposed physiological embodiment was implausible, and experimental evidence showed that it (the physiological hypothesis) was wrong.[2] The model, as a formal basis for pattern recognition and stimulus equivalence, might still have been viable if it had been logically satisfactory. The logical weakness pointed out leads naturally to the question: What *would* be a satisfactory basis for a system which recognizes stimulus equivalences?

First, since patterns with similar appearances usually have common physical or geometrical properties, it is possible that the generation of an internal representation of the patterns is based on those properties. Obvious as it now seems to be to say so, the coding of pattern properties

---

[2] This was not the only reason. Reaction against the excessively nativistic flavor of Gestalt perceptual theory was perhaps at least as important.

in this way and the *form* of the coded representation need not necessarily share anything in common with the perceptual characteristics of the coded pattern. For instance, the coded representation of "square" need not itself be square. Second, it is clear that the process of coding patterns is different from the process of recognizing the coded patterns, and the two should be dealt with separately and explicitly. In this way it may be possible to avoid the inherent danger of circularity already discussed.

Lashley, as ardent an opponent of local sign theory as Köhler, came somewhat closer to a tenable model for pattern recognition with his theory of reduplicated interference patterns (Lashley, 1942). The basic idea, never fully worked out in his published work, involved the notion that a retinal pattern of stimulation would generate in the brain a series of "interference patterns," which would be propagated over a large part of the visual cortex. One could think of these in terms of moving patterns of DC potentials, which might then interact much as do wave patterns generated on a smooth water surface into which objects are dropped; Lashley conceived of them in terms of the sympathetic activation of multiple series of timed resonating circuits. In this way he tried to reconcile to some degree two contrasting doctrines about the visual system. The first was the widely accepted tenet that stimulus equivalence is incompatible with explanations in terms of fully connected series of networks having explicit computing functions. The second was the opinion that the Gestalt alternative (of considering the cortex of the brain as simply a volume conductor) is implausible. The point of Lashley's model, of course, is to try to explain how one and the same brain state can be generated by a specific pattern of retinal stimulation independently of the particular retinal units excited. The idea that a stimulus pattern generates an interference pattern is the postulation—although in a rather vague manner—of a coding process in which geometrical properties of a pattern, presumably such as the relative positions of various contours, determine what interference pattern is generated. Propagation of that process through the cortex is supposed then to ensure that the recognition of the original stimulus pattern is not position-bound.

Lashley's realization that some sort of coding process is plausible and probable, if not logically necessary, is a clear advance over the isomorphic ideas. His notion of reduplicated interference patterns is also ingenious as a compromise between "dynamic" and "network" concepts of brain function. Nevertheless, in his model there is no explicit specification of a recognition process as such. One can still ask the question: How are the interference patterns themselves classified, or recognized? The easiest assumption to make is that each different propagated interference pattern, and the set of circuits over which it is propagated, was supposed to define the recognition of a class of inputs, perceptual category, or stimulus equivalence. But without a definite hypothesis about how particular stimulus patterns generate particular interference patterns, this has more than a hint of the circularity which was exposed in the Gestalt theory. One still wants to ask: How are the interference patterns, or outputs, recognized as being equivalent or not? The model gives no direct answer, so is no further ahead than the theory of isomorphism in this regard and can be criticized on the same grounds. It is only fair to add that Lashley was one of his own sternest critics; he wrote:

> There are numerous objections to such a theory, among which the chief is that it is too general and vague to be capable of experimental test. I seriously doubt that a cortical network excited throughout by afferent stimulation, as in the visual cortex, can develop such reduplicated patterns as I have postulated. The theory is no more than a means of emphasising the problems which must be met in any adequate account of cerebral integration [Lashley, 1952, p. 542].

A very different attempt to solve the problem of stimulus equivalence, for shape as well as for other attributes and modalities, was made by Pitts and McCulloch (1947). They addressed the general question in different language, the language of computational networks, but with essentially the same objective: How can a system with variable input, such as a human sensory system, compute "invariants" of that input, so that—to use the earlier example—a square can be recognized as such, despite variations in size, orientation, position, and so on. It was held that definition of networks which can compute such invariants is sufficient to demonstrate how a human sensory system might abstract Universals (in the epistemological sense of the word) or, to put it another way, how an observer may recognize abstract properties such as squareness or a particular tonal interval in a variety of different instances.

Pitts and McCulloch postulate networks of *formal neurons* or *modules,* which have the following properties: Each module has a number of inputs and one output, all of the same type (essentially "on" and "off" in every case) operating on a discrete time scale, with no time delay in transmission through the modules. Every module has a stable threshold for firing. A *modular net* is a set of interconnected modules, all operating on the same time scale, in which transmission delays occur only at synapses (junctions between modules). Modules and modular nets were first proposed in an earlier paper (McCulloch & Pitts, 1943) in which some important properties of such nets were proved, including a demonstration that they can always be devised to compute any of the functions of a normal two-valued (truth-functional) logic. This in turn means that they can compute values of any function in which the computation can be reduced to an *algorithm,* or procedure where the desired result can be obtained in a finite number of mechanical steps. Modular networks have a very wide field of application, as we shall presently see, which stem from their property of implementing logical functions. Perhaps the application to abstract pattern recognition is not among their immediately obvious uses.

The networks postulated for pattern recognition have inputs $\phi(x,t)$, where x defines locus of stimulation on the receptor surface, and t is time. These are discontinuous functions taking the values 1 or 0 depending on whether a "neuron" at x is firing at time t or not. The network then applies a group G of linear transformations (such as translation, rotation, and magnification) to any pattern of input stimulation $\phi_i(x,t)$. Every possible transformation in G is applied to every input pattern, and an average output value a is computed. These transformations are conceived of as occurring in parallel sheets of "neurons" in a step-by-step fashion as the transformed input pattern is relayed from one sheet to the next. Every possible size and orientation of square (if that happens to be the input pattern) in all possible positions will occur on some sheet and contribute to the final value of a. Thus the initial state of stimulation has no privileged status and does not affect the computation of a in any special way. The system is complicated by the fact that a number of different outputs, a_ξ, $(\xi_1 \ldots \; _m)$, are computed on the inputs and their transformations in order fully to specify the input class (the evaluations could be related, for example, to "squareness" or "circularity"). There are other refinements which need not be elaborated here.[3] The general idea is clear enough; the class to which a pattern belongs is defined by enumerating all the instances that can be obtained by a set of linear transformations of the original. The question of recognition no longer poses a problem *if* each class of input patterns yields unique values for the a_ξs, which can be thought of as states of particular modules within the net. In this sense, such networks really do compute invariants of their variable inputs, and thus solve the general problem of stimulus equivalence. However, Pitts and McCulloch neither attempt to *prove* that unique values for the a_ξs are necessarily computed for *every* class of input patterns, nor to specify what classes of input are classified (or misclassified) by their model for a particular sensory system. In this sense, the now familiar problem of recognition and stimulus equivalence is not completely solved, and the model is therefore too vague and general to be testable behaviorally. Moreover, it may be argued that the likelihood of such net-

---

[3] A more thorough description of the general principles of the Pitts-McCulloch networks is given by Arbib (1964, pp. 108–113), in which the description and discussion of the original paper are followed quite closely.

works being embodied in real sensory systems is remote. Lashley criticized the Pitts-McCulloch position as follows:

> The recent theory of Pitts and McCulloch has been specially formulated to deal with the problem of stimulus equivalence. Based on an analogy with digital computing machines, it assumes a precision in the arrangement and interconnections of cortical neurons which is not supported by anatomic studies. To account for equivalence of excitation in different *loci* within a functional area the theory assumes a distribution of afferent fibers from each sensory point excited to the whole cortical receptive area within which equivalence occurs, the afferents being distributed in such a way that the pattern is expanded at different levels which can then be isolated by a scanning mechanism. The histological evidence seems to rule out such an arrangement at least for the visual and sensory areas. The theory implies also a greater number of levels of transformation or neuronal shunting than is possible with the limited number of cells in the striate areas and, if I interpret it correctly, different structural patterns for each type of generalization. Its specific assumptions with regard to the functions of the colliculi and of area 8 . . . are contradicted by the facts that removal of either of these structures does not disturb the stimulus equivalence of visual perception [Lashley, 1952, p. 541; see also Lashley, 1951, p. 131ff.].

It is clear that this criticism is aimed more at the neurological interpretation of Pitts and McCulloch's networks than at their general solution of the theoretical problem of stimulus equivalence. As was pointed out before, criticism on grounds of physiological implausibility is not *necessarily* damaging to a theory, if it otherwise is satisfactory. But this cannot be claimed for the theory either since it is not really testable empirically.

FROM FIELD TO NETWORK THEORY: A CONCEPTUAL ADVANCE

The work of Pitts and McCulloch represents an important break with the earlier tradition of theorizing about systems for pattern recognition represented by the ideas of Köhler and Lashley. First, they show that there is no *necessary* incompatibility between a system's having a definite, fully connected structure and its ability to abstract invariants of its classes of inputs. This completely undermines the field theorists' position, for one of their major assumptions was that it is logically impossible to account for stimulus equivalence by computations within a network with fixed and specific connections. While that was perhaps true of the nineteenth century "telephone switchboard" notions of central nervous system operation, the generalization to *every* type of network was of course unwarranted. With the wisdom of hindsight we can see that the assumption was naïve, just as was the isomorphic postulate that the cortical representation of a pattern had in some sense to *be* that pattern. This of course does not mean that a field-type theory is wrong, only that it may now seem rather less plausible than before. In one sense the Pitts-McCulloch networks reinstate the "local-sign" concept, since their discrete input functions $\phi_i(x,t)$ "tag" each neuron of the receptor surface separately. The relative clumsiness of their networks' computational procedures is a direct consequence of the attempt to "neutralize" the local signs of input patterns: But to put it loosely, it seems to be a great waste of effort and computing capacity to enumerate and sum over all the transformations of which the network is capable on each and every input pattern. As we shall see, subsequent models for pattern recognition invariably discard this principle and base recognition of equivalent patterns on other properties, such as the detection of particular features within a pattern or the abstraction of some simple common characteristic.

A second general point about Pitts and McCulloch's work is that it provided a means of exactly specifying input-output properties of modules and modular nets. This led directly, on the one hand, to the formal theory of logic circuits, finite automata, and computers,[4] and on the other hand to the practical business of constructing machines which implement mathematical or logical statements and operations. This also, as we shall see, has enormous relevance to the investigation of pattern-recognition systems. But perhaps the single most important aspect of their work for psychologists is the fact that they introduced a precise theoretical basis for modeling brain processes in terms of modular nets. Although their influence is not always direct or readily traced, it pervades a great deal of modern theoretical psychology. It has led to a general sharpening of ideas about the specification of possible models for biological systems such as the visual system. A model as loosely stated as Lashley's notion of interference patterns, for example, would scarcely be given serious consideration these days without much more precise definition of its components and their interactions. Pitts and McCulloch's influence is basic to a whole species of *structural models* that play an important role in psychological explanation; these will be characterized shortly. In particular the theory of modular nets has led to a clearer understanding of the requirements for *effective procedures* for computing specifiable outputs from a model, given its inputs and present state. This means in our context that the requirement of exact specification can be met by asking: Could one devise a network to do this job? The concept of effective procedure is of course deeper than this, and has its principle application in the theory of recursive functions. The topic is discussed by Arbib (1964).

---

[4] A good introduction to this field is Arbib's book *Brains, Machines, and Mathematics* (1964).

It is important to notice the duality in the Pitts-McCulloch network models for sensory systems. On the one hand a mathematical formulation is given, both of the inputs to the system and of the linear transformations and other mappings that occur within it.[5] This formulation can be made quite independently of any proposed network for implementing it. On the other hand, there are proposals for a network to embody the formal specification. The two are independent, and one can always ask the question: Does the network implement the specification? If it does not, or if there are grounds for supposing the implementation to be implausible, this would not invalidate the formal model, whose adequacy must be tested in other ways. The mathematical functions proposed by Pitts and McCulloch are discontinuous functions of both x and t. Such functions were obviously chosen since they are easily represented in the inputs to a modular net which in turn are a formal representation of neural nets. However it is not necessary for the formal specification that the inputs and mappings should be discontinuous. Without too much difficulty it would be possible to rewrite it in continuous form and obtain essentially the same results. The question then would be: Could the continuous functions be modeled by a network? The answer is "yes"; such problems are routinely handled, for instance, by digital computers. With modular networks of sufficient size a continuous function can be handled to an arbitrarily close approximation. So a second prop is removed from the field-theorists' position—not only can networks compute Universals, but they can model continuous functions as closely as we please. The field-theorists' contention that a process normally continuous in space and time, like perception, can be modeled only by a continuous ("dynamic") process is thus found to be false. We see that the dichotomy is not as absolute as it seems to be at first glance; there *may* be advantages in formally specifying a perceptual model in terms of continuous functions, but an implementation of the formal model may still be possible in discrete, or digital, form. The obvious appeal of such an implementation is that it harmonizes with our present understanding of the principle means of operation of the central nervous system.

MODULAR NETS AS PATTERN RECOGNIZERS AND MEMORY UNITS

In a sense even simple logic circuits and modular nets can be considered as pattern recognizers. For example, a logic circuit that is known as an "and gate" has inputs p and q, and an output which is "on" if and only

---

[5] As a matter of fact, the rigor of their mathematical formulation leaves something to be desired, a point I was happy to have confirmed by a mathematician friend, who—like many another charitable donor—wished to remain anonymous.

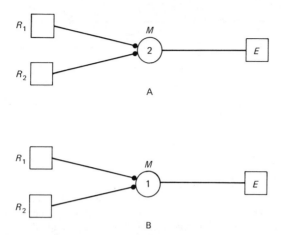

Fig. 1.1. Representations of two very simple networks. R_1 and R_2 are inputs which send single pulses on a discrete time scale to the module M. In 1.1A the module has a "threshold" of 2, each input "counts" 1, so that M is only activated if inputs from R_1 and R_2 are simultaneous. The output from M is thus a signal that R_1 and R_2 are both "on," that is, it computes the logical function "p and q" where R_1 is the representative of p, R_2 the representative of q. Similarly M in 1.1B computes "p or q." It is activated by either one of them, since it has a threshold of 1.

if p and q are simultaneous inputs. It can be said to recognize the pattern "p and q." Such a circuit is shown in Fig. 1.1A, following a common convention for its representation. Figure 1.1B shows an "or" gate, that is, one which recognizes "p or q." Given that all the units are on the same time scale, circuits are readily devised for recognizing temporal patterns also. A simple example is shown in Fig. 1.2.[6] Such simple circuits are not useful in solving the problem of stimulus equivalence for pattern recognition systems for a variety of reasons. First, each circuit is designed to recognize one, and only one, pattern. It would be possible to construct as many such recognizers as there are patterns to be recognized (assuming that this is known), but it would be a clumsy way of proceeding. There is good evidence, to be presented later, that this is not the way mammalian systems work although the visual systems of invertebrates and some lower vertebrates may do so (see Chapters 3 and 4). Second, such a system would be incapable of generalizing, or dealing with Universals in the Pitts-McCulloch sense. Third, of fundamental importance, simple logic circuits are not modifiable with use. They cannot store, learn, or profit by experience. Since biological systems do such things, this might appear to be a crippling restriction on our use of logic circuits as models. However,

[6] An introduction to logic circuits is given by Edwards (1964).

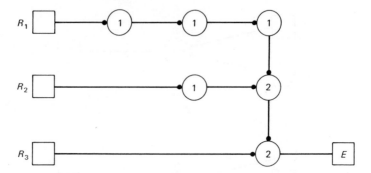

Fig. 1.2. A network which computes a simple temporal pattern. It "recognizes" the pattern R_1 followed after one unit of time by R_2, followed after a third unit of time by R_3, since this is the only input sequence which yields an output, given that transmission delays through each module are equal.

with some increase in complexity, circuits can be designed—usually involving "circles" or feedback so that a module's input can become some function of its own output—which count, store, represent, and compute probabilities, and so on. It is uncertain whether or not biological systems store information in this way, particularly over long periods of time. The hypothesis is an attractive one, however, and the concept of a "recirculating storage" for biological systems has recently been very popular. It cannot be ruled out as a possibility, particularly for short-term storage. We shall see in Chapter 2 how the idea played a leading role in one of the most important and influential theories of perceptual development yet devised.

Structural models for pattern recognizers with memory features can of course be devised with components other than modules and modular nets (or including some other components), which are nonetheless explicit in their postulated modes of operation. An example is given in the second half of Chapter 2. There is nothing sacrosanct about modules and modular nets in this regard; it is simply that we have learned largely through them to look for a new standard of precision in model building.

SYSTEMS, MODELS, AND THEORIES

A good deal of space has been devoted to the discussion of networks, since the topic is fundamental to what follows. But so far the discussion has proceeded without any explicit definition of such terms as "system," "model," and "theory." It would be as well to clarify these concepts before proceeding.

I use the term "system" for any aggregate of elements of different sorts that interact with each other but which can be considered more or less in isolation from other elements. This is a purposely vague definition that can cover a variety of situations. For instance, a "biological system" could mean an animal or it could mean a part of one; a "visual system" means those interacting elements within an organism that are primarily responsive to stimulation by light, but whose boundaries may otherwise be difficult to draw.

I shall follow the usual sense in which a mathematical model is thought of as a system whose initial properties are fully specified by a set of definitions and axioms and rules of entailment, so that once the system has been set up and shown not to involve inconsistencies, further properties can be found deductively. The deductions follow necessarily from the system, but its *usefulness* as a model depends on the extent to which the deductions (predictions) can be verified empirically in the real system that the mathematical system is used to model. Well-known examples of such mathematical models in psychology are the stochastic models for learning (see Hilgard & Bower, 1965) and the Shannon model for information transmission (see Garner, 1962). I shall use the term "structural model" to refer to a species of model, now common in psychology, in which the basic elements and their interactions are given more or less explicitly, and in such a way that input-output relations in the model can be deduced from the elements and their relationships, or "structure." The degree of specificity with which inferences can be drawn about the behavior of such models will depend almost exclusively on the precision with which the basic elements and structure are defined. To take one extreme, a model might contain the statement: "Behavior is a function of past experience and present stimulation" or, as it may somewhat grandiosely be put: $B = f(P, S)$. Such a postulate is practically vacuous, and perhaps expresses no more than a general faith in the regularity of behavior. At the other extreme, a model may be couched in exact mathematical statements, but with strong implications as to how the elements might be realized in neurological form. The Pitts-McCulloch network for computing Universals is an example. A boundary to the idea in another direction is the engineer's typical concept of a model: If a device can be constructed in such a way that its behavior is analogous in some respects to that of the real system, a model of that system has been achieved (for example, the "tortoises" of Grey Walter [1953]). Models might also be directly suggested by the discovery of particular physiological functions (for example, regulation of water intake and "thirst" by physiological mechanisms suggests the basis for a motivational model).

These examples span a wide spectrum; one might question the propriety of attempting to classify them in common. The point I wish to make is that all such models involve, initially, the concept of a "black box" with certain inputs and outputs, more or less specified, from which one proceeds to infer what the elements and their interactions could be. The process of "dissection" and "reconstruction" of the box may be more or less exact, more or less exhaustive, depending largely on how well the behavior of the to-be-modeled system is understood. On the one hand the process may lead one to a set of mathematical functions or logical formulae; on the other it might lead to mechanical, electrical, or other analogues of the system. Somewhere in between lies the psychologists' province, in which formal structural properties may be proposed, but usually in such a way that a neurological embodiment is plausible, or at least some attempt is made not to do violence to established neurophysiological facts and principles.

Clearly, in its formal aspect a structural model does not depend on neurophysiological verification of the presence of particular elements and structures, since its very formality ensures that it could be embodied in a variety of ways. On the other hand, neurophysiological evidence that certain elements and structures with similar (or identical) properties to those postulated for a particular model actually occur in some biological system may lend strong support to it. An outstanding example in the recent literature is the finding of three different cone pigments that occur in individual cones of the vertebrate retina (MacNichol, 1964), as was proposed in the Young-Helmholtz trichromatic color theory.

Clearly, model builders in psychology do not all speculate on possible physiological embodiments to the same extent, and so leave their models open to physiological disconfirmation to different degrees. But to the extent that formal specification of a model has been achieved, such evidence can never be conclusively disconfirming. Ultimately the test of a model's adequacy must be behavioral. We thus have a situation, supposedly rare in science, where positive evidence is in some respects stronger and more informative than negative.[7]

To a degree, this situation simply reflects our ignorance, both empirical and conceptual, of the relationships between physiological functions and behavior. No doubt as knowledge about neurophysiological functions increases, so will our propensity to identify formal elements of models with physiological entities increase, just as such knowledge will narrow the range of plausible models. But it would be a mistake to suppose

---

[7] I say "supposedly rare" since the standard logical analysis of "scientific laws" shows that a single negative instance can conclusively disprove a universal affirmative generalization, whereas an indefinitely long series of positive instances never *conclusively* proves it (which is the celebrated Problem of Induction). However, scientific statements are not always—perhaps even rarely—of this sort, especially when it comes to theoretical and conceptual issues (see Chapter 11).

that complete knowledge of a physiological system necessarily entails complete understanding of an associated psychological function, a point I shall take up in the final chapter. For the moment one can simply state that the closer a model's structure and properties are to known physiological structures and functions, the more likely is it to be accepted as a plausible model for the system.

Whether a particular explanatory schema in science is called a "model" or a "theory" is, it seems, to a great extent an historical accident. Newton's theory of gravitation could just as well be called "a mathematical model for gravitation." It would probably not be very productive to attempt to make fine distinctions between the uses of the two words. A general separation, however, can be made. I shall reserve the term "model" for attempts to explain the properties of a circumscribed system in terms of an explanatory schema that is fairly closely tailored to the known properties of the system, and that has some deductive explanatory power; that is, predictions can be made about the system's future behavior and at least some of its present behavior follows from (can be explained in terms of) the postulated properties of the model. "Theory," on the other hand, will be used in a wider sense to encompass both ideas about the general nature of psychological explanations (one might, for example, hold the theory that all brain functions can be analyzed in terms of modular networks) and more diversified models whose range of application may be to several different systems. Thus, for example, I would class Hebb's general ideas about cell assemblies as a theory, but the application of these ideas to a particular process, such as perceptual learning, may reasonably be called a "model" of that process. This usage is, I think, fairly commonly accepted, as is the fact that no firm boundary can be set between the denotations of "theory" and "model." One might expect a model to yield more powerful explanations than a theory (in the second sense) although its range is smaller. Both types of explanatory schema are worthwhile, and no judgment is intended on their relative merits. The history of science is replete with examples of important advances which have been occasioned by the appearance of both new models and new theories.

Pitts and McCulloch's work is a prime example of the increase in precision and power, with concomitant narrowing of the range of phenomena explained, which model building typically introduces. The trend will be obvious in later chapters, too, as various specific models are considered. It could well be said that such model building *assumes* implicitly a theory of behavior, as well as a general theory of scientific explanation; true, but that is another story which can profitably be left to the final chapter.

CHAPTER 2
Models for Pattern Recognition and Perceptual Development

One respect in which the type of modular net for abstraction of Universals described in the previous chapter is inadequate as a model for any higher (say, mammalian) visual system is its lack of modifiability with use, a property shared by the other two models we considered, those of Köhler and Lashley. In a way this is not surprising, since it is probably necessary to show how a stable system logically could recognize equivalent patterns before attempting to understand how it might *develop* that ability. This may have been an element in the Gestalt psychologists' insistence on the innateness of the forces determining isomorphism, and hence of perception itself, in addition to their strong reaction against the extreme "environmentalism" and "peripheralism" of some of the then contemporary schools of thought. Lashley was not able to tackle the problem of learning and memory in relation to stimulus equivalence adequately, and it is debatable whether Pitts and McCulloch even thought of it as a problem at the time in question.

Given that prior experience is an important factor in perception, it is of great theoretical interest to speculate on the ways in which it might affect perceptual development. This statement is too vague: We should like to model some of the processes of perceptual learning. A major step in that direction was the appearance of Hebb's *Organization of Behavior* (1949). Probably few modern books have had as deep and lasting an effect on psychological science as this one.[1]

[1] Interestingly enough, a second book, Hayek's *The Sensory Order* (1952) appeared shortly afterwards and propounds a theory that is in many respects similar

THE CELL ASSEMBLY

Hebb's concept of the cell assembly is basically simple: A set of neurons is held to be so interconnected that the firing of one neuron in the assembly affects the probability of the firing of others. Contiguity of firing within the set over space and time will tend to change these probabilities so that *organization* emerges and this organization is greatly enhanced by the (presumed) presence of closed, reverberating circuits within the cell assembly, since such circuits will amplify and consolidate the effects of contiguous firing. Such reverberating circuits are thus held to be the basis both for short-term storage and for developing longer-term structural changes. Hebb envisaged initial connections between cortical neurons as being essentially random, although this assumption is not necessary to the development of his ideas. The input to a cell assembly can be from receptors or other cell assemblies; similarly its output can be to effectors or other cell assemblies. At a higher level of development the sequential firing of groups of cell assemblies is held to organize *phase sequences,* but the basic units of the computational network which emerges are still the cell assemblies themselves.

The concept of a cell assembly thus falls within the class of structural models. It can be defined formally in terms of input-output relations and its possible internal states. At the same time, it was devised with the express aim of being as close in its characteristics as was reasonably possible to a network of real neurons as these were understood at the time. It differs from a simple modular net in that each unit has built into it (or rather into its synaptic terminals) the property of modifiability with use. While it would be possible to replace Hebb's construct with an extremely complicated modular net, in which change in synaptic "resistance" is replaced by altered probability of output from some set of modules, the exercise would probably neither increase our understanding of the cell assembly's behavior nor lead to further insight into its properties, since it would be mainly a question of "instrumentation."[2] Units that are

---

to Hebb's. One might suppose that both books represent a *Zeitgeist,* crystallizing ideas that were vaguely current, but not yet articulately expressed. Since Hebb's treatment is more definite, particularly in the proposals for models of perceptual learning and pattern recognition and their neurophysiological substrate, I confine discussion to it.

[2] A more formal statement of cell-assembly postulates is worked out by Milner (1957), who shows that, in order to work, the system must incorporate inhibitory processes. Hebb's own treatment is not highly formalized, although it is quite clear and was precise enough for his initial purpose.

modifiable with use are obvious candidates for the modeling of the visual system, whose properties are changed with experience. The interesting question is: How are the units to be put together into an acceptable model? And, in particular, to what extent can such a model explain pattern recognition and the *learning* of stimulus equivalences?

The relevant features of Hebb's solution are as follows: the "unschooled" visual system is assumed to have built into it a "primary receptive system" (not Hebb's terminology) of cortical "detectors" of certain primitive elements in the visual field, such as edges, contours, and angles. (The efficiency of these detectors may improve with use, but they are held to have an innate basis.) Their important properties, so far as his model is concerned, are that such detectors are activated originally only by the elements for which they *are* detectors, and their fields of action are strictly localized. The firing of a detector (apart, perhaps, from some spontaneous random activity) is a necessary consequence of the occurrence of a particular event at a specified place on the retina, and of no other. The building up of an organized, well-articulated perceptual field from such basic piecemeal detectors is held to occur by means of a special property of cell assemblies previously noted—namely that, through constant use, and particularly through contiguity of firing of separate units in space and/or time, the firing of one detector affects the probability of firing of others, which now or in the past have fired in conjunction with it. In this way recirculating, or reverberatory, activity is set up within sets of cells, eventually leading to permanent changes in their organization or "structure." The contiguities of firing of elements that are parts of a "visual whole" such as a geometric shape or a physical object are determined by a built-in eye-movement process, which ensures that in the early stages of visual learning the outlines of a shape, and especially its corners, are fixated one after the other, although not necessarily in a regular sequence. On this basis, Hebb shows how many properties of visual perception might be accounted for, such as the "wholeness" of perceived shape, closure, and other Gestalt-like phenomena.

Does the system also account for stimulus equivalence? That is to say, can it explain how different groups of detectors can become so associated with each other that the recognition of a *particular* pattern can occur despite the fact that different elements in the primary receptive system are activated when the pattern is projected onto different parts of the retina, in different sizes, and so forth? The difficulty for Hebb's model is the same as for any network-type model that postulates "local sign" at the receptor surface, as Hebb assuredly does. The difficulty, already pointed out several times, is to show (demonstrate, deduce from the properties of the model) that different classes of input at the receptor surface really do give rise to identifiably different outputs, and that members of particular (psychologically defined) classes of inputs all necessarily give rise to the same output and no other. In particular it is not clear whether one "detector" is supposed to be specific to one cell assembly or could function in the building up of several of them.

Three criteria at least for a model of pattern recognition and learning must be met: It must specify effective procedures for mapping input classes into specified outputs; it must give a plausible account of how the mapping is related to organization which emerges as a contingency of visual experience; and it must specify the operation of recognition. The question of whether Hebb's model for the visual system meets these criteria can be divided into two parts: First, does Hebb's statement of the model meet them? Second, if the answer to this question is negative, can the model be reformulated more adequately?

The hypothesis about the building up of cell assemblies which mediate the perception of geometrical figures such as a triangle can be symbolized by letting a, b, and c stand for the firing of the detectors of A, B, and C, the corners of the triangle. Observing the triangle in the undeveloped visual system would, under the direction of eye movements, give rise to a sequence such as: a–c–b–c–b–a. . . . At some stage, which is not precisely specifiable, the continual contiguity of the pairs a–b, b–c, and so forth, will lower the thresholds between the pairs sufficiently for the firing of one of them to fire the other, and so eventually the whole group, abc. This event is symbolized by t, a "superordinate activity" whose occurrence depends on the formation of the cell assembly abc. The sequence of events may now be envisaged as something like: a–b–a–c–t–b–c–t–a–t . . . in which the occurrence of t becomes more and more frequent as abc becomes more strongly organized. At this point the argument becomes vague—There is no clear statement about the recognition process (coding, detection, and recognition are not explicitly distinguished or defined by Hebb). Recognition seems merely to be equated with activity in "superordinate structures," yet "activity in a superordinate structure is . . . defined as being whatever determinate, organized activity results from repeated activity in earlier-developed or subordinate structures giving rise to it" (Hebb, 1949, p. 98). Thus, "perception of x" (where x is a *pattern,* or class of input, such as a triangle) is made to depend on the arousal of a particular cell assembly, or set of cell assemblies which, strictly speaking, can be identified only as "that cell-assembly set which is fired by pattern x." This is the same type of circularity which was criticized in the theory of isomorphism (Chapter 1).

While a plausible case is made out for the sort of "learning" which might underlie the setting up of a functional group of assemblies *in one location* of the cortex, the manner in which this could lead to generalization for all positions in the visual field is left completely vague. Thus,

Hebb attributes the phenomenon of stimulus equivalence to activity in cell assemblies, without specifying how cell assemblies generate *input classes* or how superordinate activity could become "general" for the whole visual projection area. The model, like the Gestalt theory, poses the problem of equivalence without giving an adequate solution to it. To say that t "signals" a triangle is not sufficient unless one can demonstrate how t can be generated in different places and at different times and still be known for what it is ("recognized").

Perhaps the model can be made more plausible by extending—or amplifying on—its hierarchical properties. Thus one might postulate that t_1 arises when *abc* is organized, t_2 when *def* is organized (where *def* is a group of different detectors associated with the identical pattern occurring in a different retinal position), and so on. The vagaries of visual search and fixation will ensure that, in time, t_1 and t_2 will fire contiguously, as will t_3 . . . t_n, where n is some unspecifiable, but large, number. One can imagine that once subsets of the t_is become sufficiently organized to fire one another (one need not assume that *all* the t_is become so organized), a further superordinate activity, T, will occur, and it is *this* that represents identification of "triangle." The recognition of T is now independent of retinal positions, which is to say that T mediates stimulus equivalence. Thus any second-order superordinate activity will generate an output that is determined solely by the contiguous firing of first-order superordinate units, and these second-order units in fact correspond to input classes, such as different geometrical figures, only because it is extremely probable that the t_is that occur in contiguity *happen to* represent different occurrences of the *same* pattern at different positions on the retina, rather than a rapidly changing sequence of *different* patterns. It would be quite possible for such a system to misclassify, but extremely improbable. For convenience of exposition, I shall call all first-order superordinate units members of the set S_1, all second-order units members of S_2, and so on. The members of S_1 that become associated, and thus generate a member of S_2, will form a definite subset of S_1, and so on.[3]

With this modification, Hebb's model seems to be capable of explaining stimulus equivalence, but there are still some problems with it. First, it seems to be rather inefficient in the sense that every part of the retina and its associated structures must be schooled separately for the formation of members of S_1. It is impossible to demonstrate that this is or is not the case, since no one knows how rapidly or slowly cell assemblies of this order would be formed, and it is quite probable, as Hebb indeed

---

[3] A hint of circularity remains, however, since we still do not have any independent method of specifying *abc, def,* and so forth, as detectors of a particular pattern.

argues, that the rapidity of learning will be different at different levels of the phylogenetic scale, in general showing an inverse relationship to it. However, it might be worthwhile to explore other possibilities, particularly as there is still the difficulty, already touched on, that there is no means of ensuring that a particular detector, say for a given angle at some definite locus near the center of the visual field, can be preempted for a particular cell assembly that generates a specific member of S_1. Alternatively, if it were held that a detector could be associated with *several* cell assemblies (would take part in the generation of several members of S_1), it is not clear how these different functions are distinguished and kept separate from each other. It is particularly difficult to imagine how this might happen in the early stages of learning. Thus we may say that Hebb's model fails to specify effective procedures for the generation of S_1.

Despite its many attractive features, then, the cell-assembly model still leaves much to be desired, so far as the explanation of perceptual learning and stimulus equivalence are concerned. As we shall see later, recent findings on the neurophysiological organization of the mammalian visual system tend to disconfirm the model too, despite some interesting similarities. On the other hand, Hebb's ideas have rightly been recognized as an important stage in the development of adequate models of the visual system, and particularly for their contributions to the problems of perceptual learning.

AN ALTERNATIVE MODEL

If one may attempt to define some stages in the development of specific models for pattern recognition (models of the visual system which incorporate properties that explain stimulus equivalence) one can, roughly but not too inaccurately, say that Köhler's and Lashley's models belong to a first generation of *field theories,* postulated on the firmly held conviction that the facts of stimulus equivalence are incompatible with any model of the visual system as an interconnected network of distinct units with discrete modes of computation and transmission. They are of prewar vintage, and were followed in the 1940s by models—represented by the work of Pitts and McCulloch and of Hebb—which attempt to demonstrate that the conviction of incompatibility was not justified. These models incorporated relatively clumsy methods of ensuring stimulus equivalence— either the group of linear transformations with enumeration over the whole system or separate learning of perceptual units over the whole primary receptive system, as previously described. A third generation may be distinguished, represented by work published in the 1950s, in which greater attention is paid to the specification of effective procedures for generating codes for different patterns and in which rather more elegant bases for stimulus equivalence are proposed. The first of these models was proposed by Deutsch (1955) and the others owe a great deal to his ideas. The two most clearly related to Deutsch's model are those of Sutherland (1957) and Dodwell (1957, 1964). I shall describe the latter in some detail in this section, not because it presents a final answer to any questions about pattern recognition, but because it illustrates the advances that are common to this generation of models, is rather more specifically worked out than the others, and, more importantly, incorporates a design for perceptual learning which the others do not. Also—as subsequently turned out—it is closer to the principles of coding and classifying of contour and shape in the mammalian visual system, as assessed by neurophysiological techniques, than are the others. Some comparisons between these models will be considered in Chapter 4.

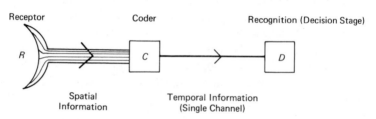

Fig. 2.1. A schematic layout for the pattern-coding model.

The overall design of the model is shown in Fig. 2.1. It is assumed that a spatial array of contour information on the retina is basically preserved and transmitted as the input to a coder. The coder is an information-reduction or computing system, which maps the spatial information in its input into temporal patterns of pulses which all occur in a single output line. This is the input to the recognizer, the function of which is to register the occurrence of particular temporal patterns in its input. Thus, initially at least, the input classes of the system are defined by the form of computation that occurs in the coder, and they are represented or registered by states (or outputs) of the recognizer. It will be shown later that the recognizer can be so devised that its outputs are modifiable with experience, and hence can model processes of perceptual learning. It should be noticed that the learning stage in this model is placed "higher up," or more centrally, than in Hebb's, a point which turns out to have important advantages, as I shall endeavor to demonstrate subsequently.

A great variety of coding systems might be devised; the present one has no unique advantages, but it seemed to account for most of the facts known about shape recognition in rats at the time it was first proposed (Dodwell, 1957, 1958), and has not been unsuccessful in generating correct predictions (see Chapter 4).

Consider a two-dimensional array of units, C, which are connected permanently to units of the receptor surface R (retina) in such a way that only contour information is transmitted to C from that surface. "Units of the receptor surface" is vague, and deliberately so, since a unit here would be unlikely to be identifiable with a single photoreceptor, and perhaps not even a ganglion cell. All that need be specified is that somewhere between receptors and coder contour information is extracted, and that the units of R output and C input are in fixed one-to-one correspondence. That is, whenever a contour is projected onto a particular fixed position on R, then and only then is a particular set of units in C activated (thus far, "local sign" is preserved). It is not necessary that topographical correspondence be preserved in the sense that the pattern of C units activated mirrors exactly the pattern of the contours at the receptors. However, topological correspondence must be maintained, and one further restriction is imposed. The units in C are connected in chains, so that each unit has at most two neighbors, one from which it receives "excitation" and one to which it transmits "excitation." Each chain is so arranged that, whenever a horizontal contour is projected onto R, the units in C which are thereby activated all lie on one chain. A distinction is drawn between "activation" from R and "excitation." "Activation" is the steady state of a unit in C induced by input from R, whereas "excitation" is its input from or output to neighbors in C, which is the type of discrete transmission on a fixed time scale characteristic of a modular net.

The array C is represented in Fig. 2.2. One set of units in C, the end-set A, have only one neighbor each on a chain, to which they transmit excitation. The elements of set A also have the property that their outputs are simultaneous; if one unit fires, they all fire. All other units in C transmit this excitation to their neighbors after constant time delays, T_p, if they are not activated from the receptors. Thus, firing of the set A induces a sweep, or scan, of the array, at a constant rate along each chain provided there are no contours projected to the receptors. If all the chains are of equal length, this sweep will reach the end-set B simultaneously. The units in B all have a common output, which is the output of the coder (the final common cable, following Deutsch's terminology). Thus, under the restrictions mentioned, the output of the coder will be a single large pulse of constant amplitude, occurring at a constant time after the output from A and depending only on T_p and the number of units on each chain, n.

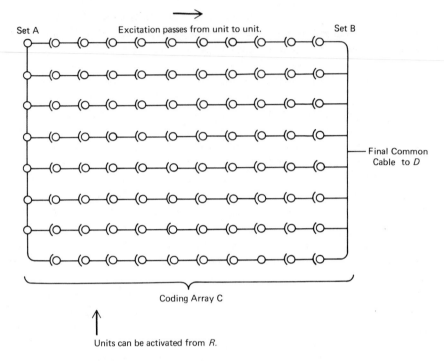

Fig. 2.2. A possible coding device (model *C*) for mapping spatial into temporal patterns.

It is assumed that when a unit in *C* is activated by the occurrence of a contour on *R*, its transmission time for excitation is increased to T_a. Thus, the occurrence of contours on *R* will alter transmission times along the chains of *C*, and hence the coder's output. To take the simplest example, suppose a horizontal contour is projected onto *R*, of sufficient length to activate *r* units on some chain in *C*. The coder's output will be an initial pulse, diminished in amplitude by one unit from its maximum, followed by a signal of unit amplitude after delay $r(T_a - T_p)$. This may be symbolized conveniently as $(1, r\Delta t)$, where the first measure of the pair specifies the amplitude, the second the time of occurrence of a signal, measured from the time base provided by the large-amplitude initial output due to all the unactivated chains. By assuming that $T_p = \Delta t = 1$, that is, that "passive" transmission time and the additional delay induced by the change of state of a unit from "passive" to "active" are each one unit in the coder's time scale, our expressions become even simpler. Logic circuits for attaining these states are illustrated in Fig. 2.3. In general, any output signal could be specified by some $f(a, t)$, where *a* and *t* refer to amplitude and time as above, both measured on discrete scales. One

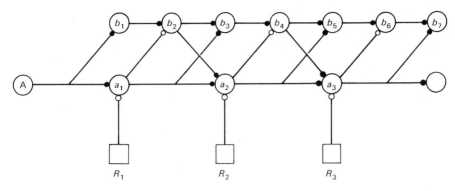

Fig. 2.3. Logic circuits for implementing the delay functions of the coder. A pulse from A goes to a_1, and b_1. If R_1 is "on," a_1 is inhibited (open circles represent inhibitory connections), but b_1 fires in the next time unit. Since a_1 is inhibited, its connection to b_2 is not activated, and b_2 fires in the next following interval. If, on the other hand, R_1 is "off," the original pulse from A fires a_1 at the same time as b_1. In the next time interval a pulse goes from b_1 to b_2, but b_2 is now inhibited by its input from a_1. Thus, when R_1 is "off" a signal passes to a_2 (and b_3) in one unit of time (traverses one cell, a_1) whereas if R_1 is "on" the signal arrives at a_2 and b_3 after two time units (traverses two cells, b_1 and b_2). The sequence then repeats itself to b_4, b_5, and a_3, depending on whether or not R_2 is "on."

may assume that A is triggered whenever a new contour occurs on R and hence activates one or more of the units in C.[4]

To show how the coder operates when a more complex set of contours is on R, Fig. 2.4 illustrates a possible state of C when a rectangle with longer sides horizontal is projected on R. (The topographical relation shown in the figure need not be preserved, of course, but makes for simplicity in exposition.) If there are n chains in C, the output function is specified by $(n - k, 0)$, $(k - 2, 2)$, $(2, n - r)$, where r and k are the horizontal and vertical lengths of the rectangle's sides specified in terms of units in C, which is quite arbitrary, and n is the number of units on a chain. This is shown diagrammatically in Fig. 2.5. Obviously, the same output function would be generated no matter where the rectangle was positioned on C, provided its orientation (longer sides horizontal) were not changed. Thus, the coder's output is unaffected by simple

---

[4] It will be seen that the coder thus satisfies the conditions for a finite automaton (Arbib, 1964, p. 8), since it has a finite set of inputs, I; a finite set of outputs, O; and a finite, although large, set of internal states, S. The next-state function $\lambda: S \times I \to S$ is determinate, provided the signal to trigger the end-set A is counted as an input, as is the next-output function $S: S \times I \to O$. In this case, however, the "output signal" mentioned $f(a, t)$ should be considered as a series of outputs, generated by a succession of internal states of the automaton.

translation, thereby solving the problem of stimulus equivalence in that regard. The output function for any set of contours can be specified, given a measure of "length" on R in terms of units activated in C, which will be constant and arbitrary. However, as it stands, the coder generates similar, if not identical, outputs for some patterns which, on common-sense grounds, we should expect to be discriminable. Thus any parallelograms of the same height, with two sides (of constant length) in the horizontal will all generate identical outputs; the same is true of a diamond and any pair of nonhorizontal straight lines of the same vertical extent. In a general way, horizontal contours appear to be the only truly distinctive properties of shapes coded so far. The difficulty can be resolved by postulating a second independent array, C_v, in which units on the same chain are activated by vertical contours falling on R. The second array is thus functionally perpendicular to the first, and the coder's output is now the two separate outputs C_h (the original C) and C_v.

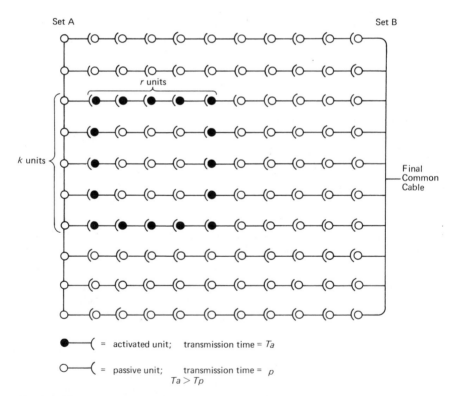

Fig. 2.4. The coding array, showing projection of a rectangle onto it. Filled circles here represent activated units, over which a transmission delay occurs that is additional to the unit delay on unactivated cells.

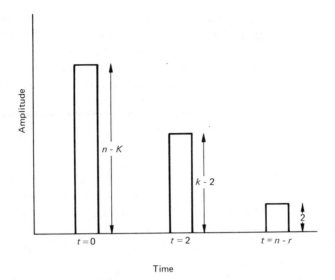

Fig. 2.5. Graphical representation of coder output for a rectangle. The amplitude of pulse registers number of chains discharging into final common cable. Time is measured on coder's time scale.

Different shapes will now, in general, generate different outputs, although some interesting confusions can occur. In particular, it is obvious that a shape having no straight contours in the horizontal or vertical orientation will tend to yield a less distinctive signal than a shape with one or more such contours. Also, the coder does not compute outputs that are invariant under rotation and change of size. In particular, simple geometrical considerations show that the coder is most sensitive to slight deviations from horizontality or verticality in a contour, while much larger rotations of a straight contour at 45° to the horizontal would not cause large changes in output. The question of size invariance for the coder's output is bound up with the question of how coarse the time and amplitude scales of the coder may be. Certainly only rather small changes in size could be tolerated unless some additional system for scaling the output in terms of the total amount of contour on R at a particular time were devised. However, the question to be asked is: Should a model of the rat's visual system provide for these invariances *ab initio?* In fact, there is evidence (see Chapter 4) that rotation of a geometrical shape which rats have learned to recognize tends to disrupt the discrimination, and that "equivalence" of the rotated shapes has to be learned. The evidence for size invariance is less definite, but there is no good reason to suppose that stimulus equivalence with respect to size variation is not at least in part a function of perceptual learning.

Separation of the operations of coding and recognizing patterns allows us to reformulate the question of stimulus equivalence rather more explicitly than has been done before: Which outputs from the coder are classified by the recognizer in the same way? The simple answer is that, provided a recognizer works on the same time and amplitude scale as the coder, it *can* be designed to "recognize" precisely all the different possible outputs of the coder. By "recognize" I mean here that the recognizer itself has a set of outputs (or states) that are in one-to-one correspondence with the set of all possible outputs from C. Alternatively, the recognizer could be designed to partition the outputs from C in particular ways—for instance, whereas the coder can generate a large number of signal amplitudes, these might be reduced to a smaller number of amplitude classes by the recognizer, each one specified by an interval on the scale of C's output. In this case the recognizer would further specify input classification, since information would be lost between the coder and it. Postulating such an addition to the coder may seem rather trivial, since it apparently adds nothing to the input classification already attained by the coder. However, I shall show how such a recognizer may be modified to incorporate a principle of perceptual learning which is by no means trivial, and which allows one to model a different *sort* of stimulus equivalence than that provided by the coder. So far, "recognition of x" is defined as the occurrence of a signal on some particular output from the recognizer, or as the state of some well-defined unit within it. Since the classification "x" is a function of the specified computations of the coder and the consequent recognizer classification, the circularity in earlier definitions of stimulus equivalence is avoided. To put it another way, we have specified *effective procedures* for generating coded representations of patterns, so that the equivalence of two patterns no longer depends merely on *asserting* equivalence. Rather, equivalence is now determined by similarity or identity in the coded representation. Of course the coding suggested may be wrong, but whether its classification agrees with the classifications of shape of any particular organism is an empirical question, which can in principle be answered.

The output from the coder consists of sequences of pulses of varying frequency and amplitude all occurring in the same transmission line (or, strictly speaking, in two lines, one for C_h and one for C_v—the recognizer for a single line will be described, since the problem is identical in principle as for the double line, only less complicated). A recognizer could be designed to accept this input, but I make use of a classifier that was proposed by Uttley (1954), whose mode of operation is very straightforward, and for which a digital input is postulated. Uttley (1954, p. 486) indicates how analogue signals (such as the coder's output) might be converted to digital form (that is, pulses of unit amplitude, on a discrete time scale) in a nervous system. There is evidence that analogue-digital conversion occurs in some neural structures (Hilali & Whitfield, 1953) so its postulation between the outputs of C and inputs to the recognizer D is not implausible. The form of conversion suggested requires that there be as many inputs to D as there are amplitudes to be distinguished in the coder output. Each input fires for one and only one amplitude, or range of amplitudes, of coder output. The simplest case, where only two amplitudes are classified, is sufficient to illustrate the classifier's mode of action. In this case D has two inputs, labeled j and k. These are connected to a set of modules that are so arranged as to register (a) the initial arrival of pulses in either input, and (b) the temporal patterns of impulses on either or on both inputs. This is achieved by feeding each input into series of simple modules and then to "coincidence counters," which are modules with thresholds equal to 2. Possible logic circuits for this are shown in Fig. 2.6, which follows Uttley's original classifier in

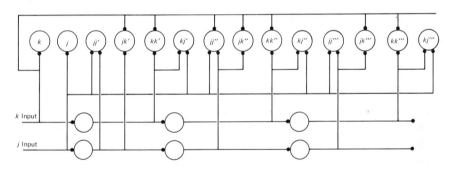

Fig. 2.6. The recognizer for outputs from model C. All units except those labeled j and k are "coincidence counters" and require two simultaneous inputs to fire.

design, although different symbols are used. To see how *temporal* patterns are recognized, consider the module labeled jj'. It will register if, and only if, an impulse on the j input is followed by a second pulse on j within time τ, the constant "synaptic delay" for all units. Similarly, the module jk' fires only if an impulse on j is followed within time τ by one on k. (The primes refer to the number of delay units separating a pair of pulses.) The delay τ could be the same time unit as that of the coder, or some integral multiple of it, in which case additional modules would be required in the delay lines of Fig. 2.6. In either case, simple and specifiable relations hold between coder outputs and recognizer states. It can be seen that the recognizer shown in Fig. 2.6 will discriminate all possible patterns of two inputs up to delays of 3τ. For patterns involving more than two impulses, more than one counter (excluding the initial j and k counters) will fire. An hierarchical recognition principle can be added, whereby a module $jj'jk''$, for instance, will register only when both jj' and jk'' are firing simultaneously, which happens only if an inpulse in k is followed by one in j after 2τ, followed by a second pulse in j after a further time τ. In this case jk''' would also fire, so that at a third level a module $jj'jk'''$ would be activated. The principle is simple enough, and can be carried to any desired level of complexity, although it becomes complicated to draw, especially if more than two inputs are shown. The restriction that $2U\tau > n\Delta t$, where U is the number of delay units in the recognizer, is required if the system is to operate unambiguously, that is, a "clearing time" of no more than $n\Delta t$ can be tolerated if spurious coincidences between different sequences of coder outputs are to be avoided.

"Equivalent stimuli" are now defined as sets of contours on R all of which fire the same set of modules in D. The only remaining vagueness concerns the "coarseness" of the scaling between R and C and between C and D. There is little enough evidence on the difference limens of the rat of the type that would be required to specify the scalings, and the imprecision is therefore inevitable. The model as proposed is essentially noiseless, but could operate under some random perturbations such as undoubtedly occur in real sensory systems. Also, the restriction that all chains in C have equal numbers of modules is implausible. Relaxing this slightly would do no more than convert the output pulses of C into some less tidy form, such as distributions of pulses with normal probability density over time, if the variation in n over chains were itself normal. Limited integration over time before the digital conversion could handle this, provided the variance over time is not large with respect to the interval between to-be-discriminated pulses. However, such minutiae may be disregarded for our present purposes. The main point is that an effective procedure for computing equivalent input classes to R, or equivalent stimuli, has been specified and is independent of perceptual learning; but it restricts equivalence to cases of translation without rotation or magnification, let alone more complicated matters such as equivalence under perspective changes.

CODING AND PERCEPTUAL LEARNING

The model so far described has no "memory"; its performance is quite independent of its previous states, and as such is an inadequate model for the visual system even of a rat. To show how the system can be extended to incorporate a type of perceptual learning, the notion of a conditional probability computer can be introduced. The idea is, again, due to Uttley (1958a,b, 1959). Consider the hierarchical classification system of Fig. 2.7, which can be thought of as a schematic version of *D* as shown in Fig. 2.6. The lines *a, b,* and *c* represent digitalized inputs

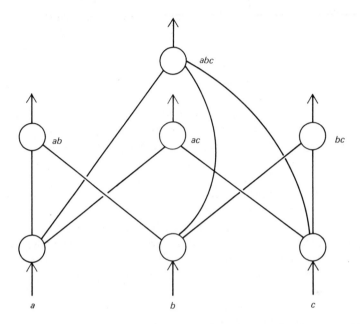

Fig. 2.7. A recognizer with three levels of classification. The second and higher levels of unit are coincidence counters for two or more simultaneous inputs.

from *C,* the open circles coincidence counters. Simultaneous inputs at, for instance, *a* and *b* will activate the three counters *a, b,* and *ab.* Simultaneous inputs at *a, b,* and *c* will activate all the counters. Suppose now that each counter has a limited memory such that each time it counts its state is altered step-wise, but gradually tends to revert to its initial condition. (A simple physical analogue is a leaky condenser to which a standard charge is applied each time the unit counts.) Suppose, further, that the system is so arranged that two counters in approximately the same state (with equal charges) will count if either one of them is activated. For example, if *b* has almost always been activated at approximately the same time as *a,* then if *a* is activated (but not *b*) the *b* and *ab* counters will also be activated. By choosing a suitable criterion for "same state" such a system computes conditional probabilities at a specified level. (The probability that *b* occurs, given *a,* determines whether or not the *b* and *ab* counters register when *a* occurs alone.) The details of these computers and the related "conditional certainty" computers are given by Uttley (1958a,b, 1959). It will be seen that the notion of "association by contiguity" is the same as Hebb's; it is clear that such computers will "recognize" patterns, conjunctions of patterns, and conjunctions of patterns occurring in rapid succession. Such conjunctions of patterns must lead to "generalization" or "inference" by the system, and this is all that is needed in order to complete a type of perceptual learning, since in its normal environment an organism is in constant visual contact with stimuli which fluctuate in size, shape, locus of stimulation of the retina, and so on. How does it "organize" or "recognize" a stable visual world, however?

The proposals that perceptual organization is entirely learned or that it is entirely built-in are both implausible, and to say that it is partly learned is vague enough to avoid the issue unless further specifications are made. By specifying which equivalences are built in, which learned, and how the two are related, one can avoid such ambiguity. If one imagines a particular object in the environment of a young organism, say a circular disk, then as the organism approaches the object, moves around, over, or away from it, the apparent size, shape, and orientation of the object will change, but these changes will be orderly and will give rise to orderly changes in the output from C, and hence to orderly sequences of counts in the units of D_m (the recognizer with memory). Many of these sequences will occur in fairly rapid succession (as when the organism locomotes) and eventually will give rise to "inferential learning" when the conditional probabilities become high enough and stable enough (see Uttley, 1958a,b). That is, when one member of the sequence is registered in D_m, if its counter's state is sufficiently close to the states of some other counters in the system, these will also register. D_m will therefore build up a system of internal classification which is dependent on the organism's history, to the extent that regularities in the perceived environment will be matched by regular patterns of activity in D_m. Thus, two types of stimulus equivalence have been incorporated into the model—one due to the ways in which C processes incoming patterns, which gives rise to "low-order equivalence" because outputs from the coder are identical or very similar, the other due to experience of regular sequences of signals from C, which builds up higher orders of equivalence within D_m. Thus, for example, in this system the equivalence of a pair of circular contours is explainable in terms of the nearly identical outputs they generate in C. On the other hand, the "equivalence" of different perspective views of a circular disk, which may generate quite different outputs from C, is explainable in terms of "perceptual learning," which means, in this context, the regular conjunction of sequences of different signals from C, giving rise to "organization" in D_m. Such higher-order equivalence can be thought of—if rather speculatively—as the basis for perceptual organization and the stability of the visual world.

COMPARISON WITH THE CELL ASSEMBLY MODEL

In what respects does this model for pattern recognition-with-memory improve on Hebb's model? It offers an explicit and precise solution to the problems of equivalence and learned equivalence, and defines recognition of equivalent patterns unambiguously. It will be remembered that two very real difficulties with Hebb's model were pointed out—first, that separate "learning" had to occur for any particular shape over all of the primary receptive system, and second, that the possibility that one and the same "detector" might enter into several larger cell assemblies (generators of S_1) was left vague, and the problems of specifying how this might occur were not discussed. In this sense, effective procedures for generating S_1 were not provided. In the present model, despite a very limited form of built-in equivalence, the generation of S_1 does not require any separate learning over parts of the field. S_1 is "built-in" as a first layer of registers (shown schematically in Fig. 2.6), and S_2 can be considered as some set of registers in D_m above the first layer, whose exact position cannot be ascertained without further assumptions about the number of input lines to D_m, and so forth. (Incidentally, a "layer" will not correspond exactly to a line of registers such as those shown in Fig. 2.6.)

To see what an enormous advantage this is, consider the learning of equivalence for a square of a given size in all orientations in the two models. In Hebb's, the cell assembly or assemblies of S_1 for the square itself have first to be organized over the whole primary system. Then—or perhaps partly contemporaneously—the assemblies for a new orientation have to be built up, again separately for each location. The organization in one area will not contribute anything at all to the organization in others, at least until a very late stage, when a large number of units in S_1 and at least some in S_2 have been formed. The whole process would have to be repeated, although very probably not in the exact sequence here described, for yet another orientation, and so on. The complexity of the operation is staggering to imagine. In the present model, however, learning of the equivalence of different orientations is much more economical, since the formation of units of S_2 proceeds for all locations *simultaneously*. Thus, far from requiring separate learning of the equivalence under rotation for each and every different retinal position, occurrence of *any* sequence of signals caused by change of orientation of the square will contribute equally to formation of a unit in S_2, even if it occurs in a part of R that never received that particular pattern before, because the coded output from C is not position-specific. Once the relevant unit in S_2 is formed, generalization over the whole of R will be complete. The second awkward feature of Hebb's model does not occur here, since the generation of specific codes for specific shapes in a specified orientation is built in, thus ensuring the effective generation of S_1 over the whole of R despite the fact that one and the same units in R (and C) contribute to the outputs for different patterns.

A further word about stimulus equivalence and the postulated two forms of equivalence is in order. Having criticized earlier theorists for failing to come to grips adequately with the problem of equivalence, it is perhaps incumbent on me to spell out yet again the way in which I think the solution proposed is an improvement on its predecessors. The skeptic could argue thus: A cell-assembly theorist states that two visual patterns are equivalent if they give rise to the same pattern of cortical activity, and Dodwell states that two patterns are equivalent if they cause the same unit in the recognizer to fire; it is difficult to detect any real difference in the two positions. So stated there is little difference, of course. The difference becomes clear only when one looks at the specificity of the postulated coding and recognition functions. One way of showing this would be to attempt to build machines incorporating the principles of operation of different models; another way would be to ask under what conditions an isomorphist or cell-assembly theorist could assert that two patterns are equivalent (say, for the rat) other than by looking at them? I can assert that certain patterns will be equivalent despite an obvious difference in appearance for the human observer, if I believe that the coding principle is correct (see, for example, Chapter 4). Thus the model—or, more important, the *type* of model—here proposed is testable in ways that were not previously possible, since rather specific predictions can be made, not just about equivalence in general, but in terms of patterns having certain well-defined properties. The idea that equivalences (or at least some forms of equivalence) are learned is scarcely new, but to attempt to demarcate the boundary between "built-in" and "learned" equivalence certainly is not a feature of most models. The force of this point will perhaps emerge only in subsequent chapters, as the proposed lines of demarcation become clearer.

The model is still incomplete in the sense that nothing has been said about responses, and surely to be realistic any theory about pattern recognition systems should be able, at least in principle, to show how the formation of input categories is related to responses and response classes. An earlier proposal (Dodwell, 1964) that "response generators" are associated with the units of D_m, and that the strengths of such associations are determined by reinforcement history, still seems plausible. However, detailed discussion of the topic is deferred until Chapter 10, where pattern recognition is considered in the context of discrimination learning theory. Some more specific proposals for integrating D_m into a discrimination learning model are there developed.

OTHER CODING POSSIBILITIES

A further generation of models for pattern recognition and stimulus equivalence is not so readily described or characterized; probably the two points which will most influence new developments are, first, the neurophysiological findings on mammalian visual contour processing (see Chapter 3) and, second, the now generally accepted notion that pattern recognition occurs by the detection—and subsequent integration—of *local* pattern features. Thus a model which considers a constant coding or computing function over the whole array (visual field) like model C, may seem to be behind the times. On the other hand it has not been established that a reasonable model for specific sorts of equivalency coding, and particularly for *learned* equivalence, can be set up on another basis. Obviously enough the model described in the preceding section by no means exhausts the possibilities for pattern coding on the basis of a constant computing function for the array. An indefinitely large number of coding systems could be devised readily enough, but in fact only one other general coding principle has been seriously entertained by psychologists for pattern recognition in animals. This is coding by contour separation.

Deutsch (1955) proposed a structural model for shape coding that would account for a number of features of shape recognition. It is based on the idea that shape is coded in terms of the distances between contours in every part of the shape. For instance, the code for a pair of parallel lines would depend only on the perpendicular distance between them; the code for a square would be simple also, since the perpendicular distance from any one side to another is constant. On the other hand a pair of nonparallel straight lines or a triangle would have more complicated codes, since the distance between contours would vary in different parts of the pattern. Thus the model is quite similar in principle to (although very much more explicit than) Lashley's theory of interference patterns, since the coding occurs in terms of *internal* properties of the shapes; it is independent of position, orientation, and—to some degree—of size. Contour separation (distance) is coded into time delays of signals in a final common cable, amount of contour at a given separation into amplitude of signal. The model was designed specifically to account for six assumed properties of the rat's ability to recognize shapes—the three just mentioned (independence of position, orientation, and size), and the facts that mirror images tend to be confused, that rats have difficulty in discriminating squares from circles, and that the ability to recognize shapes survives destruction of large parts of the striate area. Deutsch's model meets this specification, but it can be argued that the six properties are not characteristic of the rat's visual system (Deutsch, 1960a; Dodwell, 1957, 1958). In particular, rats can, under appropriate circumstances, discriminate square from circle, but change of orientation of a shape (that is, rotation in the plane normal to the line of vision) tends to disrupt recognition (Fields, 1932). Fields showed, however, that rats can *learn* to generalize from one orientation of a triangle to another, which indicates again that a model of this type is incomplete unless some system for perceptual learning can be incorporated into it.

Deutsch has proposed two other models, one designed specifically for the octopus (Deutsch, 1960a) and one which is more general (Deutsch, 1962). Both are based on the same principle of coding by contour separation, and evidence is quoted from histological studies on the octopus and the bee, mainly by Cajal (1917); this evidence is suggestive of the sort of neuronal networks that might compute such intercontour distances. Similarly, Sutherland has proposed several bases for contour coding, but principally a model that computes contour separations in a figure horizontally and vertically, each independently of the other (Sutherland, 1957). Again, anatomical evidence reported by Young (1960, 1961) supports the notion that separate horizontal and vertical outputs play an important part in the visual coding of the octopus (Sutherland, 1964; Young, 1964, especially p. 147 ff.). The octopus is by far the best-investigated animal so far as shape discrimination is concerned, a large number of experiments having been reported by Sutherland and his associates. More recently, Sutherland (1963b) has proposed a revised model which appears to account for most of his results, and which makes use of recent neurophysiological findings. This model will be discussed in Chapter 4, following a review of the neurophysiological evidence in Chapter 3.

The relative merits of these various models have been debated, perhaps at too-great length, and certainly inconclusively (Dodwell, 1961, 1962; Sutherland, 1960). All of them are at best oversimplifications of the real systems they attempt to model, and it seems probable that attempts to model the visual systems of mammals and invertebrates in the same way are misconceived. The anatomical and histological evidence adduced by Deutsch and Sutherland (pre-1963) comes from studies of invertebrate visual systems, and it seems quite possible that for, let us say, insects and cephalopods, pattern coding is based on contour separation (see, however, Chapter 4). Recent work with microelectrode recording in mammalian visual systems (principally in the cat) suggests very strongly that a different principle operates there, as we shall see in the next chapter.

This is not too surprising, since the anatomy of both retinal and central structures in vertebrates is quite different from the organization in lower forms like the octopus and the bee. (Some of the principle differences are described and discussed by Young, 1964, Chapter 7.) While differences in structure do not necessarily entail differences in function, diversity of function seems more probable where the structural differences are greater than they otherwise would be.

CHAPTER 3
Neurophysiological Evidence on Contour Coding

Structural models of the visual system provide useful guides to research in the sense that they predict properties of the system that can be tested in discrimination experiments. Since most models of this sort are devised with a possible neurological realization in mind, it is important to review neurophysiological evidence on contour and pattern coding. In increasing measure such evidence must assume a role in our theorizing about the structure and operations of visual systems, since recent findings appear to come close to discovering the basic elements that generate coded representations of pattern features. These findings place considerable constraints on the sorts of processing which may plausibly be incorporated into a model for pattern recognition. This chapter considers the most apposite neurophysiological work on pattern and contour coding, especially in mammalian species.

ELECTRICAL RESPONSES OF THE VISUAL STRUCTURES

More than a century ago, Holmgren discovered that the eye responds to stimulation by light with gross changes in the electrical potential existing between the cornea and the back of the eye. This response, the electroretinogram, has been widely investigated but can as yet tell us little about the coding or processing of contour and pattern information, simply because it is a "macroscopic" response. Recording from the optic nerve *in toto,* pioneered by Adrian and Matthews (1927) is limited in the same sort of way. Important advances were achieved by Hartline and Graham (1932) and Hartline (1938) in recording from individual cells and optic nerve fibers, and at about the same time Granit and Svaetichin (1939) developed their method for recording from individual retinal ganglion cells. This makes possible the investigation of microresponses and the analysis of the functions of individual neurons within the visual system. As techniques have improved it has been possible to achieve progressively finer placement of recording electrodes in complex structures such as the retina and the lateral geniculate bodies, culminating in recording from individual neurons of the visual cortex (Hubel & Wiesel, 1959; Jung, 1959; Jung & Baumgartner, 1953). To attempt to review all these developments in detail would be well beyond the scope of this book, so I shall confine myself to those findings which are most relevant to an understanding of how contour and shape are coded. Discussion of the older techniques is available in standard reference works such as Davson (1962) and important work (up to 1962) in physiological optics is reviewed in a number of papers in Volume 53 (1963) of the *Journal of the Optical Society of America*. A fine account of Granit's outstanding contributions to the field is available in his Nobel Prize address (1968).

RESPONSES FROM INDIVIDUAL OPTIC NERVE FIBERS OF THE COMPOUND EYE

The first recordings from individual nerve fibers in a visual system were achieved with limulus (Hartline & Graham, 1932); the technical problems are less formidable here than in other species, particularly vertebrates, since the optic nerve of limulus is long, and the fibers large. Moreover, the interpretation of responses is more straightforward than for the optic nerve fibers of more complex vertebrate visual systems. Limulus has a compound eye, and the cell bodies whose axons constitute the optic nerve are positioned right in the ommatidia, which are the receptor units. Recordings are made from the axons of the so-called eccentric cells, whose dendritic processes receive inputs from the retinular cells, which are believed to be the true photoreceptors (Hartline, Wagner, & MacNichol, 1952; Miller, 1957). Thus the recorded signals can be considered as rather more direct effects of light stimulation than signals from third-order neurons in the vertebrate optic nerve. One may thus expect to find simpler principles in operation than in the vertebrate system, where two synaptic layers, with rich lateral connections and a considerable degree of convergence, have already been crossed before impulses are recorded.

Figure 3.1A shows schematically the recording arrangement and is taken from a later publication. In the original work with limulus, Hartline and

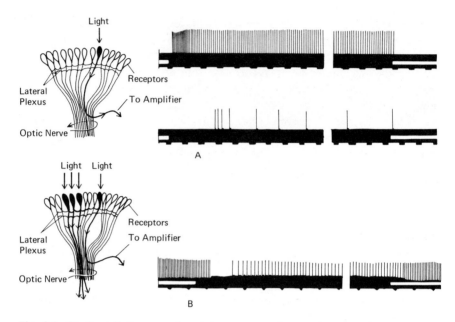

Fig. 3.1. On the left the experimental arrangements are shown, and on the right the oscillograms of action potentials in a single optic nerve fiber of limulus. The action potentials are the typical "spikes" of electrical activity which are propagated along the axons of nerve cells. (A) For the upper record the stimulating light was 10,000 times the intensity of that used for the lower record. The latency of response is much greater, and the frequency of discharge much less, in the lower record. Signal of exposure to light blackens out the white line above the ⅕-sec time marks which appear along the base of each record. The "break" in each record represents an interruption of about 7 sec, during which the stimulating conditions remained constant (from Hartline, Wagner, and MacNichol, 1952). (B) Inhibition of the activity of a single steadily illuminated ommatidium, produced by illumination of a number of other neighboring ommatidia. The oscillograph record is the discharge of impulses in the optic-nerve fiber coming from the one steadily illuminated ommatidium. In this case the interruption of the white line above the ⅕-sec time marks signals the illumination of the *other* ommatidia. Thus the first (left) part of the record represents the single-fiber response to light, which is inhibited—completely for about ⅕-sec—by illumination of nearby receptors (from Hartline, Wagner, & Ratliff, 1956).

Graham were able to demonstrate frequency coding of intensity and other properties characteristic of sensory nerve fibers whose receptor elements are subjected to steady stimulation. Subsequently Hartline demonstrated that the rate of optic nerve firing is a function of the product of intensity times duration for short light flashes, and that dark adaptation increases sensitivity, effects which are commonly attributed to the photochemistry of the light receptors. (This and related work is summarized by Hartline, 1940.) Spatial summation had been demonstrated physiologically for the vertebrate retina by Adrian and Matthews (1927), but no such effect is observed in limulus. In fact one might suppose that no spatial interactions at all are obtainable, since the eccentric cell fibers are directly linked to each receptor complex (ommatidium) without synaptic interruption. On the contrary, spatial effects can be obtained, but they are purely inhibitory. Figure 3.1B shows the effect of stimulating neighboring ommatidia on the discharge rate of one which is stimulated by steady illumination. Such inhibitory effects are greater, the closer the inhibiting units are to the one from which recordings are made, although effects can be obtained over some distance. Moreover, the inhibitory effects are themselves summated and reciprocal—the more neighbors stimulated, the greater the effect on the original. It has been established that the inhibitory effects are mediated by neural connections in the lateral plexus just posterior to the receptors, which is indicated on the left in Figs. 3.1A & B. What is the point of such an inhibitory mechanism? Clearly if a fiber fires maximally when it, but none of its neighbors, fires, the system gives priority to the detection of spots or contours, and in general to sharp changes in the spatial distribution of stimulation. This was elegantly illustrated by recording from individual fibers as a bright edge was passed over the field of the compound eye (Ratliff & Hartline, 1959). The resultant firing patterns are shown in Fig. 3.2. Similarly, sharp transients are obtained to sudden temporal changes in illumination, and these also have a lateral inhibitory effect, as shown in Fig. 3.3. Thus the system is designed to detect sudden changes, both of spatial and temporal patterns of stimulation and of their interactions.

Even at the comparatively lowly level of limulus, we see a processing arrangement that selects and "sharpens" contour information. Are similar effects demonstrable in the vertebrate retina, or elsewhere in the visual system? The anatomical arrangements are so different that one might suppose different sorts of coding occur. This is indeed true, the structures are more complex, and so are the coding processes, but we shall see that inhibitory activity still plays a fundamental role: One that is similar to its role in the limulus system, in sharpening and selecting contour information.

RESPONSES FROM SINGLE UNITS OF THE VERTEBRATE EYE: THE RETINAL RECEPTIVE FIELD

Recording from the optic nerve of limulus is simpler than the same operation on the vertebrate eye; the more difficult feat was first achieved by Hartline (1938), who obtained results of great interest and importance, principally on the frog. He found that a single optic nerve fiber could

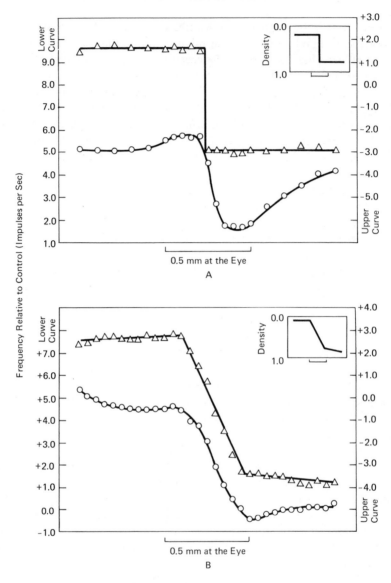

Fig. 3.2. The discharge of impulses from a single receptor unit in response to simple patterns of illumination in various positions on the retinal mosaic. (A) "Step" pattern of illumination. The demagnified image of a photographic plate was projected on the surface of the eye. The insert shows the relative density of the plate along its length as measured prior to the experiment. The density of the plate was uniform across its entire width at every point. The upper (rectilinear) graph shows the frequency of discharge of the test receptor, when the illumination was occluded from the rest of the eye by a mask with a small aperture, minus the frequency of discharge elicited by a small control spot of light of constant intensity also confined to the facet of the test receptor. The scale of

42

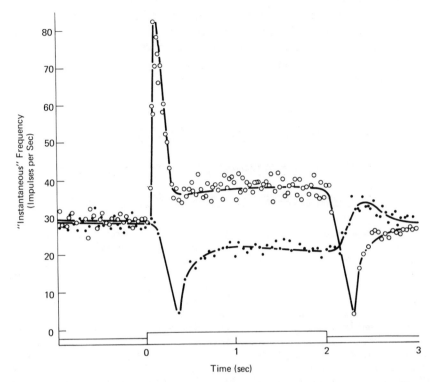

Fig. 3.3. Simultaneous excitatory and inhibitory transients in two adjacent receptor units in the lateral eye of limulus. One receptor unit, (filled circles), was illuminated steadily throughout the period shown in the graph. The other unit, (open circles), was illuminated steadily until time 0, when the illumination on it was increased abruptly to a new steady level where it remained for 2 sec and then was decreased abruptly to the original level. Accompanying the marked excitatory transients in one receptor unit are large transient inhibitory effects in the adjacent, steadily illuminated receptor unit. A large decrease in frequency is produced by the inhibitory effect resulting from the large excitatory transient; during the steady illumination the inhibitory effect is still present but less marked; and finally, accompanying the decrement in the frequency of response of the element on which the level of excitation was decreased, there is a marked release from inhibition (from Ratliff, 1961).

Fig. 3.2. (*Continued*)
the ordinate is on the right. The lower (curvilinear) graph is the frequency of discharge from the same test receptor when the mask was removed and the entire pattern of illumination was projected on the eye in various positions minus the frequency of discharge elicited by a small control spot of constant intensity confined to the facet of the receptor. The scale of the ordinate is on the left. (B) A simple gradient of intensity (the so-called Mach pattern), following the same procedure as in A (from Ratliff & Hartline, 1959).

be activated only from a circumscribed, but fairly large, area of the retina, and this he defined as the fiber's *receptive field*. Responses were typically of three different kinds: the well-known "on," "off," and "on-off" effects, illustrated in Fig. 3.4; any one fiber gave only one type of response. The new order of complexity, as compared to the limulus responses,

Fig. 3.4. Oscillograph records of the action potentials in three single optic nerve fibers of the frog's eye, showing three characteristic response types. As in Fig. 3.1 the action potentials are the "spikes" at the top of each record, time is marked at the base of the record in ⅕ sec, and "light on" is signaled by interruption of the white line above the time marker. (A) The "on" response. Discharges in this fiber occurred only when the stimulating light was turned on, and continued steadily while it was on. There was no response when the illumination ceased (the apparent "off" response at the right end of the record is from other sources, shown by the fact that its spikes are smaller in amplitude than those of the relevant fiber). (B) The "on-off" response. This fiber discharged both at the onset and termination of stimulation and did not show maintained discharge during illumination. (C) The "off" response. Response was only to cessation of illumination (from Hartline, 1940).

scarcely requires comment. Hartline's evidence suggested that the receptive field was of a fixed size, remaining unchanged under varying conditions of adaptation and illumination. However, he did show that the central portion of a receptive field had a lower threshold of stimulation than the periphery, and that all optic-nerve receptive fields were circular or slightly elliptical in shape. Most important, in view of subsequent developments, Hartline showed that spatial summation of activity occurred over the receptive field, whichever of the three types it happened to be. Spatial interaction of this sort is not surprising in a system with at least two layers of synaptic junctions and the rich lateral connections and degree of convergence between photoreceptors and ganglion cells which are typical of the vertebrate retina (Fig. 3.5). A receptive field may be as much as 1 mm in diameter, an area large enough to contain at least 1,000 receptors in the frog retina. However, the fields overlay each other, and it is not known whether a single rod or cone can contribute to more than one field, so the degree of true convergence cannot be estimated.

Hartline's findings were substantially confirmed by Barlow (1953) for

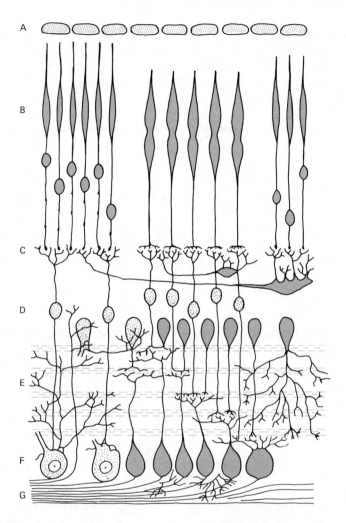

Fig. 3.5. The structure of the human retina, simplified and shown schematically. Other vertebrate retinas are similar in general organization. Light strikes the retina first at layer G and travels from bottom to top in terms of this diagram. Layers are: (A) Pigment layer, which plays no direct part in transducing light signals into neural signals, (B) rods and cones, the photoreceptive units which capture light quanta and thereby generate neural signals, (C) synapses between the rods and cones and bipolar cells (D); some synaptic connections with horizontal cells also occur at this level (two such cells are shown). The major function of the bipolar cells is to mediate between the photoreceptors and the ganglion cells (layer F), whereas the horizontal cells and amacrine cells (shown in layer E) mediate lateral interactions. The difference between horizontal and amacrine cells is that the latter synapse with ganglion cells. Layer G shows the axons of ganglion cells, which exit from the eyeball and form the optic nerve [redrawn from F. E. Cady and H. B. Dates *Illumination Engineering* (2nd Edition), New York: Wiley, 1928].

the frog and by Kuffler (1953) for the cat, both using Granit's technique for recording from retinal ganglion cells. However, Barlow showed that most receptive fields have a clear plateau of maximum sensitivity at their centers, the threshold rising rapidly toward the periphery. Moreover, in "on-off" fields, although the thresholds for "on" and "off" activity are usually very close at the centers and periphery, there are often intermediate zones where the threshold for one type of response was as much as 100 times the threshold for the other—perhaps the first indication that the "on-off" response is not unitary, but can be separated into two different components. Barlow also found that illumination of an area greater than the size of the receptive field tended to inhibit responses, and that this inhibition is more powerful for the "off" than the "on" effect. This was confirmed by shining two spots of light, one at the center of the receptive field, and one about 1 mm away (that is, apparently outside the receptive field). Inhibition of the response to the central spot was clearly demon-

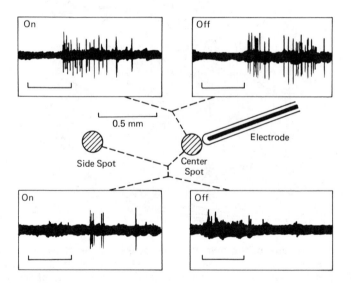

Fig. 3.6. Discharge of ganglion cell produced by central spot in retinal receptive field (upper records) inhibited by side spot (lower records) (from Barlow, 1953).

strated, as is shown in Fig. 3.6. Such "antagonistic" interaction, but from within a single receptive field, was demonstrated by Kuffler (Fig. 3.7) who also showed, by exploring a field with a small light spot, that all three types of response may be obtained from the same receptive field in the cat (Fig. 3.8). The distribution of the three types of response is not random, but follows the well-defined pattern shown in Fig. 3.9.

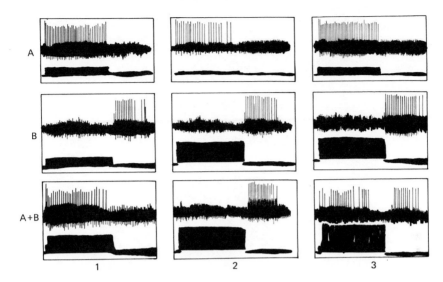

Fig. 3.7. Antagonistic interactions within the receptive field of a cat ganglion cell. Col. 1: (A) Strong "on" response occurs to a spot of light (radius 0.1 mm) shone near the ganglion cell, close to the center of the receptive field; (B) "Off" response occurs to a larger spot (diameter 0.4 mm) shone in the field's periphery; (A + B) When both spots were on simultaneously, the peripheral "off" response is inhibited. Col. 2: Same series, but with A reduced in intensity and B increased. In this case the "on" response of A is inhibited. Col. 3: same series, but with both spots "strong." In this case, A + B shows mutual inhibition of the two responses (from Kuffler, 1953).

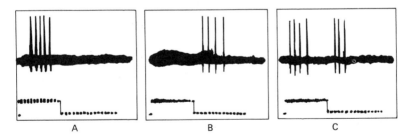

Fig. 3.8. Specific regions within receptive field; 0.2-mm-diameter light spot moved to three different positions within receptive field. A light flash to the region near the electrode tip in (A) causes only "on" discharges in the ganglion cell, while the same stimulus 0.5 mm away is followed by "off" responses (B), and in an intermediate position an "on-off" discharge is set up (C) (from Kuffler, 1953).

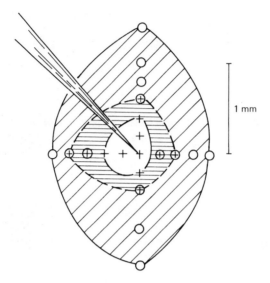

Fig. 3.9. Distribution of discharge patterns within receptive field of ganglion cell (located at tip of electrode). The exploring spot was 0.2 mm in diameter, about 100 times the threshold at the center of the field. Background illumination was approximately 25 mc. In the central region "on" discharges (+) are found, while in the diagonally-hatched part only "off" discharges occur (○). In the intermediary zone (horizontally hatched) discharges are "on-off." A change in conditions of illumination (background, etc.) also altered discharge pattern-distribution (from Kuffler, 1953).

In general, ganglion cell receptive fields in the cat are from 1 to 2 mm in diameter, approximately circular and with an "on" center and "off" periphery, or vice versa. Where suppression of one area by another occurs, it is generally the "on" center that inhibits the "off" surround (or the "on" surround that inhibits the "off" center), although there is some evidence that two "off" areas may be mutually inhibitory (Kuffler, 1953, p. 59).

OPERATIONS AND INTERACTIONS WITHIN RECEPTIVE FIELDS

The mechanism of the three sorts of response has been further clarified by Wagner, MacNichol, and Wolbarsht (1963), working with goldfish. They have found retinal units that code *color* information in receptive fields of the general type already described. However, in this case the field will yield "on" responses for one region of the spectrum and "off" responses for another when the whole field is illuminated. More precisely, in one case the center of the field may apparently give "on" responses to green light, and no response to light of longer wavelengths, whereas the periphery gives "off" responses to red light and no responses to light of shorter wavelength. The cutoff point on the spectrum where the response type changes is quite sharp (Fig. 3.10). By careful exploration of such fields with very small spots, of the optimum "on" and "off" colors, "on" responses (from an "on-center" field) could be obtained over the whole, or nearly the whole, field, but with a very low threshold at the center and a high threshold elsewhere. "Off" responses, on the other hand, which were also elicited over the whole field, had a more even threshold throughout (Figs. 3.10 and 3.11). The net result, given the mutual antagonism of "on" and "off" responses, would be the apparent "on" center and "off" surround described. The same arrangement held in "off"-center fields. It seems reasonable to assume that a similar arrangement of "on" and "off" units exists in the color-nonspecific fields, although it is impossible to prove this since response-specific stimuli (giving only "on" or only "off" signals) are not available. However, the arrangement shown in Fig. 3.8 seems to be most common in the receptive fields of the cat, and is nicely accounted for if one assumes that the narrow "on-off" annulus is the region where "on" and "off" thresholds have similar values. More-

 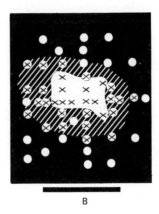

A	B

Fig. 3.10. Receptive field response pattern of "on"- (A) and "off"- (B) center color-coded ganglion cells. The circular stimuli have the following parameters:

	A	B
Intensity	$23\mu W/cm^2$	$18\mu W/cm^2$
Wavelength	550 mμ	600 mμ
Diameter	300 μ	153 μ
Duration	0.5 sec	0.5 sec

"×" indicates an "off" response; ○ indicates an "on" response. Pure "on" regions are shown in black, and "on-off" regions are hatched. The bars under each diagram represent 1 mm on the retina (from Wagner, MacNichol, & Wolbarsht, 1963).

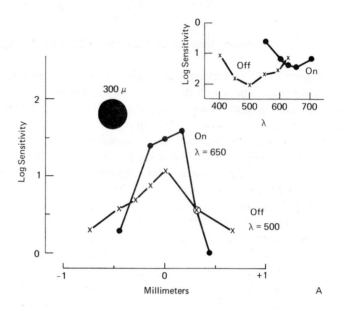

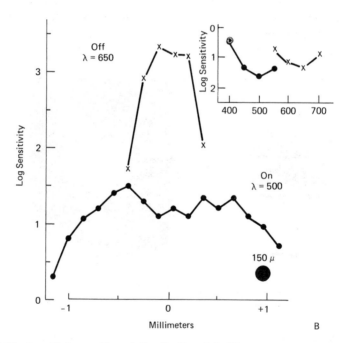

Fig. 3.11. Sensitivity profiles of the "on" and "off" component responses across two receptive fields: (A) "On"-center and (B) "Off"-center colour-coded ganglion cells of the goldfish retina. In the upper-right corner of each panel is the spectral sensitivity for both "on" and "off" systems. The exploring spots were of the wavelength giving maximum responses. Spot sizes are also shown. The lower panels show sensitivity across the receptive fields in terms of the intensity of light required to give a constant discharge rate: That is, the *reciprocal* of the intensity is plotted, so the higher a point on the curve, the less light is required to evoke a given response (from Wagner, MacNichol, & Wolbarsht, 1963).

over, an arrangement of the Wagner-MacNichol-Wolbarsht sort would account for changes in receptive-field "type" with changes in adaptation or strength of stimulation (Kuffler, 1953). This rather neat explanation of "on-off" characteristics of receptive fields is unfortunately somewhat obscured by a recent finding of Daw's (1967, 1968). Working also with the goldfish, Daw demonstrated that the retinal receptive fields are actually as much as five times larger in diameter than MacNichol et al. reported, and that their findings hold only for the central portion of a field. Daw showed that in the larger periphery there is strong spatial summation, and spots of light are ineffective in evoking responses from that region; he showed also that the periphery is color-specific, giving the same type of response as the central area but for the complementary color. Thus, if the center gives an "on" response to a red spot, the periphery gives a reinforcing "on" response to green, and so on. The fields are thus detectors of color contrast as well as for contoured features, or spots. How the two sets of findings (MacNichol et al. on the one hand, Daw on the other) are related is not yet known and awaits further experimental analysis.[1]

We can say, however, that the overall response of a receptive field depends on the position, wavelength, and intensity of light falling upon it even though, as Daw's work shows, the exact extent of a field may be difficult to establish. The state of adaptation within a field is also important. Barlow, Fitzhugh, and Kuffler (1957) found that consistent changes occur in the cat's receptive fields during dark adaptation; surprisingly enough the fields seem to get *smaller* as dark adaptation proceeds and generally to show only one type of response when well dark-adapted. This is probably because the thresholds for both center and periphery fall during dark adaptation, but the former fall much more than the latter (Hubel, personal communication). In the same vein, Kuffler found in his earlier studies that changes in receptive field characteristics occur with changes in background illumination. The precise limits of a field are usually indeterminate because thresholds become high at the periphery, and the use of intense stimuli entails problems of light scattering. Receptive fields do, however, differ consistently in the sizes of their centers, the limits of which are more readily established; generally smaller field centers are found near the fovea, and larger ones towards the periphery, at least in the cat (Wiesel, 1960) and spider monkey (Hubel & Wiesel, 1960). Presumably this arrangement is common to all visual systems with well-defined central areas for detail vision.

[1] It is perhaps worth pointing out that color coding in more central units in mammalian visual systems (Wiesel & Hubel, 1966; De Valois, 1960; Michael, 1966) seems to correspond to the MacNichol type ("on" center to red, "off" periphery to green, and so forth) rather than the Daw type chromatic coding.

We thus see that vertebrate retinas have a system for the extraction of information about sharp changes in illumination since the receptive field response will tend to be greatest when the states of illumination are different in its center and periphery. Also the process of *lateral inhibition* obviously plays a fundamental role, as it does in the visual system of limulus. However, so far we have seen no evidence that contours as such are coded in a particular way, or that the system is designed specifically to extract information about contours. To show that such specific coding is indeed built into the mammalian visual system, we turn now to consideration of the brilliant series of investigations by Hubel and Wiesel on receptive field organization. Working principally with cats, they have extended the technique of single-cell recording to the lateral geniculate bodies and to the visual cortex.[2]

In order to facilitate understanding of the following pages by readers unfamiliar with the gross anatomy of the mammalian visual system, a highly schematized diagram of its major components is given in Fig. 3.12. Transduction of the optical information on the retina into the electrochemical energy of nervous discharge is accomplished via the photoreceptors, intermediate retinal structures, and ganglion cells (Fig. 3.5). The receptive field properties of retinal ganglion cells have already been described; the information output from these cells is transmitted—probably without essential modification—through the optic nerve and optic tract to the lateral geniculate bodies of the thalamus. The amount of crossing of fibers at the chiasma varies between species, the arrangement illustrated in Fig. 3.12 being the complete mixing characteristic of man. The lateral geniculate bodies (l.g.b.'s) are "relay stations" between the retinas and the visual cortex of the brain, each l.g.b. having a well-defined six-fold layered structure. Cells in each layer synapse with fibers from only one eye, but adjacent layers receive their inputs from corresponding regions of the two eyes, which suggests very strongly that these structures perform some sort of "binocular mixing" function. The axons of l.g.b. neurons form the optic radiations, which transmit directly to the visual cortex where they synapse with cortical neurons.[3] The primary (striate) visual cortex also has a layered structure, but there are rich interconnections among neurons both within and between layers, so that the morphology suggests extremely complex relations between the activities of different cells or groups of cells.

---

[2] It is not established that the properties to be described are common to all mammals, or that there may not be differences of detail in different species. However, the main features are certainly found in cat, monkey, and rabbit.

[3] A certain proportion of the l.g.b. neurons have axial connections with other parts of the brain, but these do not concern us here.

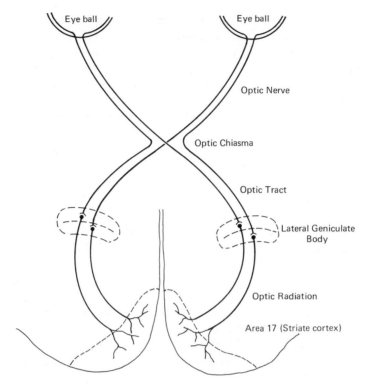

Fig. 3.12. Macrostructure of the visual system of man, shown schematically. All mammalian systems are somewhat similar, although the amount of fiber crossing, convergence at the l.g.b.'s, and representation of the half-retinas in the cortex vary in different species. The diagram is highly simplified, and only two of the l.g.b. layers are shown. No attempt is made to give an accurate representation of terminal arborizations within area 17.

The major sites from which electrophysiological recordings are made correspond to the different levels of neurons within the system—the retina (principally ganglion cells), the lateral geniculate bodies, and the visual cortex. As we shall see later, recording at the cortical level is not limited to the striate area, but has also been achieved successfully in the adjacent so-called visual association areas.

RECEPTIVE FIELD CHARACTERISTICS FOR CELLS OF THE LATERAL GENICULATE BODIES

The earlier work of Kuffler on ganglion cell receptive fields was confirmed by Hubel and Wiesel (1962) and essentially the same type of organization for single units in the lateral geniculate bodies (l.g.b.'s) discovered. That is to say, the receptive fields for l.g.b. cells are all more or less circular, with an "on" center and "off" surround, or vice versa, and the parts of the field are mutually inhibitory. As with ganglion cells, the fields are defined by exploring the retina with a small spot of light to determine those areas that cause activity in the particular cell from which recordings are being made. The l.g.b. fields are nearly always uniocular; that is, a particular cell can be fired from only one eye, and the functional arrangement corresponds to the well-established anatomical organization, in which different layers of cells are fed by fibers from the two eyes, and the cells which receive from corresponding parts of the two retinas are "lined up" in the different laminae, one above the other (Hubel & Wiesel, 1961). Moreover, electrode penetrations that are perpendicular to the layered structure of the l.g.b. encounter successive units within a layer, all of which have receptive fields in the same part of the retina. Other workers have claimed to find binocularly driven cells in the l.g.b. (for example, Bishop, Burke, & Davis, 1962b) and there is evidence that cells in the interlaminar regions receive fibers from both eyes. However, it is clear that binocular interaction in the l.g.b. is relatively unimportant, in the sense that very few cells are driven in a similar manner by both eyes. Some recent evidence (Suzuki & Kato, 1966) suggests that the nondriving eye may affect a unit in the l.g.b. only indirectly by postsynaptic inhibition.

It is of great interest to note that in some cases Hubel and Wiesel made simultaneous recordings from an optic tract fiber (a ganglion cell axon) and a geniculate cell, the optic tract fiber being one of the inputs to the geniculate cell from which the recordings are made.[4] This situation is shown in Fig. 3.13A, where the geniculate cell response is distinguished from that of the optic tract fiber in terms of amplitude and polarity. The two responses to a spot of increasing size demonstrate a "sharpening" of response to light spots at the l.g.b., further clarified in Fig. 3.13B, which shows that the threshold for response to a large-diameter spot rises steeply for the geniculate cell but not for the fiber. The "sharpening" effect is common to all the simultaneous pairs studied, and, in general, geniculate cells are even less readily triggered by diffuse light than are ganglion cells. Such findings, as Hubel and Wiesel point out, make it fairly certain that there must be multiple inputs to the geniculate cells, and that the receptive fields for such cells are not simple replicates of the ganglion cell fields.

---

[4] The fact that the particular optic tract fiber was an input to the particular l.g.b. cell from which recordings were taken is proven by the fact that the former so often triggered the latter.

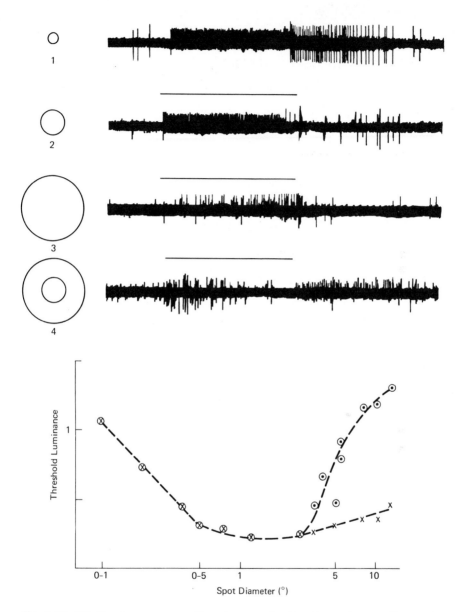

Fig. 3.13. (A) Simultaneous recordings from an "on"-center optic tract fiber and an "off-center lateral geniculate cell. The fiber signals are the small, upward, positive spikes characteristic of fiber responses; the l.g.b. cell responses are the larger positive-negative spikes. On the left is the stimulus used, on the right the corresponding responses. The dark bar above the records shows when the stimulus was on (duration 1 sec). 1, 2, and 3 are centered light spots, 1, 2, and 8° in diameter. 4 is an annulus, inner diameter 2°, outer diameter 8°. (B) Thresholds for an "off"-center l.g.b. cell ($\odot$) and an associated optic tract synaptic potential ($\times$) measured for various spot diameters (from Hubel & Wiesel, 1961).

RECEPTIVE FIELD CHARACTERISTICS FOR CORTICAL CELLS: CONTOUR CODING

Turning now to the visual area of the cerebral cortex, we find that recording from single cells has revealed processes of contour information extraction of amazing precision, not hinted at by the known morphology. Hubel and Wiesel's 1962 paper on recording from the cat's visual cortex is the most important single contribution to our understanding of the neurophysiological basis for contour coding, and has strongly influenced psychologists' thinking about modeling of the system. The authors write:

> What chiefly distinguishes cerebral cortex from other parts of the central nervous system is the great diversity of its cell types and interconnections. It would be astonishing if such a structure did not profoundly modify the response pattern of fibres coming into it. In the cat's visual cortex, the receptive field arrangements of single cells suggest that there is indeed a degree of complexity far exceeding anything yet seen at lower levels in the visual system (Hubel & Wiesel, 1962, p. 106).

Indeed, one might go further and suggest that it is even surprising that receptive fields for single cells can be mapped at all at the cortex. With so many cell types and such complicated interconnections between them, one might suppose that the interactions between cells and cell types would be so intricate and involved as to defy analysis, particularly when recordings are made from only one cell at a time. On the contrary the system, insofar as it has been investigated, turns out to have an economy, and even simplicity, that is truly remarkable.

For many cortical neurons in the primary visual area (17) it is possible to define a receptive field in the way already familiar for lower visual centers, that is, to map out "on" and "off" areas with a spot of light shone on to the retina. These Hubel and Wiesel call "simple receptive fields." As before, their "on" and "off" areas are mutually antagonistic, but various field shapes are found, none of which is circular. Figure 3.14C–G shows the most commonly found field shapes. The static stimulus for any receptive field that is maximally effective is one which covers all the "on" area and none of the "off," or vice versa, so it is immediately obvious that these cells respond selectively to straight contours (bright slits of light) in a particular orientation and position on the retina, in most cases to isolated contours on a featureless background, or in some (G, for example) to light-dark edges. About two-thirds of the receptive fields classified were of types C, D, and E; that is to say, the associated neurons fired selectively for narrow slits or isolated contours. Exploring the units' responses with contoured and/or moving stimuli shows that

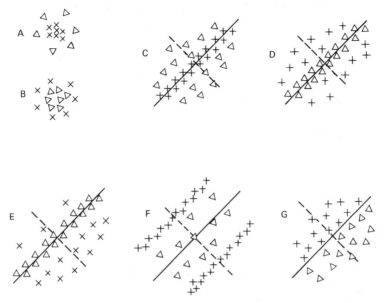

Fig. 3.14. Common arrangements of lateral geniculate and cortical receptive fields: (A) "On"-center geniculate receptive field; (B) "Off"-center geniculate receptive field; (C–G) various arrangements of simple cortical receptive fields; "×" areas give excitatory responses ("on" responses); "Δ" areas give inhibitory responses ("off" responses). Receptive field axes are shown by continuous lines through field centers; in the figure these are all oblique, but each arrangement occurs in all orientations (from Hubel & Wiesel, 1962).

the cells are sensitive to quite small changes of contour orientation, a change of 5–10° being sufficient to reduce the response greatly, if not to abolish it. Moving stimuli, either spots or contours, are particularly effective, but in the case of contours the orientation is again critical, as is the direction of movement, which must be perpendicular to the field orientation. No doubt movement responses, and particularly responses to the movement of a "correctly" oriented contour across the field, are particularly effective because of the synergistic properties of the system. A contour moving across field C of Fig. 3.14 in a direction perpendicular to the field's axis, for instance, would elicit an "off" response on leaving the surround, but simultaneously an "on" response on entering the central portion.[5]

---

[5] Hubel and Wiesel talk of "excitatory" and "inhibitory," areas of a receptive field, and this is the usual terminology, rather than "on" and "off" areas. However, the latter terminology seems preferable, since in fact both types are a form of excitation, and they are mutually antagonistic, or inhibitory. "On" activity is then both excitatory *and* inhibitory, depending on the measurement or operation in question.

An even higher stage of organization is represented by the so-called complex fields. Some cells were found whose different regions could not be mapped with a spot of light, since they gave either very little response at all or an "on-off" response. However, such cells could be fired by patterned stimuli of the type that are characteristically optimal for simple fields—that is, by contours or edges in specific orientations. But the most striking difference between simple and complex fields is that in the latter the strict localization required for optimal (static) stimulation no longer holds, and summation of "on" and "off" activity occurs only in a special way. Figure 3.15 shows the response of a typical complex field. On the left the stimulus used is shown in relation to the center of the field; a horizontal slit projected to the upper half of the field elicits "off" responses only, and the same stimulus projected at the center or lower elicits "on" responses. It should be emphasized that summation within a field occurs only in one special way—widening the slit (as in F and G) causes a response decrement, and in fact a slit only $\frac{1}{8}°$ across is optimal. However, summation in the horizontal dimension *does* occur; that is, a horizontal slit less than the width of the field elicits a smaller response than one that extends across the whole field. This field is less common than the type which gives a uniform response over the whole field, such as "on" activity to a horizontal contour anywhere within it (Fig. 3.16). The latter type made up over 55 percent of all the complex fields accurately mapped. Other common types are activated by an edge, or a dark bar (as opposed to the light slit usually used). As in simple fields, the orientation of the stimulating contour is critical, as is illustrated in Fig. 3.16. Complex fields, even more than simple fields, tend to be most responsive to movement of an appropriately oriented contour, and in some cases there is a preferred direction of motion (for example, up-to-down, rather than down-to-up). The movement sensitivity is again always for a direction perpendicular to the contour's orientation. While there is a variety of complex fields, they all share in common the main features described; that is, they respond scarcely at all to diffuse illumination or spots of light, and the "preferred" stimulus is always a contour or edge in a specific orientation. Exact location of the contour within the field is not critical. Better responses are elicited by narrow contours and sharp edges than by less-sharp gradients, and summation occurs only for contour length in the preferred orientation. Movement selectivity is also high. It is as if the complex fields have as inputs the outputs from a set of simple fields all of the same type, as indeed Hubel and Wiesel suggest. Thus the responses of the complex field of Fig. 3.16 would be expected if its inputs were a series of simple fields like C in Fig. 3.14, with a common orientation but different positions, and if its threshold were high enough to ensure that it was fired

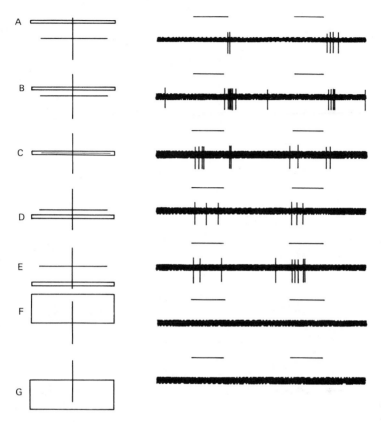

Fig. 3.15. Responses of a cell with a complex receptive field to stimulation of the left (contralateral) eye. The receptive fields located in the area centralis. The diagrams to the left of each record indicate the position of a horizontal rectangular light stimulus with respect to the receptive field, marked by a cross. In each record the upper line indicates when the stimulus is on. (A–E) stimulus $\frac{1}{2} \times 3°$, (F–G) stimulus $1\frac{1}{2} \times 3°$ (4° is equivalent to 1 mm on the cat retina). The cell was activated in the same way from the right eye, but less vigorously. Positive deflexions upward; the duration of each stimulus was 1 sec (from Hubel & Wiesel, 1962).

only by an optimal, or near-optimal, discharge from one or more of that set. Actually, a further qualification is required, since this complex field responds only with "on" activity, and the maximum "on" and "off" responses of the simple fields are usually of about equal strength. There are some further difficulties of a similar nature which might lead one to question the "simple hierarchical" arrangement, although that arrangement seems to be a natural one to account for the main findings.

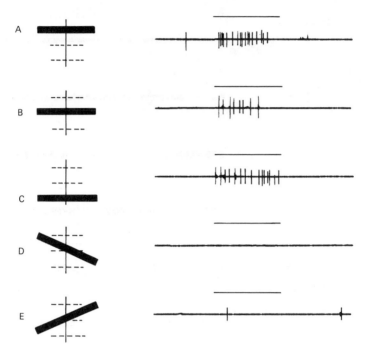

Fig. 3.16. Cell activated only by left (contralateral) eye over a field approximately $5 \times 5°$, situated $10°$ above and to the left of the area centralis. The cell responded best to a black horizontal rectangle, $\frac{1}{3} \times 6°$, placed anywhere in the receptive field (A–C). Tilting the stimulus rendered it ineffective (D–E). The black bar was introduced against a light background during periods of 1 sec, indicated by the upper line in each record (from Hubel & Wiesel, 1962).

BINOCULAR EFFECTS AND CYTOARCHITECTURE FOR CORTICAL CELLS

Another great difference between cells in the visual cortex, as compared to the l.g.b., is that a high proportion of them—over 80 percent—are responsive to stimulation of both eyes, and a few give a good response *only* when both eyes are stimulated. Again, a clear and specific organization is found. The two receptive fields for a particular cell are always found in closely corresponding parts of the two retinas, are always of the same type and size, and always have similarly oriented principle axes. The modal "binocular" cell is about equally driven by stimulation of either eye; there is otherwise a preponderance of cells that are more responsive to the contralateral eye than the ipsilateral one (although quite a few cells "prefer" the ipsilateral eye), and this is true for both simple and complex fields. Also the phenomenon of "recruitment" is frequently observed; the response of a cell to proper stimulation of both eyes simultaneously is greater than the sum of the individual effects. Thus we see that the coding is highly precise and specific, not only for each eye separately, but also for the functioning of the two eyes simultaneously when identical patterns are projected to corresponding parts of the two retinas. Moreover, and this is a very important point, the mutual antagonism of "on" and "off" processes also holds for binocularly driven cells. If "on" activity is generated from one eye and "off" activity from the other by stimulating the two receptive fields appropriately, the two processes inhibit one another, and the cortical cell is silent or responds only weakly.

How are the cells for different receptive field types distributed in the visual cortex? One might suppose that the different types and different orientations are randomly distributed, so that in each part of the visual area detectors for each type of contour information are equally represented. On the contrary, an amazing degree of precision in organization occurs, and again—so far as is yet known—the principles of this organization are beautifully clear and simple. Figure 3.17 shows the reconstruction of an electrode track through the visual cortex of a cat. The crosslines indicate receptive field orientations, and it is immediately clear that in the first part of the track, where its path is normal to the surface of the brain, all the field orientations are the same. After passing through the white matter this situation no longer holds, although neighboring clusters of units still have the same orientations. This is typical of all the probes, and indicates that the primary visual area is organized into columns, each of which consists of units with similarly oriented fields. There appears to be some clustering of field *types* within a column, too, although this is not particularly regular. Both these arrangements would clearly facilitate the sort of integrative action between simple and complex fields discussed above, especially since the fields for units within a column all tend to be in the same retinal region and show a considerable degree of overlap. However, penetrations within a single column do not reveal precise superposition of the fields of neighboring units or an orderly progression of the position of the fields with recordings from neighboring columns, so it may be concluded that, at the cellular level, no exact topographical representation of the retina is present in the cortex; earlier anatomical evidence had established a gross topographical correspondence, of course (see discussion in Chapter 7). The cross-sectional shape and area of columns has been shown to vary considerably (Hubel & Wiesel, 1963a), but there is evidence that in monkeys the columnar arrangement is even denser and more precise than in cats. Thus, there can be little doubt that it plays an important role in detail vision and sensory integration.

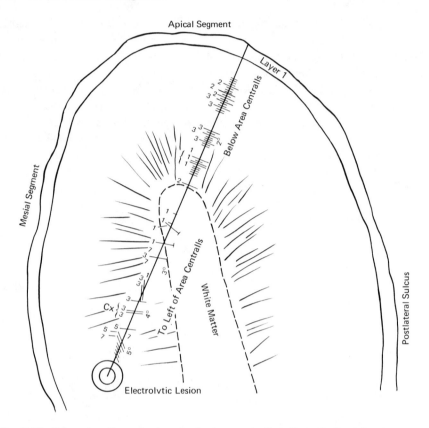

Fig. 3.17. Reconstruction of microelectrode penetration through the lateral gyrus of the visual cortex (area 17). Successive recordings were made as the electrode tip was pushed in, step by step. The longer lines crossing the electrode track represent single-unit responses of cortical neurons, the field axis being shown by line orientation. Lines perpendicular to the track are for vertically oriented fields. The approximate position of fields on the retina is indicated, and brackets show simultaneous recordings. The shorter lines represent regions in which unresolved background activity was observed (from Hubel & Wiesel, 1962).

THE CODING SYSTEM IN VERY YOUNG KITTENS

The system for contour coding so far described is present in all essentials in the kitten at or very soon after birth. In a series of papers (Hubel & Wiesel, 1963b, 1965b; Wiesel & Hubel, 1965a, b) it was established that recordings from kittens soon after the eyes had opened showed the familiar types of receptive fields for cortical cells, although the responses were more sluggish than in the adult. Forced disuse of one eye, either by suture or a light-diffusing occluder, leads to impairment of the system, and in the former case to atrophy of cells at the l.g.b. The impairment is most severe in very young kittens (if the closure is maintained for some weeks) and there is practically no recovery of function.[6] No similar impairment is found in a normal adult cat if one eye is occluded for a similar length of time. The conclusion is, of course, that the system requires use in the young organism to maintain its properties, although it is essentially "built in." By producing squint artificially, Hubel and Wiesel also showed that it is not simply *amount* of stimulation that is required to maintain the system, but stimulation that is congruent to the two eyes. A kitten with squint should receive, on average, about equal stimulation to the two eyes. Yet a severe impairment of the system can be demonstrated in terms of a change in the proportion of binocularly driven cells (from about 80 percent to 20 percent), although both eyes give completely "normal" cortical-unit responses in other respects. It is as if a cell simply loses its connections to the nondominant input, if that is incongruent with the dominant input. This is further evidence of the high degree of specificity and delicacy of the processing system.

CODING IN CORTICAL CELLS IN THE HIGHER VISUAL AREAS

In a further paper (1965a) Hubel and Wiesel continued their exploration beyond the striate, primary, visual cortex in cats (area 17) into the so-called visual association areas, 18 and 19. Their neurophysiological findings accord well with the anatomical divisions which are shown in Fig. 3.18. Whereas in area 17 (called visual area I) nearly all units had receptive fields of the types described as simple and complex mixed together, visual area II (or 18) had a great preponderance of units with large complex fields (over 90 percent) and no simple field units at all. A new type of field, to be described shortly, and termed "hypercomplex," was discovered here (area II) and formed about 50 percent of the units' fields in visual area III (or 19).[7] Again, no simple fields were found for cells in visual area III. Futhermore, the hypercomplex fields themselves could be divided into two categories, of lower and higher order, both types being found in both visual areas II and III.

The hypercomplex field units represent a new level of contour information processing, in one sense more specific than that of ordinary complex fields, but also—for the higher-order type—at a higher level of abstraction.

---

[6] Recently the "sensitive period" has been narrowed down to between the fourth and sixth weeks of life, at which time deprivation of normal vision even for two or three days leads to markedly abnormal physiology (Hubel, personal communication).

[7] Subsequently a few cells with hypercomplex fields have been found in area 17, for both the cat and monkey (Hubel & Wiesel, 1968).

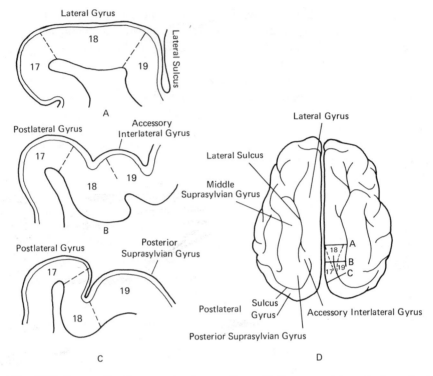

Fig. 3.18. Composite diagram showing on the right the general layout of cerebral cortex of cat, indicating the boundaries between visual areas 17, 18, and 19. A–C show three sections through the visual cortex (also identified in D) which give an idea of the cortical folds (from Hubel & Wiesel, 1965*a*).

They share with other cortical units the characteristics of being mostly binocular, with the receptive fields of both eyes in homonymous areas and of the same type; of being fired by specifically oriented contours, and of being sensitive to movement. Indeed one gets the impression that most hypercomplex field units are *primarily* responsive to highly specific moving contours. The high degree of specificity of a low-order hypercomplex unit's response is demonstrated in Fig. 3.19A–D. Such a unit is called a "stopped-edge" unit, and the reason for this description becomes obvious enough if the responses elicited by different contour arrangements are compared. Figure 3.19A shows that the field has an excitatory region for the edge oriented at 2 o'clock–7 o'clock, which is indicated by the left half of the interrupted rectangle. The right half of this rectangle is "inhibitory," as is demonstrated in Fig. 3.19A4–5. Also, 3.19B particularly shows that the unit is not simply a "corner" detector. Summation clearly occurs along the contour in the preferred direction (3.19A1–3), which is cancelled by its excursion into the antagonistic region (3.19A4–5 and 3.19B3–6). In 3.19B one sees that the inhibitory effects of the right-hand region of the receptive field are also orientation-specific. The greatest inhibition occurs when the contours on the two parts of the field are similarly oriented. Figure 3.19C shows summation of inhibition within the right-hand part of the field, as does 3.19A4 and 5. Finally, 3.19D shows how a "step" in the contour affects the cell's firing. Putting the characteristics illustrated in 3.19 together, one can see why Hubel and Wiesel characterized this cell as a "single stopped-edge" detector. The new complexity of its response characteristics scarcely needs comment.

A remarkable characteristic of hypercomplex fields is that they do not demonstrate "off" effects, although they all have regions of well-defined inhibitory power.

A second hypercomplex field (also low-order) is shown in Fig. 3.20. This field's response is highly selective, for a "double-stopped" contour (compare 3.20A and 3.19C) of a specific width (3.20A) orientation (3.20B) and position (3.20D). Interestingly enough, this cell responded well both to a bright edge on a darker field and to the reverse arrangement (3.20A and D). This characteristic is found only occasionally in ordinary complex field units and it represents an even higher level of abstraction; contour per se is registered, rather than a brightness change of a particular type (light-dark or vice versa).

An example of a hypercomplex unit of higher order is shown in Fig. 3.21A–C. This is again a unit primarily responsive to a moving edge, in this case, double-stopped. Clearly, the unit is not selective for positions within the field (3.21A) but is for width (3.21B). Surprisingly, in view of previous findings, this same field was also responsive to a double-stopped edge at 90° to the original, both in orientation and movement (3.21C). Ability to respond to two contours at 90° to each other appears to be a common feature of higher-order hypercomplex field units.

Hubel and Wiesel point out that, as before, many features of the hyper-complex units can be understood if they are thought of as units whose inputs are the outputs of lower units: For example, one might think of the single-stopped unit of Fig. 3.19 as having inputs from a set of units with complex fields that are excitatory for a light-dark edge in the appropriate orientation over the left half of the field, and a similar set of inputs from antagonistic complex field units for the right half. High-order hyper-complex field units may similarly be thought of as having inputs from low-order hypercomplex units. Further evidence in favor of such a scheme is found in the fact that units in visual areas II and III are arranged in the same sort of columnar structure with similarly oriented fields as in visual area I. However, there are still some problems with this sort of explanation, although it may be correct in principle. The difficulty

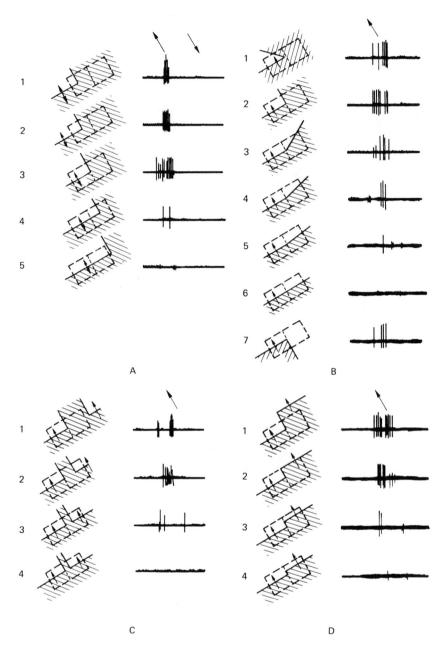

Fig. 3.19. (A) Recordings from a hypercomplex cell in visual II on stimulation of right (ipsilateral) eye, with strong ocular dominance. Receptive field, $2 \times 4°$, is indicated by interrupted rectangle. The stimulus consisted of an edge oriented at 2 o'clock–7 o'clock with dark below, terminated on the right by a second edge intersecting the first at 90°. (1–3) Up-and-down movement across varying amounts of the activating portion of the field; (4–5) Movement across all of the

of reconciling the mutually inhibitory functions of "on" and "off" activities at lower levels with proposed inhibitory functions that do not involve "off" activity at the higher levels was mentioned before. It is also not clear how the time-course of "on" and "off" activities to moving stimuli in lower units affects excitation and inhibition of hypercomplex units, which are, it seems, principally responsive to moving contours.

At all events, Hubel and Wiesel have demonstrated in a most remarkable manner how contour information is processed, to a very high level of abstraction, in the visual system of the cat. Clearly they have not said the last word on investigation of contour coding by recording from single units in the visual system. As they themselves point out, still more complex receptive units may yet be discovered, and how far this process can go is anybody's guess. At some stage of investigation one surely must expect to find units whose activity is dependent on, or at least influenced by, perceptual learning. This *could* be true of the units with hypercomplex fields since the presence of the different sorts of unit has as yet been verified in newborn kittens only up to the level of complex fields. However, it seems rather likely, in view of the common cytoarchitectural arrangement of units in all three visual areas investigated, that the properties of hypercomplex units are also essentially innate.

OTHER EVIDENCE ON SHAPE AND MOVEMENT DETECTORS

It is rather unlikely that precisely the same sorts of arrangement for contour coding and movement detection exist in other species—even in other mammals—and perhaps other principles will be found to operate

---

Fig. 3.19. (*Continued*)
activating portion and varying amounts of the antagonistic portion. Rate of movement was 4°/sec. Duration of each sweep was 2 sec. (B) Stimulation with two intersecting edges moved up across the receptive field as shown. Inhibition is maximum when the right (antagonistic) half of the receptive field is stimulated with an edge having the same orientation as the optimum edge for the left (activating) half (6). Duration of each sweep was 2 sec. (C) Each time an optimally oriented stopped edge was moved up across the activating (left) part of the receptive field at optimal speed (2°/sec), a second edge was simultaneously moved up to the right of the first, at varying distances. The antagonistic effect, first noted about 2° from the boundary between the two parts of the field, increased the closer the edge was to this boundary. Duration of each sweep was 2 sec. (D) The two halves of the field were stimulated simultaneously by two edges separated by a step of varying height: Antagonistic effects were first seen when the step equaled the width of the field, and increased as the step was narrowed to about ½°, after which no change was seen. Duration of each sweep was 2 sec (from Hubel & Wiesel, 1965a).

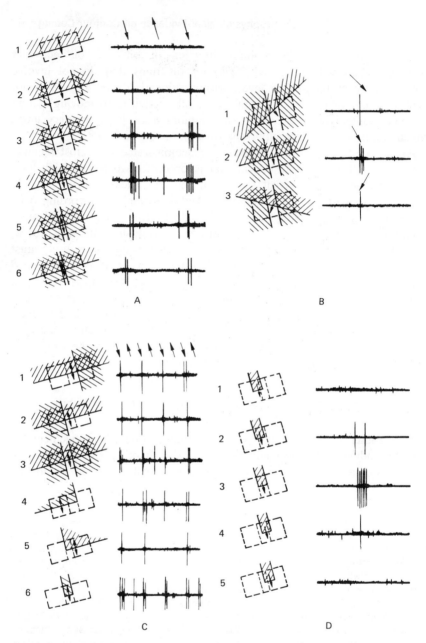

Fig. 3.20. (A) Recordings from a cell in area 19 of the right hemisphere to stimulation of left eye. Receptive field was about 8° below the center of gaze, about 13° long and 6° wide. Rapid (30°/sec.) up-and-down movement of a long edge with dark above evoked no response (1). Responses to downward movement began to appear when the stimulus was limited in its length (2, 3), and became maximal when a 2½°-wide region in the center was stimulated (4), at which point an occasional response occurred even to upward movement. Further

in the cat's visual system too. For example, although it is generally agreed that the commonest type of l.g.b. cell in the cat has a circular "on" or "off" field with opposite surround, a few other types have recently been reported by Bishop and his associates, including some that are directionally sensitive (Kozak, Rodieck, & Bishop, 1965; Spinelli, 1966[8]). Although such units have not been discovered in the retina of the cat (Rodieck & Stone, 1965a), they have been found in the retina of the rabbit (Barlow, Hill, & Levick, 1964), frog (Maturana, Lettvin, McCulloch, & Pitts, 1960), and pigeon (Maturana & Frenk, 1963), as well as more centrally in the visual systems of several species. Similarly, it has already been pointed out that the organization of receptive fields for ganglion cells in the frog is not the same as in the cat and is different again from that found in rats (Brown & Rojas, 1965). Baumgartner, Brown, and Schultz (1965) have reported *cortical* units in the cat whose receptive fields are radially symmetrical (that is, are apparently circular), at least for some types of stimuli, suggesting perhaps that further investigation of cortical-unit field types in visual area I may be worthwhile. Finally, MacIlwain (1964) and subsequently Levick, Oyster, and Davis (1965) have found that both ganglion cells and l.g.b. cells can be influenced by stimuli falling many degrees outside their receptive fields, as usually defined—a finding that may be thought to cast some doubt on the concept of a circumscribed receptive field for each ganglion cell and higher unit that has become so firmly established in the last few years.

At a slightly greater remove, the well-known investigation of shape and movement detection in the frog of Maturana et al. (1960) should be mentioned. They found five main types of detector units, all retinal ganglion

---

[8] Some doubts about the firmness of this evidence have been expressed (Hubel, personal communication); see Barlow, Levick, and Westheimer (1966).

Fig. 3.20. (*Continued*)
narrowing made the response weaker (5 and 6). Duration of each sweep was 1 sec. (B) Effects of varying the orientation of the edge. Duration of each sweep was 1 sec. (C) In 1 and 2 portions of the field to the right and left of the $2\frac{1}{2}°$-wide center were blocked separately, to show that the more important antagonistic region is to the right. The equivalent experiment was repeated in 4 and 5, using dark corners. In 6, which corresponds to 3, a dark tongue was used instead of an edge blocked to either side—a dark tongue moved in from above (6) is equivalent to a light tongue moved out from below (3). Duration of each sweep was 2 sec. (D) A dark tongue $2\frac{1}{2}°$ wide crossed the receptive field from above downward, in different positions. Maximum excitation occurred when the central (activating) strip of field was stimulated. Varying the position by $\frac{1}{2}°$ either way greatly reduced the response. Duration of each sweep was 1 sec (from Hubel & Wiesel, 1965a).

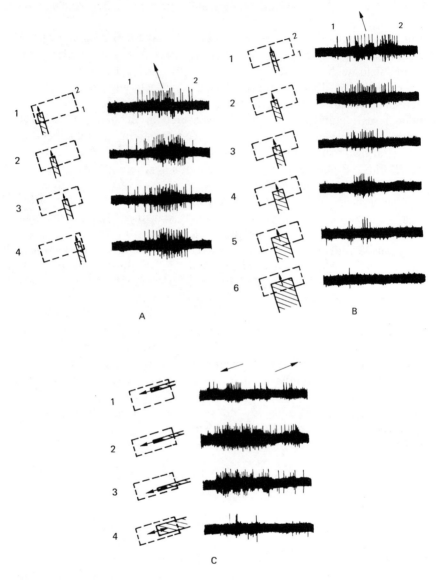

Fig. 3.21. (A) Responses of a cell recorded in area 19, right hemisphere. Region from which responses were evoked, $4° \times 1\frac{1}{2}°$, is indicated approximately by the interrupted rectangle. (A) Responses to a dark tongue $\frac{1}{2}°$ wide introduced from below in four different positions, at a rate of about $0.5°$/sec. Duration of each sweep was 5 sec. (B) Effects of varying the width of tongue. Movement from below up over the center of field was at a rate of $0.5°$/sec. Widths are (1) $\frac{1}{4}°$, (2) $\frac{1}{2}°$, (3) $\frac{3}{4}°$, (4) $1°$, (5) $1\frac{1}{2}°$, and (6) $2°$; optimum width is $\frac{1}{2}°$. Duration of each sweep was 5 sec. (C 1–3) Responses to a dark $\frac{1}{4}°$ tongue moved across the field from right to left in various positions as shown, at a rate of $1°$/sec. (4) Response to a $1°$ tongue moved across field. Duration of each sweep was 10 sec. (from Hubel & Wiesel, 1965a).

70

cells, whose axons terminate in different layers of the optic tectum. Essentially, all processing appears to go on at the ganglion cell level. The authors relate this, reasonably enough, to the high survival value of quick detection of a few features of the visual environment for the frog, and the fact that its retina has many more cells than the tectum (in a ratio of about 15:1). Comparing this with the very different arrangements discovered in the cat, Hubel and Wiesel say:

> At first glance, it may seem astonishing that the third-order neurones in the frog's visual system should be equalled only by that of sixth-order neurones in the geniculate cortical pathway of the cat. Yet this is less surprising if one notes the great anatomical differences in the two animals, especially the lack, in the frog, of any cortex or dorsal lateral geniculate body. There is undoubtedly a parallel difference in the use each animal makes of its visual system: the frog's visual apparatus is presumably specialized to recognize a limited number of stereotyped patterns or situations, compared with the high acuity and versatility found in the cat. Probably it is not so unreasonable to find that in the cat the specialization of cells for complex operations is postponed to a higher level, and that, when it does occur, it is carried out by a vast number of cells, and in great detail (Hubel & Wiesel, 1962, p. 150).

In other words, we have here an example of the well-established biological principle of encephalization. Where the process of detection and recognition is "postponed" until the cortex is activated, a far higher degree of flexibility is achieved.

At an even further remove, we may consider again briefly the coding of contour and movement by the eye of limulus. Here pattern coding is 100 percent peripheral, so far as is known: One might even say that particular patterns of stimulation over the whole compound eye impose transient receptive fields for each receptor as they occur. It is very doubtful whether such "fields" have much in common with vertebrate ganglion cell receptive fields; but it is also intriguing to discover that the limulus optic fibers can be "programmed" to give the three types of response— "on," "off," and "on-off"—characteristic of more developed systems, by appropriately controlled external patterns of stimulation (Ratliff, Hartline, & Miller, 1963).

The field of single-unit recording in the visual system is under intensive investigation, and no doubt new findings will make us review and revise our concepts of visual coding for shape and movement. Already the scheme of things is a good deal more complicated than was at first envisaged, and a number of quite elaborate coding activities seem to occur fairly far peripherally even in the mammalian system. Also, specific codings for other sorts of feature, particularly movement and binocular disparity (see Chapter 7) have started to emerge. However, it seems unlikely that very profound changes will have to be made in the general coding scheme for the cat discovered by Hubel and Wiesel, whatever changes of detail and emphasis may be called for.[9] It will be of enormous interest to know how far these same principles operate, in general and in detail, in higher visual systems closer to that of man. So far, the little evidence available indicates that the arrangement of receptive fields and of cytoarchitecture are quite similar, in general, at least in cat and monkey. Almost as intriguing is the question whether the same sorts of principle apply over a fairly broad range at the upper end of the phylogenetic scale (for all mammals, for instance). So far, there is little enough evidence on this point, but what there is suggests an affirmative answer.

[9] One argument we can dismiss at once: It has been maintained that, on detailed investigation, many of the receptive field types turn out not to be quite as simple and symmetrical as was at first thought by Hubel and Wiesel, so therefore the cortical units for those receptive fields cannot have the sorts of simple coding functions that have been suggested for them. The argument is irrelevant because, even if there is less regularity in the system than was at first claimed (and conversation with a number of neurophysiologists in the field has convinced me that there is wide disagreement on the point), this does *not* show that the detecting or computing functions are more complicated. What it more plausibly suggests is that the computations are carried out by "noisy" modules; and the argument then becomes trivial since it is known that computations carried out by modules having a given noise factor (unreliability) can be made arbitrarily reliable by increasing the size (and redundancy) of the network. See Arbib (1964), pp. 83–90.

CHAPTER 4
Relations Between Neurophysiological and Behavioral Evidence on Contour Coding

SOME PRACTICAL DIFFICULTIES FOR SPECIFYING SHAPE CODES

A large number of experiments on discrimination learning in animals have been reported, many of them quite relevant to the question of shape recognition. Older studies (up to about 1961) are summarized and discussed by Sutherland (1962). There are considerable problems in trying to devise discriminanda that can be used to obtain unambiguous evidence about the shape-recognition characteristics of a particular species; these problems arise mainly from the fact that it is difficult to ensure that the experimental subjects really base their discriminations on those aspects of the stimulus display which are of interest to the experimenter. For example, it is easy enough to train a rat in a jumping stand to discriminate between a circle and an equilateral triangle with a horizontal base (Lashley, 1938), but it is by no means certain that the discrimination is necessarily based on the bare recognition of the two shapes. Thus, the rat might base its discrimination on parts of the display only, for instance, approaching any shape with a horizontal base and avoiding others; it might base it on a difference in brightness (although this is usually controlled) or "brightness gradient," where the shapes have different amounts of contour in different quadrants (a triangle has an asymmetrical gradient, a circle a symmetrical one, for example); or it might base it on something

73

as indefinite as what one might call "subjective size." It is not even possible, in some cases, to be sure that the discrimination is visual, as cues based on smell have not been adequately controlled. These are the more obvious possibilities, and no doubt there are others. The point is that, unless very careful control is exercised, and other possibilities are eliminated, no firm statement about *shape* recognition per se can be made. In this regard most of the reported studies on shape recognition in animals are more or less deficient, although they may be cited in favor of one hypothesis or another. It may even seem that the range of potential discriminanda is so great, and the possibilities are so ill-defined, that any attempt to ensure that discrimination is based purely on pattern, or shape, is doomed to failure. I do not believe that this is so: If the patterns are chosen carefully, and adequate controls instituted, unambiguous evidence may be found. The best chances of getting clearly interpretable findings exist when the patterns used are outlined shapes (rather than filled in) presented on a background that is homogeneous, when the patterns are symmetrical about both their horizontal and vertical bisectors, and when some care is taken to find out whether parts, rather than the whole shapes, are the effective discriminanda. (Some examples are given later.)

Because of the ambiguity about what the effective discriminanda really are, an ambiguity which is almost always potentially present, there is good reason to look for physiological evidence to bolster up a psychological model. Although there has been some success in attempting to correlate structure and function in this way, there is still plenty of room for improvement in achieving a fit.

COMPARISON OF PATTERN-RECOGNITION CHARACTERISTICS BETWEEN SPECIES

In a general way, the Hubel and Wiesel findings suggest the sorts of coding to be expected in mammals, at least, and behavioral findings may suggest some sorts of characteristic to look for in neurophysiological research, especially where differences between species are found. It has long been known, for instance, that rats discriminate easily between horizontally and vertically oriented striped patterns or single contours; however, if the same patterns, oriented at 90° to each other, are set at 45° to the horizontal, the discrimination becomes very difficult. This is true also of the octopus (Sutherland, 1957), but not of the cat (Sutherland, 1963) or the rabbit (van Hof, 1966). There is other evidence that horizontal and vertical contours are particularly important in the rat's shape recognition system (Dodwell, 1957), evidence which was the main ground for proposing the contour coding model (labeled model C for convenience) outlined in Chapter 2. This does not strictly entail the proposition that contour and edge detectors like Hubel and Wiesel's simple receptive field units—if they exist in the rat—should be nonrandomly distributed with respect to orientation, having many with horizontally and vertically oriented fields, few in other orientations. The finding of such nonrandom distributions may, however, seem more probable, in view of the behavioral evidence, and it would be most interesting to have the question settled. For the cat and rabbit, the behavioral and neurophysiological findings accord with one another: Both species have receptive fields in all orientations; both can discriminate between bars or stripes out of the horizontal-vertical orientations.[1]

Pattern Discrimination in the Octopus

In a limited sense, this accord is true of the octopus too. In a long series of experiments with octopuses, Sutherland and his associates have shown quite conclusively that horizontal and vertical extents of a shape are often important in determining the characteristics of shape recognition and the transfer of a discrimination from the training shapes to various novel stimuli. Young (1964) summarizes his own evidence showing that the cells which transmit excitation from the plexiform zone of the optic lobe of the octopus (where retinal receptors make synaptic connection with cells in the optic lobe) have dendritic fields in that zone that vary in orientation and length. Their positioning is not random, but shows signs of predominantly horizontal and vertical orientation (in terms of the normal orientation of the eyes).[2] However, there is no real evidence that these cells behave like the edge or contour detectors of Hubel and Wiesel, although Young assumes that they may do so. Indeed there seems to be no evidence at all that receptive field arrangements like those in vertebrate visual systems are found in the octopus or other invertebrates (Young, personal communication). It seems just as likely that the plexiform zone cells act as "intercontour distance" detectors, as Deutsch suggests (1960a). The predominantly horizontal and vertical orientations would still be useful in explaining the behavioral evidence on shape recognition in the octopus.

[1] However, there is recent evidence for primacy of horizontal and vertical detectors in the cat when moving light slits are used as stimuli (Pettigrew, Nikara, & Bishop, 1968a).

[2] The visual system of the octopus is like that of limulus, in having direct transmission from the retinal receptors, and no retinal ganglion cells. Apparently no investigations have been made to find out whether lateral inhibitory mechanisms of the limulus type also exist in the octopus, however.

It would be most interesting to know whether units that have receptive fields in the now-accepted meaning of the term can be found in the optic lobe of the octopus (or in similar structures in other invertebrates). Only then would it seem reasonable to make direct comparisons between neurophysiological, anatomical, and behavioral findings on the octopus—and other invertebrates—and vertebrates. Although we have seen evidence of "sharpening" in selectivity for contour information in limulus, this does not ensure by any means that such information is coded and preserved in the same way as in systems organized on the receptive field pattern.

Some behavioral evidence does suggest, however, that the extent and orientation of contours are important in shape recognition and preference in the octopus. Sutherland (1963b) has found that the octopus shows a consistent preference for certain shapes over others, despite varied prior training in shape discrimination. The training and transfer shapes shown in Fig. 4.1 illustrate this. Training on any of the pairs in the left column tends to yield the same ordering of transfer shapes, shown in the right column. Thus, if an octopus is trained to choose cross (7) and avoid square (8) it will, in transfer tests, tend to order the shapes A–L from top to bottom in terms of preference. If the original training is the reverse, the transfer preferences are also reversed. This evidence suggests that discrimination is based on a single dimension of change, although it is difficult to specify what it is. Sutherland identifies it tentatively with "openness-closedness." This is not meant to be a precise description of the dimension, but it can be seen that, with some exceptions, the "open" shapes tend to be more "spikey" than the "closed." Where differences in order are found for identical shapes in different orientations (such as A, B) the effect may be attributable to the well-known anisotropies in the visual system of the octopus (Sutherland, 1960). Possibly the visual coding is selective of features of this sort ("spikes," or thin contours) but an alternative explanation might be that the system is designed to detect some other feature, more complex and as yet unidentified, similar to the "convexity detector" of the frog (Maturana et al., 1960), which has particular survival value for the octopus. Although this is a speculation, it seems to be not improbable, considering the rather primitive arrangements in the visual system of the octopus as compared with those of even the frog. On the other hand, it should be mentioned that similar orderings on an "openness-closedness" dimension have been found not only in the goldfish, but also in the rat (Sutherland & Carr, 1962; Sutherland, Carr, & Mackintosh, 1962).

Rather different evidence comes from an experiment on reduplicated patterns (Sutherland, Mackintosh, & Mackintosh, 1963). It was found that the two shapes shown in Fig. 4.2 are readily discriminable by the octopus, a finding which is inconsistent with any notion of counting and

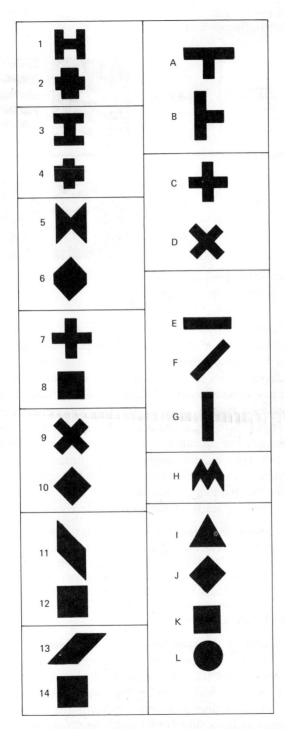

Fig. 4.1. Training shape pairs (on the left) and transfer shapes (on the right) used by Sutherland (1963b) in his transfer experiments.

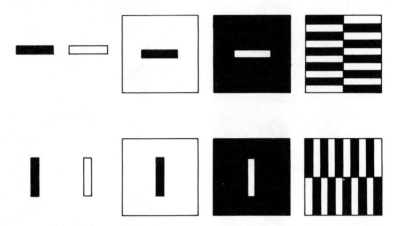

Fig. 4.2. Training shape pairs used in the experiments of Sutherland, Mackintosh, & Mackintosh (1963).

summing a shape's "extent" both horizontally and vertically, "openness-closedness" (if this is the relevant factor in the previously described experiment), or any ratio of contour length to area. The natural interpretation is that the octopus learns to discriminate between horizontal and vertical contours, and has a coding system designed to detect these. The interpretation is strengthened by the fact that the reduplicated patterns are more easily discriminated than the single horizontal and vertical bars, suggesting that the former generate signals that are stronger or more redundant than, but of the same type as, the single bars. A further piece of evidence favoring the view that contour detection as such is important is the finding that presenting the training shapes of Fig. 4.1 as outlines, rather than filled-in block shapes, leads to surprising differences in behavior.

> If, after training, an outline version of any of the original training shapes (odd numbers) is presented, it is always treated in exactly the same way as the animal had learned to treat the original open shape. If an outline version of any of the original closed shapes (even numbers) is presented, there is either no transfer at all, or the animal tends to respond to it in the same way as it had been trained to treat the original "open" shape (Sutherland, 1963b, p. 120).

Perhaps "openness" is the same as "amount of contour" for the coding system of the octopus, and presenting outlines, rather than block figures, simply sharpens contour detection in some way.

However this may be, Sutherland has proposed a revised model (1963b) in which contour detection plays an important role. The suggestion is that retinal receptive fields, like Hubel and Wiesel's simple receptive fields, exist for units in the optic lobe of the octopus, but with a nonrandom distribution of orientation (horizontal and vertical predominating). Thin contours and "spikes" would then fire such units selectively, as suggested in Fig. 4.3, if it is assumed that excitatory and inhibitory parts of the field summate antagonistically, as they do for vertebrate receptive fields. Such a model seems to account for pattern discrimination evidence in

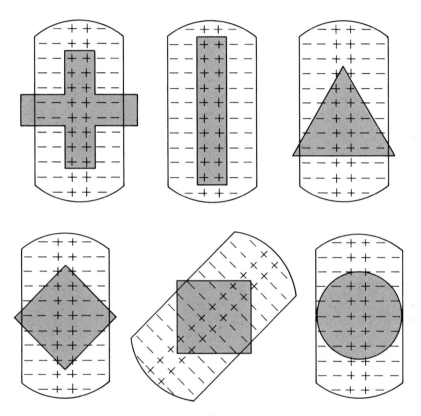

Fig. 4.3. Relationships between various shapes and the hypothetical receptive fields in the visual system of the octopus, postulated by Sutherland (1963b).

the octopus quite well. As a formal model it cannot be criticized for lack of neurophysiological support, but it would be more plausible if it were known that units with the proposed properties exist in the optic lobes of the octopus. There is also some difficulty about the relative sizes (in terms of retinal extent) of the postulated fields and the to-be-discriminated shapes. As we have seen, the octopus does seem to select for contour extent, and Hubel-and-Wiesel-type fields are selective for sharp boundaries—either edges or isolated contours. But, unless retinal projections of the to-be-discriminated shapes are small in relation to receptive field size (as is conveniently suggested in Fig. 4.3), such a system would not work at all with filled-in (block) figures, since uniformly illuminated surfaces tend not to affect receptive field units. Quite obviously, since the working of the model would be highly dependent on the size of the retinal projection, viewing distance and size of stimulus display should be critical variables. In general, such a system must have difficulty with small shapes (poor resolution) if the receptive fields are large, and must be lacking in discriminative power for large shapes if the receptive fields are small. A mixture of sizes is a possibility, although not very economical. There is much to be said for a system that extracts contour information *before* further processing (Dodwell, 1961). As yet there is no clear anatomical or physiological evidence on the octopus to show how contour information is coded. In this sense there is still a wide gap between the neurophysiological and behavioral findings.

Pattern Recognition in Mammals

Some experiments on rats and squirrels carried out recently in my laboratory are indicative of the sorts of contour coding that occur in the visual systems of these animals. I shall describe two of them briefly, since they show how fairly "pure" measures of shape coding may be obtained by behavioral methods, despite the sorts of difficulty described at the beginning of this chapter about ambiguities in the interpretation of such findings. They also illustrate the sort of convergence between neurophysiological and behavioral findings which one hopes will come increasingly to light. The first set of experiments is concerned with an effect first described by Krechevsky (1938). He trained rats in a jumping stand to discriminate between columns and rows of squares, as shown in Fig. 4.4A. Columns and rows were appropriately balanced as positive and negative training shapes in two different groups. Transfer tests were then run to determine the preference between the training-positive shape and a set of smooth, equally spaced stripes in the same orientation (Fig. 4.4B). The animals' preferences were anomalous, in that they consistently preferred the stripes to the original training shapes in both groups. On most theories of discrimination learning, and certainly on any "continuity" theory (for example, Spence, 1936), one would necessarily predict that the training-positive shape would be preferred over other, novel, shapes. This experiment we repeated (reported elsewhere in Dodwell, 1965, 1970), but care was taken to ensure that the anomalous transfer really did occur as a result of discrimination training and was not attributable to some other factor. Krechevsky's original result is inconclusive, because it is conceivable that rats have some initial preference for smooth stripes over "interrupted" stripes, so that the "anomalous transfer" is not transfer

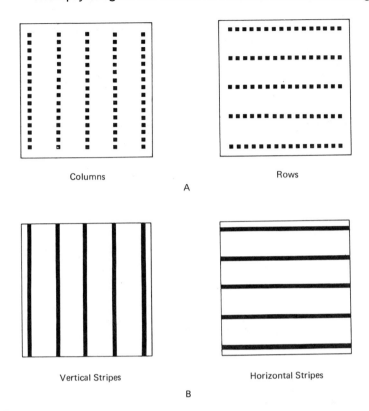

Columns   Rows

A

Vertical Stripes   Horizontal Stripes

B

Fig. 4.4. (A) The patterns of rows and columns used as original training shapes in Dodwell's (1965) experiment on anomalous transfer. (B) The transfer shapes.

at all. It could be that the apparent brightness of the patterns is not equivalent, although they were equated for amount of white surface. Also, it is possible that the anomalous preference was simply preference for a novel pattern, although this may seem rather unlikely. These possible alternatives were excluded in my experiment as follows:

1. All rats were given preference tests after learning to jump in the stand but before training on rows and columns. The preference tests were between rows and horizontal stripes, and between columns and vertical stripes. Very few showed any preference; those that did showed slight preference for stripes, and none showed preference for stripes in both orientations (all rats were given the tests for both orientations).

2. Rats which showed some preference for stripes in one orientation were placed in the group which had as its positive training shape the *opposite* orientation (for example, an animal which showed preference for vertical stripes over columns was trained with rows positive).

3. All rats were tested with the training-positive shape and the stripes of the same orientation and also with the training-negative shape and the stripes in its orientation.
4. The brightness (and width) of the stripes was varied in different transfer test series for each rat.
5. Fresh stimulus cards (with the same patterns) were introduced from time to time, to ensure that discrimination was not based on idiosyncratic features of particular cards, such as scratches.

The main features and findings of the experiment are summarized in Table 4.1. The results were clear-cut. Anomalous transfer occurred with

Table 4.1. Experiment on Anomalous Transfer in Rats: Design and Results

Training Shapes		Transfer Using Positive Training Shape	Preference	Transfer Using Negative Training Shape	Preference
Positive	Negative				
Rows	Columns	Rows (+) and horizontal stripes	Horizontal stripes	Columns (−) and vertical stripes	Columns
Columns	Rows	Columns (+) and vertical stripes	Vertical stripes	Rows (−) and horizontal stripes	Rows

both the positive and negative shapes, and was statistically reliable; rats trained with rows positive subsequently preferred horizontal stripes to rows, and those trained with columns positive subsequently preferred vertical stripes to columns. The transfer effect with the negative training shape was anomalous in that the negative shape was *preferred* to stripes in the same orientation. In some sense, then, smooth stripes in the appropriate orientation were "more negative" than the negative training shape. In those rats which showed an initial preference the negative-shape anomalous transfer occurred in opposition to it (alternative 2 above). This result disposes of both the "initial preference" and "novelty" arguments. It was found that varying the brightness of the stripes had little effect on anomalous transfer. Thus it is clear that we have a genuine case of transfer as a result of training on rows and columns.

A similar experiment has been run with squirrels in a jumping stand, with essentially the same results, except that here the effect is somewhat confounded by the very pronounced preference for horizontal lines found in all squirrels captured and trained at maturity, as reported elsewhere

(Dodwell & Bessant, 1961). Very recently we have also demonstrated the effect in squirrel monkeys, using a panel-pressing task (Dodwell, Litner, & Niemi, 1970). The effect is not apparatus-specific, since we have also obtained it in rats in a modified form of WGTA and in another new form of discrimination apparatus to be described shortly. Although the effect is obtainable here, it is not as pronounced as in the jumping stand.

How is the anomalous transfer effect to be explained? It can be predicted from model C of Chapter 2, but perhaps it is more plausible to attribute it to coding by Hubel-and-Wiesel-type simple receptive fields. Such fields, it will be recalled, show summation of output in the preferred orientation of the field, in the sense that the longer the vertical contour falling within the limits of a vertically oriented field (for example), the stronger the output from its associated cortical cell. Clearly, the output for vertical fields would be stronger for vertical stripes than for columns, and the output of horizontal fields stronger for horizontal stripes than for rows. Similarily, there would be more summation of horizontal contours than of vertical contours in the row pattern and vice versa for the column pattern. Thus the original discrimination would be between the relative outputs of horizontal and vertical fields, and the anomalous transfer—both for positive and negative training shapes—follows immediately. To make this clear, reconsider the case where rows are the positive training shape, columns the negative. In training, the rat learns that stronger outputs from horizontal detectors signal the positive shape; stronger outputs from the vertical detectors signal the negative shape. During transfer tests, the horizontal striations now give a stronger signal on the horizontal output detectors than the rows (training-positive shape) and are therefore treated as the positive shape. Similarly the vertical stripes give a stronger output than the columns, and are therefore treated as the negative shape. If this interpretation is correct then the series *vertical stripes–columns–rows–horizontal stripes* form points on a continuum in a single dimension, the classical situation for demonstrating relational learning. It should be emphasized that the interpretation is plausible only if one can make the definite postulate about how these stimulus patterns are coded. (See Dodwell, 1970.)

Of course, it is not yet established that the cortical receptive field units of the rat are similar to those of the cat, but the overall similarity in the gross features of the two visual systems suggests that they probably are. So far, I have not been able to obtain the anomalous transfer effect in rats for orientations other than horizontal and vertical, a finding which again reinforces the probability that field orientations are nonrandom in the rat. The anomalous transfer effect is not critically dependent on stimulus parameters such as the relative distances between squares in the rows and columns. The arrays shown in Fig. 4.4A have a center-to-center ratio of 4:1. I have repeated the experiment with ratios down to 1.5:1, in which case the difference between rows and columns is much less obvious than in Fig. 4.4A, and still obtained the same effect. I have also found (unpublished data) that the anomalous transfer is a "macropattern" effect, in the sense that the nature of the pattern elements is apparently not too important. Training on rows and columns of small circles or of triangles yields the same transfer effects. Thus the finding is quite robust and not limited to a particular species, apparatus, or method of training, nor to one particular stimulus display—although, of course, it is probably limited to a class of displays which can be tentatively identified. The identification is tentative since the receptive field interpretation of the findings is not as yet conclusively demonstrated. But still an explanation of the effect in terms of model C, or in terms of receptive field characteristics, is clearly an advance on the vague notion of "Gestalt forces of cohesion" postulated by Krechevsky so many years ago to account for his results.

Another experiment, carried out by R. R. Niemi,[3] addressed specifically the question of whether contour separation is an important factor in shape coding in the rat, as compared with contour orientation. There appear to be no relevant experiments reported that are uncontaminated by other potential discriminatory factors such as brightness differences. The experiment was run with the aid of a new form of discrimination apparatus, which consists essentially of an alleyway about 27 in. long, with a lever at one end and two display panels at the other. The rat starts a trial by pressing the lever, which switches on the display projector, and then turns to observe the display. If the panel with the positive shape on it is pushed, food (or other) reinforcement is delivered and the negative shape switched off, and a new trial can be started by pressing the lever again. If the panel displaying the negative shape is pushed, both displays are switched off, and there is a "time out" before the next trial can be initiated by a lever press. The apparatus and recording can be fully automated. The patterns used in the experiment are shown in Fig. 4.5. They were carefully designed so as to have exactly equal contour lengths and

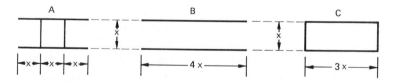

Fig. 4.5. Pattern used in Niemi's experiment on stimulus coding (from Dodwell & Niemi, 1967).

[3] Reported in detail in Dodwell & Niemi (1967).

widths (and hence overall brightness), to be symmetrical about both horizontal and vertical bisectors, and to differ only in the following respects: Contour separation is constant in both A and B (that is, a line perpendicular to any contour in either pattern, if it interests another contour of the pattern, will intersect it at a constant distance), but A and B differ in the numbers and extent of horizontal and vertical contours. A and C have equal numbers and extents of horizontal and vertical contour, but different amounts of contour separation (the distance between the vertical contours in C is three times the distance between the verticals in A). B and C differ in both respects, and were not used as a training pair in the experiment.

The intention was to find out if there is any difference in the ease with which rats learn to discriminate between A and B, as compared to A and C. If the AB discrimination turned out to be difficult, and the AC discrimination easy, this would be evidence that contour separation is probably an important factor, but the presence of specifically oriented contours is not. If, on the other hand, AB were easy and AC difficult or impossible, the reverse argument would hold. After appropriate shaping and pretraining, rats were trained to discriminate between A and B or A and C. Both tasks were learned by all eight rats to a high criterion, or until 400 trials had been completed, with counterbalancing for order, positive figure, etc.

The findings were surprising but unequivocal. Figure 4.6 shows the results for one group, averaged over four rats and over days (thus each

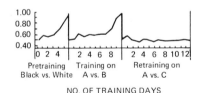

Fig. 4.6. Results of training on pairs of the patterns shown in Fig. 4.5 (from Dodwell & Niemi, 1967).

point represents 160 responses). This is the group that learned AB followed by AC, but the other group showed very similar behavior. That is, AB was readily discriminable for both groups, but AC was not, at least within the length of training used. Thus the failure of the AC discrimination shown in the third panel of Fig. 4.6 cannot be attributed to an order effect, such as "attentional blocking." The final two days of training on AC for this group was given with reversed positive- and negative-stimulus values, to see whether such a change would bring about any changes in the animal's behavior. It did not. Following the successful learning of AB, transfer tests were run to determine whether part-shapes were effective discriminanda, and whether changes in overall brightness made any difference. The results were negative, indicating that the discriminations were made in terms of the whole shapes, and it was the contour configuration that determined choice. The experiment has been replicated, both using the shapes shown in Fig. 4.5 and using each shape rotated through 90°. The findings in both cases were very similar to those reported here. One may thus assert with some confidence that the orientation of contours within a pattern is an important feature for shape discrimination in rats, and therefore probably is coded quite specifically, whereas separation (or distance) between contours is far less salient, and therefore probably is not so specifically coded.

Of course, these findings do not necessarily mean that contour separation plays no part in the shape-coding system of the rat, but they do lend support to the hypothesis that it is not a very potent cue, and is unlikely to be the principal basis on which different configurations of contours are recognized. It is not known how general the present finding may be, but we hope to find out by using these same shapes in other orientations and using different shapes sharing some of their properties. It is also quite possible that, after further training, the rats would discriminate the pair AC despite the lack of any sign of discrimination both in the group as a whole and in individual animals. It is possible that "failure of attention" to a difficult discrimination occurs, and this seems not unlikely in an apparatus where no punishment is given (except for the "time out" after wrong choices). However, it should be emphasized that the steady 50 percent correct choices over large blocks of trials on the AC pair is not attributable to position habits, which might be expected to be prominent if the visual cues are not attended to. Further investigation of such questions might be worthwhile, perhaps with additional indicators of response strength such as latency.

The second panel of Fig. 4.6 illustrates a finding that has not been commented on in the literature, but which turns up rather frequently in discrimination-learning experiments. As early as the second day of training there is a tendency for correct responses to be made at a probability somewhat greater than .5. This is not simply an artifact of the group learning curves, since it appears in many of the individual records and over many experiments, with too great a frequency to be a chance phenomenon. It is found also in other species, perhaps even more clearly than in the rat; and the level is commonly around .6 for a number of trials prior to the rapid rise in proportion of correct trials usually found just before criterion is reached (Fig. 4.6). This is a curious phenomenon which I shall return to later (Chapter 10).

The main result of this experiment can be considered as a good test between Deutsch's various models for coding by contour separation and model C, although the evidence is not conclusive, as I have already pointed out. Its implications are really wider than this, however. It scarcely need be pointed out that the finding is consistent with a model based on Hubel-and-Wiesel-type fields, in which detection of contours in particular orientations is bound to play a prominent role. Moreover, so far there is no neurophysiological evidence at all that "contour separation detectors" exist in the vertebrate visual system, although some attempts appear to have been made to find them. Intuitively it seems obvious that the distances between contours must play *some* part in pattern recognition; the attempt to define that role clearly through behavioral investigation should prove rewarding.

THE COMPLEMENTARY ROLES OF NEUROPHYSIOLOGICAL AND PSYCHOLOGICAL STUDIES

The investigations described in the previous two sections show that behavioral experiments can throw light on the pattern-recognition functions of visual systems. Their role complements, but in a sense might be considered ancillary to, direct investigation of brain processes. J. Z. Young, an anatomist, argues against the view that behavioral studies should play a subsidiary role:

> By discovering what figures the animals can and cannot discriminate it is possible to assess what is being measured, and this is clearly a first step in the search for the mechanisms that measure them. The task of examining the nervous system with microscope and microelectrode must then continue the work if the mechanism is to be understood. This analysis should, in turn, suggest further experiments on the possibilities and limitations of the capacity of form discrimination. It is difficult to see that there is any advantage in pursuing any of these types of study in isolation, or any justification for claims of precedence for psychological, anatomical, or physiological methods (Young, 1964, pp. 192–193).

Nevertheless, there *is* a sense in which neurophysiological findings, particularly in single-unit recording, are more definite and "real" than the psychological findings. It is not easy to pin down what the greater "reality" is, since psychological findings are often quite definite even though usually stated in terms of probabilities rather than a two-valued "either-or" generalization. On the one hand, it has to do, no doubt, with the fact that single-unit recording establishes definitely the presence of a particular receptive field type, and hence information-reduction process, whereas the psychologist has to infer what the process is less directly, and several processes might fit the behavioral findings equally well. On the other hand, the psychologist also has much more difficulty in ensuring that responses are made to those aspects of the discriminanda he wants to investigate, and cannot always be sure that a particular discrimination can be classed as "shape recognition." In recent years there has been a considerable improvement and tightening up of experimental control and a noticeable tendency to use patterned stimuli varying in very few dimensions, or even only one, such as orientation. It is encouraging that definite and interpretable data can be obtained from such experiments.

Single-unit recording studies have yielded such a wealth of information that one could go even further than the argument of the previous paragraph, and suggest that there is scarcely much point in pursuing behavioral investigations with animals any further, since the contour- and shape-coding system has been "solved," at least for mammalian vision. Several lines of argument can be marshaled against this position.

In the first place, the neurophysiological techniques are suited to finding out a lot about isolated elements of the system but do not lend themselves to study of its integrated action. This point cannot be pressed too far against series of studies like those of Hubel and Wiesel which demonstrate, or at least suggest very strongly, a hierarchical arrangement whose integrative functions are defined. However, even there, the single-unit method has not yet gone beyond the point of discovering "local property" detectors, albeit of a surprisingly high level of abstraction and specificity. It would be rash to try to predict what new marvels may be revealed by exploration of cortical areas even more remote from the primary visual cortex than areas 18 and 19. But one may hazard a guess that, if further superhypercomplex receptive field units are found, they will be progressively more difficult to interpret in terms of the part they play in a pattern classification, or stimulus equivalence, system. Inherent in the receptive field concept is the notion of "local property" detection, although "local" is not so specific as in the old "local sign" concept, particularly where complex fields are concerned. The enormous advances in knowledge of visual coding functions over the past few years is largely attributable to the fact that the processes tapped by microelectrode recordings *are* local. But the problem of stimulus equivalence is not—or not just—a problem of local property detection. It is a problem of configurational matching or recognition, and this seems to be to some degree learned, at least in mammals. So far it has been established that the main features of the receptive field contour-coding system up to the level of complex receptive field units are present in newborn kittens, but it is not known whether this is also true of hypercomplex receptive field units. It would be interesting and important to know more about how such units are affected by experience, but this would be unlikely to shed very much light on the general problem of the recognition of configurations.

A second line of argument is that present-day electrophysiological techniques, in particular microelectrode recording from single cells, will not easily yield clear evidence about the nature of perceptual learning. One may learn what features of a coding system are present at particular points in an organism's history, but such methods are not likely to tell us how changes arise or, in general, how a complex system for the recognition of patterns is elaborated. Greater understanding of the *development* of biological pattern-recognition systems will probably still come from behavioral studies, although it would be foolish to try to prophesy what will or will not be discovered as innovations in electrode recording techniques occur. At least it seems inconceivable that all the questions one could raise about perceptual learning could be answered without recourse to behavioral investigation.

Third, there are questions about the functioning of visual systems quite closely related to the general question of pattern recognition that can be investigated *only* by studying the organism's behavior. I have in mind questions about selectivity of learning or attention-like processes, the limits of animals' discriminating capacities, ability to transfer a discrimination to novel stimuli, and so on. This does not imply that no neurophysiological findings could be relevant to such processes, but only that they would not be fully interpretable without supporting behavioral evidence. Thus psychologists need not be intimidated by the great steps forward achieved recently by neurophysiologists working on visual systems. Their findings are bound to influence profoundly our theorizing and experimentation, but can scarcely supplant the large field of legitimate psychological enquiry into the visual behavior of organisms.

One may suggest that the discovery of hypercomplex fields of the type described in Chapter 3 actually makes the search for a model for shape recognition, which can be reconciled with the neurophysiological findings, more difficult than it would otherwise have been. For instance, if nothing more elaborate than the complex-field unit were discovered, one could readily envision a system in which several complex-field units fed information to a higher unit in such a way that that unit would be optimally fired by a collection of contours in particular orientations relative to each other, thus defining "recognition" of particular geometrical shapes, and so on. But the hypercomplex units so far discovered are not at all like this. Their specificity for contours of particular lengths (single- and double-stopped edges) and moving in particular directions at particular speeds seem hard to reconcile with the requirement—or rather the assumption— that information about collections of contours in various orientations should be integrated if shapes are to be coded in a specific way in the system. It is possible that this could happen at a yet higher level of hypercomplex unit, yet this too is problematical. A very common, although not universal, property of the hypercomplex field units is that they respond mainly when the appropriate contour's movement is perpendicular to its orientation. Thus, to take an extreme example, two such units which fire for mutually perpendicular contours could not simultaneously fire a unit at a higher level. Synergistic activity would in any case be dependent on complex series of head and/or eye movements. Indeed assuming that the same principle holds as before, namely that higher-order units' firing seems to be based on the outputs of several lower-order units, it is clear that the system would be highly movement-specific, and this seems biologically inflexible and uneconomical. Also it is at variance with the fact that while making shape discriminations animals apparently do not make elaborate and specific scanning movements with the head that depend on the particular shapes being discriminated, although this matter seems not to have been studied at all. (Certainly in my own experiments, I have never noticed any gross movements of this sort.) The extent to which large eye movements occur, or are important, in shape discrimination in animals is likewise unexplored.

If the pattern discerned so far in Hubel and Wiesel's work should be continued at a higher level, it seems likely that the findings will be of limited use in trying to elaborate a model for pattern classification and stimulus equivalence. The higher-order complex units' outputs would be simply too specific ("abstract" in the wrong way) to be understood readily as the "building blocks" for such a system. It would perhaps even be difficult to specify just what the adequate, let alone the optimal, stimuli for such units would be. Moreover, up to now it has been found that all higher units' activity (at the cortical level) seems to be best understood as depending on inputs from lower units *with the same orientation,* or in the case of some hypercomplex fields, two mutually perpendicular orientations. It seems obvious that at some stage information from units in several orientations must be integrated, but evidence of this is entirely lacking. Is it unreasonable to suggest that this may be where perceptual learning comes in, and that systems which perform this function may be found even further from the primary visual area? Probably such systems would no longer consist of single units with circumscribed processing operations like those of the receptive field units. Perhaps circuit-like arrangements are here the "building blocks" for visual integration that can transcend the "local property detection" characteristic of receptive field organization. Whether systems of this sort (see Chapter 2) could be detected and analyzed by present microelectrode techniques is another matter.

In other words, perhaps it is wrong to think of the receptive field organization as being the basis for anything but a "primary receptive system" of local property detectors in the sense suggested by Hebb (see p. 18), and that a model for shape recognition and perceptual learning should not at present expect more support from the neurophysiological findings. This is a matter which will be taken up again in connection with computer simulation of pattern recognition and the concept of trainable machine pattern-classifying systems.

There are thus several large and unresolved questions about the usefulness and interpretability of the neurophysiological findings vis-à-vis shape recognition models. To recapitulate, these are (1) the problem of transcending local property detection features of receptive field processing, (2) the problem of increasing specificity, especially movement specificity, in higher complex-field units, (3) the question of visual learning, and (4) the lack of any demonstrated integrative activity for differently oriented contours. These difficulties hardly suggest, of course, that we should ignore the neurophysiological findings when attempting to devise models for pattern recognition, but the argument does show that there is still ample scope for model building and experimentation aimed at gaining more insight into the contour-coding processes of the visual system. Eventually, no doubt, behavioral and neurophysiological analyses, working, as it were, from "both ends," will reach a high degree of accord, but there is still a long way to go.

CHAPTER 5
Computer Simulations of Pattern-Recognition Systems

USE OF COMPUTERS FOR PATTERN RECOGNITION

Perhaps the difficulties discussed at the end of the previous chapter will be seen in better perspective after some systematic attempts to devise pattern-recognition procedures by computer simulation have been discussed. One great advantage in approaching the problem of pattern recognition in this way is that it forces the designer to specify effective procedures for the operations of the model he wishes to construct. Indeed the successful computer simulation of a model is the most straightforward way of ensuring that effective processing procedures have been specified for it. It is a remarkable fact that, although a great deal of work has been done on pattern-recognition systems by computer scientists, and many programs have been devised to this end, most of it has gone on in fairly complete isolation from psychological and neurological research in the same field. Psychologists can learn much from this work, and one hopes that, conversely, computer scientists can profit from the investigations of psychologists and neurophysiologists. Some attempts to bridge this gap have of course been made, most notably by Uhr, in his book of readings, *Pattern Recognition* (1966).

Computer scientists who have investigated pattern-recognition systems have usually been interested in producing devices that will speed up, or otherwise improve, the efficiency of data intake by a computer. For example, the direct reading of print from a page into the machine has obvious advantages over transcription onto punched cards or tape by a human operator. Very rarely has any attempt been made to incorporate into such procedures features that have any known relation to biological pattern-recognition systems. Nor is there any reason to think that the attempt should be made, given that the programmer's only aim is to produce an efficient system of transcription into his machine. Nevertheless, there is a surprising degree of similarity between many concepts and procedures devised by computer scientists, on the one hand, and the models proposed by psychologists and the processes discovered by neurophysiological researchers, on the other. One may hope for rapid progress as the deliberate simulation of biologically oriented models for pattern recognition by computer proceeds. So far, most attempts to stimulate these processes by machine analysis have consisted of designing special purpose instruments, such as those of Uttley (1954) and Taylor (1957, 1959).

The question of what we mean by pattern-recognition programs for computers needs further consideration. In an obvious sense *any* device for data input involves pattern recognition of a sort since "reading" from punched cards, for instance, involves "recognizing" the pattern of card perforations and their translation into machine language. The class of problems of interest is that which involves nonspecific inputs, and some ability to generalize—that is, to tolerate changes in position, size, orientation, and perhaps irregularities or sloppiness in the to-be-recognized patterns. (Recognition of handwritten characters is a prime example.) The problem here is basically the same as for the modeling of a biological system: What transformations should be performed on a very large ensemble of potential input patterns to reduce them to a specifiable set of categories? Furthermore, what part can training procedures play in the development and improvement of correct character identification? For obvious reasons, computer pattern-recognition programs have been concerned mainly with the recognition of letters and numbers, although most can handle other patterns of similar complexity.

In nearly all pattern-recognition applications, the machine "reads" the to-be-recognized pattern from a raster, or matrix of photocells.[1] Let us suppose that the raster in question is a 10×10 matrix, which is small, and will not give good resolution for a complicated figure. Even so, if we wanted the machine to detect every possible pattern of "stimulation"

---

[1] Happily, it is not necessary for us to consider the details of how this is done, or how in detail the computer performs its subsequent operations. It is possible to describe and illustrate the processing involved in a general way, and indeed the detailed execution of the program might be carried out by a variety of means. In this sense the computer program is itself a structural model (formally specified) and how it is embodied in a particular machine's language and mode of operation is to a great extent irrelevant to an evaluation of the program as a model for a pattern-recognition system.

and assuming that each photocell has only two states ("on and off" or "white and black") there would be 2^{100} patterns to be recognized, virtually an impossible task if the machine must have a separate "store" or "recognizer" for each pattern. Thus, some degree of reduction, or computation, is necessary in order to handle the potential inputs. This data reduction should obviously be aimed at forming input classes which lead to useful character recognition. "Useful" here begs the question of how the classification should be done, but clearly we can choose our own criterion of usefulness; for example, we might want to devise a system that would "recognize" the same constellation of points (less than 10×10) no matter where it occurred on the raster (generalization of position). We might require that certain features be detected regardless of orientation, others not, and so on. We ask further: How may the categorization actually be done? And can programs be devised so that machines can be *trained* to recognize new sorts of pattern? Given an enormously large potential input and relatively few categories, misclassification is certain to occur, so procedures are needed which make it as infrequent as possible. Even more satisfactory would be systems which profit by their own mistakes; that is, which learn to improve their own performance over trials.

I shall attempt to show how such problems are tackled by describing briefly three different pattern-recognition programs. Obviously anything like an exhaustive review of the many suggested systems—or even their main principles—would be a very major undertaking. The particular three are chosen for the following reasons: (1) they appear to be representative of work in this field, although all are quite old (1959, 1961); (2) they show interesting similarities in principle to psychological models; (3) they work effectively, each by a quite different procedure; and (4) fuller descriptions of all three are readily available in Uhr (1966), for the reader unsatisfied by the cursory treatment they will receive here. Furthermore, the first, an "arbitrary" system, illustrates a simple procedure, and shows how changes in parameters of the system can be investigated. The second, based on "feature detection," shows how more intricate processing gives greater scope for complex discriminations and suggests more "cognitive" applications. The third, an "adaptive" system, demonstrates how a system may be devised which learns to improve its own operations.

An Arbitrary System

The system proposed by Bledsoe and Browning (1959) is arbitrary in that no attempt is made to detect particular features of different patterns or to perform elaborate computations on the initial input. In this sense, the system is particularly simple in its operations. The input is by means of a 10×15 raster, that is, 150 photocells. These are connected, at random, into 75 exclusive pairs, so that each photocell is connected to one, and only one, other cell. Figure 5.1 shows the raster with a large letter "I" imposed on it, and two of the randomly connected pairs of cells. The cell outputs are binary, 0 or 1, according to the state of stimulation,

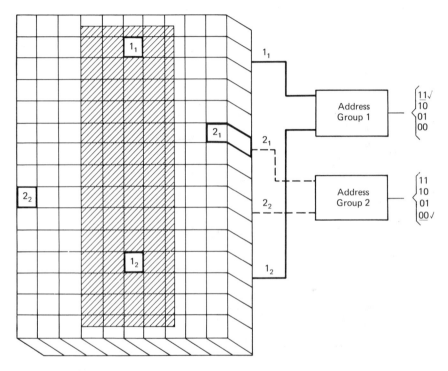

Fig. 5.1. The Bledsoe and Browning system "learning" the letter "I" in the central position. Only two of the 75 pairs of detectors are shown, together with the states recorded (from Bledsoe & Browning, 1959).

so each cell *pair* has four possible states, also illustrated. Each cell pair is assigned four 36-bit positions in the computer memory, so that the state of every cell pair can be recorded under 36 "conditions." These conditions correspond to the 10 digits and 26 letters of the alphabet the machine is to recognize. "Learning" the different characters consists of recording in the relevant memory positions the states of all cell pairs when the corresponding pattern is on some particular part of the raster. The same character may now be "learned" in a new location on the raster; that is, the states of all 75 cell pairs are again recorded for the new location, but in the *same* memory positions (conditions) since it is the same character that is being learned. This is illustrated in Fig. 5.2. The learning stage (first mode of operation) is of course completely under the investigator's control. It may not appear to be a very sensible way to instruct the machine, since, if enough different positions for the characters are tried, most of the cell pairs will have been in two or more

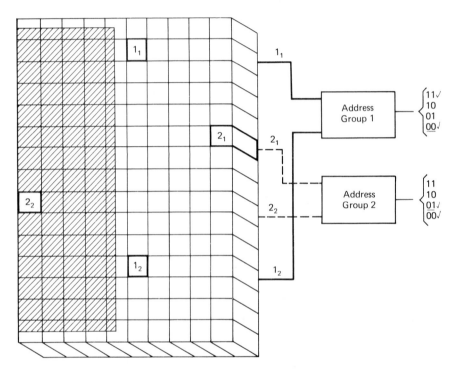

Fig. 5.2. The system "learning" the letter "I" in a different position. Notice that the "memory" for the previous position (Fig. 5.1) is still stored, and remains so during "learning" (from Bledsoe & Browning, 1959).

different states at one time or another for one pattern. However, we notice that for most patterns some cell-pair states will be impossible. For the I of Fig. 5.1, for example, the pair of cells labeled 1 must both be on or off together, and this would be true for any other pair that happened both to be in the same column of photocells. Such pairs, then, can never have states 01 or 10. These states will never be recorded for them in the memory positions corresponding to I. This is the basic discriminative feature of the system.[2] The machine is "instructed" in this way with all

---

[2] One notes that in this system rotation of shapes will almost certainly disrupt discrimination, if rotations were not included in the original "learning" conditions.

36 characters, which is called "learning one alphabet." The "amount of instruction" is a parameter of the system, since the machine might be "taught" each character in only one position or in several positions. We shall see later how this affects its discriminative capacity.

What happens when the machine has learned the characters it is to recognize? It is then presented with a character, and in its second mode of operation the resulting states of the 75 cell pairs are *compared* to all the *recorded* states for those pairs in all 36 positions (but, of course, the new states are not recorded there). The machine "recognizes" the new character by choosing the "condition" or memory location with whose states it shows the greatest correspondence. The highest possible "score" would be 75, when all states for the new character agree with all the corresponding recorded states in memory, and the lowest possible score would be zero, when there is no agreement. Both extremes are rather unlikely contingencies.

Despite its simple and arbitrary character, the system is 100 percent successful in the recognition of typewritten characters, and can achieve fair discrimination of hand-printed characters. Even handwriting can be read, although for the system outlined here only about 30 percent of the material is correctly recognized. However, there are various ways in which it can be modified; for instance, instead of connecting photocells in pairs, they might be connected in triples, quadruples, or any other higher number n-tuple, up to a limit set by the size of the raster used. For higher n-tupling, the coupling can no longer be "exclusive," and one photocell can contribute to several outputs. Figure 5.3 shows the relation between the degree of coupling of photocells (n), the amount "learned," and the ability to read. There are several interesting features. In the first place we notice that $n = 1$ rapidly leads to very poor reading if too much "learning" is attempted. The condition $n = 1$ is a very drastic constraint on the information given to the machine, so its inability to discriminate well is not surprising. Increasing n is a way of increasing the machine's ability to detect structure, or regularities, in the patterns to be recognized, in the sense that it increases the probability that particular characters will be associated with occurrence and nonoccurrence of certain n-tuple states. It will be remembered that this is the principle discriminative feature of the system. It should be noticed especially that the greater the degree of "organization" (or the larger n is) the more can the system cope with "experience." This generalization must, of course, be contingent on some other parameters of the system. However, Fig. 5.3 illustrates a feature of computer simulation that is of prime importance. It would have been difficult if not impossible to prove the relations shown in Fig. 5.3 from the principles of operation of the system, but a set of computer runs easily demonstrates them. By changing parameters of the system,

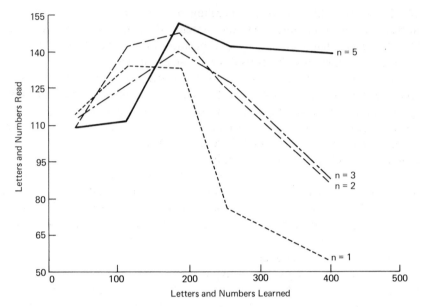

Fig. 5.3. The effect of varying the amount of coupling between inputs (n). Note that when each cell records separately (and hence has only two possible states) ability to discriminate deteriorates rapidly if too much learning is attempted. From $n = 5$ discriminative capacity remains high (from Bledsoe & Browning, 1959).

or by adding new features, properties of a model can be explored by computer simulation quite rapidly and straightforwardly, a process which may disclose new and unexpected features of the model.

As well as changing parameters of the system, one may seek to improve discriminative power in other ways. For example, Bledsoe and Browning consider the effect of "positioning" and "rotating" the character to be recognized to a standard position before processing. This, not unexpectedly, leads to some improvement in performance on hand-printed characters. More dramatic is the effect of recognition by *word context*. Essentially this consists of comparing an unknown word's scores, letter by letter, with the machine's representation of a number of common words of the same length, and choosing the word that shows highest overall agreement with the unknown word as correct. The tremendous improvement in recognition made possible by this means is illustrated in Fig. 5.4, for which a "vocabulary" of the 677 most commonly used short English words was used. Again an important principle is illustrated: Recognition can be improved by taking account of a *new order* of information, in this case information about the characteristics of common words, and

Message
THE COMPUTATION IS DONE BY THE USUAL MACHINE

For *n* = 2 (11 Alphabets)
Letters
TKU GXMPYTYTTEN LU DEYT FY TTU UUEET MNQHTUU

Context
THE COMPUTATION IT DONE BY THE GREAT MACHINE

For *n* = 5 (11 Alphabets)
Letters
TKE GVMSUTUTIVN 2U DVUM BY TKU USMAD MNCHTUE

Context
THE COMPUTATION IS DONE BY THE USUAL MACHINE

Fig. 5.4. Dramatic illustration of the improvement in performance when word context is taken into account (lines 3 and 5) compared with recognition letter-by-letter (lines 2 and 4) (from Bledsoe & Browning, 1959).

its logic is the same as that which underlies the associationistic properties of many psychological models.

We see, then, that an apparently crude and arbitrary means of processing leads to a quite efficient method of pattern recognition. An estimate of similarity between a pattern and a set of stored characters is made without excessive load on the computer's memory. The to-be-recognized patterns do not have to be identical with those already recorded, but there is no provision for the learning of "new" patterns. The behavior of the system under various changes of parameter or with the addition of new features is readily explored. As a system for pattern recognition it works well, but as a possible model for a biological pattern-recognition system (which was not its original purpose) it leaves something to be desired. The random pairing of photocells in the original version seems appealing and parsimonious from the biological standpoint, but visual systems certainly have a more structured and organized basic processing arrangement, especially in vertebrates. However, a bit of rearrangement of the coupling would yield a system surprisingly close to some models proposed by psychologists. If the coupling were not random but under the restriction that all *n*-tuples are in the same row of the raster and adjacent to each other, with $n = 1, 2, 3, 4,$ or 5 (for example), this would give a "horizontal extent" detection system quite like those proposed by Sutherland and Deutsch for the octopus, although it perhaps would not read letters and numbers efficiently.

A "Feature-Detection" System

The second computer pattern-recognition system to be described is much more elaborate than Bledsoe and Browning's and was developed by Grimsdale, Sumner, Tunis, and Kilburn (1959). The feature of main interest is the complicated processing and classification of contour characteristics which it performs. This involves the division of any pattern into a number of segments or "groups," each of which is characterized with respect to length, curvature, and orientation. The relations between the segments are also characterized (where they join, which ones are "figure ends," and so forth). The two sets of properties together are then constituted into a "statement" of the pattern, and are compared to the statements of standard patterns in the machine's permanent store. If a pattern statement agrees with one of the standard statements, it is "recognized." If not, the machine indicates the degree of the similarity to one or more standard patterns, and if so instructed can add the new pattern to its standard repertoire. The system is thus much more explicit and articulated than Bledsoe and Browning's and capable of development for the recognition of new and more complicated patterns. This does not mean that it is necessarily a better, or more efficient, pattern recognizer than the other for a fixed number of simple patterns. However, our interest is more in principles of operation than efficiency, and we shall see that some of the principles of processing used by Grimsdale et al. have interesting similarities to the coding principles discovered, or suggested, by other workers both in physiology and psychology.

Since the processing, or coding, is so elaborate in this system, only some of its features are discussed, but one hopes that these will be sufficient to convey a general idea of its nature and scope. Patterns are presented on a 64×40 raster and scanned horizontally, element by element. The object of the scan is to detect segments, or smooth contours, in the pattern, and to this end it has predetermined criteria for deciding which parts of a pattern belong to one segment. These criteria include changes in curvature, abrupt changes in horizontal extent, "separation" or intercontour distance, and the like. The sort of join between one segment and another is also recorded. Some examples of figures segmented by the system are given in Fig. 5.5. One sees that different orientations of a figure may produce different segmentations (Fig. 5.5B and D) but this does not disturb the assembly of an identical statement for the two patterns at a later stage. As the scan proceeds from point to point, small imperfections in the contours are ignored, as are isolated spots. This built-in "noise factor" ensures that only regular pattern points are recorded as pattern components. Similarly, when a group or segment has been formed and found to be nontrivial (not too small), its edges are "smoothed" by an averaging process, so that the slope and curvature of the segment can be evaluated. When the recording and analysis of segments is complete, they are assembled according to the sorts of join tabulated during the scan (see Fig. 5.6). Some compression of the description is made, so that each segment length is expressed as one of 32 values (a

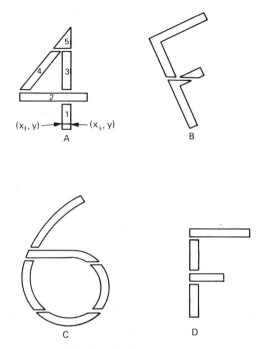

(x_f, y) (x_s, y)

A   B   C   D

Fig. 5.5. Example of groups, or segments, formed by the Grimsdale et al. pattern-processing system (from Grimsdale et al., 1959).

5-bit description) and likewise for orientation. One "criterion" segment is chosen—if possible a long, straight one—and the positions and orientations of other segments are expressed in relation to it. Thus the actual position and orientation of the original figure (provided it was all on the raster) are immaterial. Again we see how a certain amount of "generalization" may be built into the processing, but here it is much more explicit than in Bledsoe and Browning's system. A concise statement of the pattern in terms of these various features is compiled and compared with the standard set of patterns previously stored by the computer. This could be done in several ways, aimed at improving efficiency, but the principle is in every case the same—the comparison is made in terms of the coded features such as number of segments, number of "ends," and relations between segments, or "joins."

This system is much more articulate than the previous one, in the sense that pattern features are analyzed, compared, and coded individually. The details of the search and analysis on the original pattern are quite reminiscent of some descriptions of possible procedures in human pattern recognition (for example, Attneave, 1954), and clearly the detection of

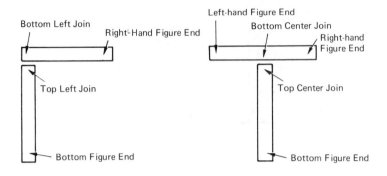

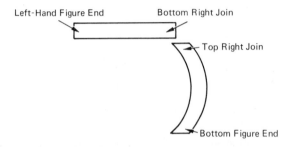

Fig. 5.6. Examples of the types of join and end coding (from Grimsdale et al., 1959).

segments looks quite analogous to the sort of contour coding found in the cat's visual system, although the details of the processing are, of course, different. The system can also be called potentially "cognitive" in that it would be easy to extend it in such a way that the coded statements themselves become the "building blocks" for the elaboration of more complex classifications. This might be done, for example, in terms of a classification-with-memory system like Uttley's (1958), or any other that computes conditional probabilities between sequences of symbols. For computer modeling, as for psychological theorizing, the border between "concept development" and "discrimination learning" is ill-defined at best, and probably rather artificial. The system of Grimsdale et al., would be only the first stage in such a potential model, of course, but further development poses no problems in principle. Some suggestions along these lines have been made by Clowes (1967a,b). The development of more cognitive models by computer techniques is also discussed by Licklider (1967) and Neisser (1967), and explicit simulation of cognitive behavior such as problem solving is an active field (see, for example, Reitman, 1965; Minsky, 1969).

An "Adaptive" System

Our third example is a system devised by Uhr and Vossler (1961), which is self-adapting in its operations and in many ways is more subtle than the previous two. Also, it was developed with certain findings in neurophysiology and psychology in mind, and may thus be considered as an explicit attempt to model the visual system as pattern recognizer.

Input to the computer is digitalized as before, this time on a 20 × 20 raster. The input is "examined" by a series of 5 × 5 "operators," confined to that smallest rectangle on the raster within which the pattern lies. Each operator consists of an array of cells, some of which are functional and some not. The functional cells have two possible states, "on" and "off" (symbolized by 0 and 1). Examples of possible operators are shown in Fig. 5.7; they may either be chosen by the programmer, or generated at random by the computer. Each operator scans the input systematically,[3] and records a "hit" each time its own cell states match the part of the pattern it is on. Thus, for example, the fifth operator in Fig. 5.7B would score hits on parts of patterns containing horizontal contours and with no other features below them. This operator will also *tend* to score for any horizontal contour, but this is contingent on the presence or absence of parts of the pattern in the positions occupied by 0s in the operator. We notice that operators may have different numbers of nonblank cells and hence be more or less explicit as detectors. Each "hit" by an operator is recorded together with its position in the pattern, and these together constitute a "characteristic" of the pattern. The set of all characteristics is the system's representation of the pattern in question. Such a system may be expected to recognize typed characters with ease. The characters of interest, and hence the ones mainly explored, are handprinted capitals with some degree of variation in orientation. A variable number of operators may be used, at the investigator's discretion—more operators produce more information about the pattern, but at the cost of increased computing time and storage load. Thus the number of operators to use is a question of efficiency and need not concern us. However, a second *type* of more powerful operator is used, once the computer has learned to recognize some patterns. This is a combinatorial operator—that is, one which selects some binary logical operation, such as conjunction or disjunction, and applies it to a pair of the simple operators in use. The choice of one of 16 possible combinatorial operations (*a* and *b*, *a* and not *b*, *a* or *b*, and so forth), and of the simple operators to be combined, may be done randomly or by a more efficient method, which selects pairs of opera-

---

[3] The process is easily visualized by imagining the operator as a sheet of cells that is superposed physically on the raster, and moves across it, step by step, although this obviously enough is not the computer's mode of action.

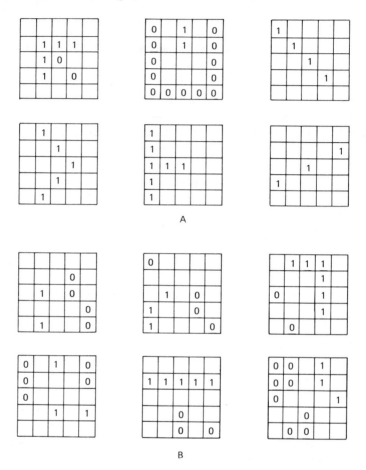

Fig. 5.7. (A) Examples of typical preprogrammed operators in the Uhr and Vossler model. (B) Examples of operators generated by the program. Notice that operators may be more or less explicit. In general, the more cells that are filled in the operator, the more explicit will be its detecting operations. Compare, for instance, the upper-middle operator with the one on the lower right in A.

tors that tend to differentiate between patterns but not between different examples of the same pattern. This again is a question that does not affect the principles of operation, and its details need not concern us here.

The two types of operator, simple and combinatorial, produce the "characteristics" by which the computer attempts to recognize the input pattern. This is done, as in the previous system, by comparing the list of characteristics with the lists for patterns previously encountered, which are stored in memory. Each characteristic for the new pattern is compared with the characteristics of the first stored pattern, and a "difference score" computed separately for each characteristic. These difference scores are combined in a special way so that an overall difference score between the two patterns is computed. The process is repeated for each pattern[4] in memory, and the resulting overall differences are compared. The smallest overall difference score is selected and the new pattern identified with the stored pattern that gave rise to it. The most important new feature of the system now comes into play. Each characteristic is weighted differentially, and after a pattern has been recognized the system examines the characteristics of stored patterns and adjusts the weights in such a way as to improve discriminative power, as follows. The weights are modified for the characteristics of those patterns which had overall difference scores close to those for the correct pattern. If the pattern recognition happens to have been wrong (as determined by the man, not the machine), the characteristics of the one or more patterns which gave difference scores *lower* than the correct one are also adjusted. The correct pattern is compared with each of the close competitors individually, and in terms of each separate characteristic. If the "choice" by a particular characteristic is correct (that is, if it alone would have identified the correct pattern), its weight is increased. If it would have identified the wrong pattern, its weight is decreased. If it would have yielded no information (by being the same for both patterns) its weight is decreased with probability $1/8$. In the case of a close competitor (yielding a difference score close to but greater than that of the correct pattern), the weights are adjusted only in that pattern's characteristics. In the case of incorrect recognition, however, weights are altered for *both* patterns, which means that if several patterns had lower scores than the correct one, the weights of characteristics in the correct pattern will fall suddenly. If the weights associated with an operator become too low, that operator is replaced by a new one, which could be either randomly generated or chosen by the programmer, as before. The first time a pattern is encountered, its characteristics are simply stored; the second time it is encountered the characteristics are replaced with probability equal to $1/2$. Thereafter, characteristics are replaced with probability $1/4$. This means that new operators are continually being tried, and the system never becomes static. Also the differential-weighting system ensures that characteristics which discriminate well will tend to be retained longer than those that are indifferent, while characteristics which tend to give rise to wrong classification are discarded. Particularly if a new pattern is incorrectly classified, the operators for

[4] More accurately, one should say for each pattern *class*, since it is assumed that the system will build up a classification of previously encountered patterns, each of which is "named" or identified in a specific way.

recognizing that pattern, that is, the operators which give rise to the stored characteristics of the correct pattern, have a high probability of being replaced. The system is designed to concentrate on difficult discriminations since it is only when a set of overall difference scores are close to each other than the likelihood of the associated operators' being replaced becomes higher than normal. The system thus displays a form of evolution by selection of the fittest discriminators, with the added feature of speeding up the rate of "mutation" of operators where it is advantageous to do so.

This system shows excellent ability to recognize printed letters after relatively few passes of the complete set through the machine, and also gives quite good results for hand-printed capitals, "segmented" handwriting (that is, handwriting split into words by a criterion built into the system), and other patterns of similar complexity. In most cases it is able to recognize unfamiliar patterns fairly well (that is, patterns it "knows," but which have not been passed through the machine previously in a particular format). On the whole, allowing the system to generate its own operators seems to work better than specifying them initially. Thus the system is moderately successful at recognizing "distorted" patterns and undoubtedly there is plenty of scope for its further development in a number of ways, such as by altering the complexity of the initial operators, changing the differential-weighting and replacement rules, and so on. However, since the system is offered explicitly as a model for visual recognition, we should principally be asking the question: Is it an adequate model of vision?

There is no easy and straightforward way to answer that question. In the sense that the system recognizes, and, furthermore, *learns* to recognize, spatial patterns of some complexity, it obviously is successful. In terms of the "input-output" criterion—the performance of the system—the answer is that the system is adequate and as good as many others that have been proposed. On the other hand, although Uhr and Vossler make a case for the plausibility and "naturalness" of the assumptions about the primary detectors—the operators—in a general way, there are some aspects of the system's organization which run counter to well-established neurophysiological facts. I have in mind, for instance, the fact that the primary detection system in vertebrate visual systems appears to be fixed in its operations and not modifiable in the way Uhr and Vossler's operators are. Despite the ingenuity of their ideas, in this sense they cannot be held to model real visual systems adequately. Flexibility in highly developed visual systems seems most liable to occur at a higher stage of processing. Furthermore, the form of coding, in mammalian visual systems at least, appears to be much simpler in its initial stages, being confined so far as we know to the detection of straight contours in various orientations. How information coded in this way is later processed to extract properties of curvature, angles, and so on, is a real problem, but it can hardly be solved by proposing that the initial coding takes a different form.

COMPUTER SIMULATIONS AND VISUAL-SYSTEM MODELING

Comments of this type may seem unduly harsh, since some of the neurophysiological evidence was reported only at about the time the system was presumably being developed.[5] However, it is well to enter a caveat, since some rather extravagant claims are currently being made for the overriding virtues of computer simulations as models for biological pattern-recognition systems. Uhr, for example, claims that computer simulations are the first class of attempted solutions to the problems of pattern recognition worthy of serious consideration:

> We now have a large number of computer programs and analog computers . . . that do in fact recognize patterns. For want of anything that we could seriously call scientific theory, that was more than suggestive verbiage, these programs must be taken seriously as the first attempts toward developing a good theory. They are in fact theoretical models of the traditional sort. They may well be bad models in that they are inelegant, without great power, or . . . contraverted by the empirical data. But bad theories, with their power to make things clear and lead to their own downfall, are far better than no theories at all (Uhr, 1966, p. 367).

The second sentence of this quotation will not be disputed here in detail— one hopes that the greater part of this book is sufficient evidence of its bias as an overall assessment of the field of pattern recognition. It may be as well to discuss the matter from the opposite point of view and point out some serious weaknesses in computer simulations as models for biological pattern-recognition systems. The general point that computer simulation can be a very powerful method of modeling is, of course, not to be questioned. As a means of translating ideas, hypotheses, or even "hunches" about how pattern recognition might occur into precisely stated sequences of operations which can actually be performed, the method is undeniably potent. It forces the investigator to sharpen his ideas, and will prove whether they work or not. As anyone who has written programs knows, it can be hard work. But the computer's two chief advantages, (1) that it forces the investigator to be precise in his statement of a problem and his proposals for its solution, and (2) that it is able to give rapid evaluation of those proposals, are props to scientific theorizing and not a substitute for it. Whether a computer simulation yields

---

[5] See also the argument about "neurophysiologizing" in Chapter 1.

a good model or not must be decided on the same grounds as are used to evaluate any other model: Are its assumptions realistic? Does it model adequately those features of the real system which are of greatest interest and importance? Does it predict new phenomena which can be investigated in the real system? Looked at from this point of view, most of the computer models for pattern recognition are seriously lacking in the qualities any other acceptable scientific model is expected to possess.

Computer models almost invariably neglect whole classes of evidence—usually behavioral—which should be taken into account, a sad comment on the compartmentalization of investigation into pattern-recognition systems. They also tend to be quite unspecific; a computer model may be held to model "the visual system," and yet it is clear that different sorts of model are appropriate for different sorts of visual systems. (See Chapters 3 and 4.) Computer models are also too general in another and more important sense. One can see this by asking the question: Under what conditions could a computer model be *refuted?* One could say that most of them are too clever, by half—the question of devising a system that will recognize patterns is no longer theoretically interesting; that it can be done has been shown time and again. A general purpose recognizer may be too powerful, capable of ad hoc refinements to do any job we can think up for it. Biological visual systems are not like this. What is needed is a new breed of models that perform recognition in particular ways, that generate particular properties that are similar to properties of the systems they are supposed to simulate. If we want to model a real visual system we should pay at least as much attention to what it cannot do as to what it can, since it is here that definitive tests of the system's properties can be made. This consideration played a major role in the construction of some of the psychological models for pattern recognition discussed earlier. There is no doubt that computer-simulated models can improve on them, but only if the right questions are posted before new models are designed.

It can be argued that there simply is not enough exact evidence about the properties of biological pattern-recognition systems, especially within one species, to make such a venture possible. It is true that there is a paucity of such evidence, and some of it is conflicting, but little information is not the same as no information, and there is an accumulating body of knowledge about the neurophysiology of vision that should be taken into account in designing a structural model. It seems to me that there is now sufficient evidence on receptive field organization, with some supporting psychological findings, to circumscribe effectively a class of models of pattern recognition for simpler mammalian visual systems which would be worth simulating by computer. Even where definite information is lacking, there may be strong indications of the sort of organization that should be incorporated. Consider, for example, the "primary detection" of pattern features. It seems clear that, over a wide range of mammalian species, this is "built-in," and quite inflexible; and yet such organisms show a considerable capacity for learning to recognize quite complex patterns, which suggests that elaborate processes for perceptual learning should be incorporated at a relatively late stage in a model (see Chapter 2). Would a computer model based on such principles display new and unexpected recognition properties which could be investigated experimentally with animals? To take another related example: Most computer models assume a relatively fixed memory, or "criterion list," against which incoming patterns are evaluated. It seems most probable that learning in perception is organized in a hierarchical fashion (it must be admitted that the evidence here comes mainly from human perceptual learning) and it would seem sensible to simulate this form of organization in pattern-recognition models. There is no doubt it can be done, as Uttley's special purpose machines so well demonstrate.

The possibilities are almost limitless. The point I wish to emphasize is that we need specific models for specific systems, which are open to empirical test. The danger with computer models seems to me to be the fascination of their complexity and efficiency. The modeler may be so impressed with this, or with the nice realization of a clever idea—the highly satisfying sense of achievement in seeing his ideas "really work"— that he loses sight of the scientific objective of simulation by computer, which is to help us to understand real visual systems. Thus, while computers open up a whole new field of exploration of pattern-recognition models, they do not absolve us from the hard work of thinking out the sorts of property a model must have if it is to prove its scientific worth. As Selfridge so nicely puts it:

> Of course we must hope that success is in some degree a continuous function of the variables incorporated in its description; but before we can hill-climb, we must find the hill. I am afraid that is a point that has been neglected (Selfridge, 1962, p. 3).

Having said this, one may still view with satisfaction the fact that computer scientists have devised methods and procedures for pattern recognition which are in some cases remarkably analogous to concepts and findings in psychology and physiology. Such "convergence of operations" is bound to make one feel that, on the whole, investigations are proceeding along the right lines. But one should not lose sight of the equally important fact that psychology and physiology are still the data sources for the discipline, and without them computer modeling of pattern recognition would be rather vacuous as an aid to understanding visual systems, no matter what its other, technical, advantages may be.

CHAPTER 6
Pattern Perception in Man

MODELING COMPLEX SYSTEMS

The kinds of elementary contour-coding and pattern-recognition systems discussed up to now are too simple to be directly applicable to the visual performance of which human beings are capable. Systems like model C, the neurophysiological coding processes, or the computer models may be useful in furthering our understanding of the recognition of contour elements and simple shapes but are manifestly inadequate for the analysis of, let us say, the recognition of different faces, different breeds of dog, or various styles of architecture. Part of Uhr's argument in favor of model simulation by computer is that earlier models were too simple, as well as being insufficiently precise; computer modeling is recommended on the grounds that it *forces* the model builder to be precise and can handle very complex problems. Computer modeling may well play a leading part in the analysis of pattern recognition in higher visual systems, including man's, but the problems to be faced are not simply those of complexity. If it were only a question of devising systems to recognize very complicated patterns, perhaps refinement of the sorts of system described in the last chapter would suffice. But there are other features of pattern-perception systems of prime importance, which pose a different sort of problem.

There are at least four basic problems which face the theorist who attempts to devise structural models for human pattern recognition. First is complexity, already touched on; second, even in the adult, pattern recognition is highly adaptable and has the power to transcend gross distortions in its normal input; third, there is the extent to which human perception is selective and dependent on prior experience and special conditions of motivation or interest; fourth, there is the "phenomenological" question.

110

Obviously the four problems are not independent, but each merits some separate discussion, if only to circumscribe more clearly the field within which structural models can make a valid contribution. It should be clear that I do not claim that the problems are present only for human pattern recognition. To some degree they are problems for infrahuman organisms too, and the closer one approaches man on the evolutionary scale, the more acute the problems become. I discuss them in relation to human vision, because it is here that they are most clearly manifested, and solutions to—or ways of evading—the problems for human vision will for the most part apply a fortiori to other organisms. In man, language and other symbolic processes give a range, subtlety, and power to his cognitive behavior which far exceed anything found in other species. To this extent one recognizes a real discontinuity in the sorts of behavior to be explained, but this is not the same as claiming that explanatory models or principles for human vision are irrelevant to other organisms.

Complexity

Here one may include such straightforward things as the fact that human beings can discriminate between objects and patterns of many different sorts, and can base their discriminations on a wide variety of different factors. Even in rats and squirrels, for example, one finds that the recognition of patterns may be based on discrimination of the whole shape, on parts such as the lower halves, on special features such as corners or straight edges, or sometimes apparently on one feature, sometimes on another. In humans, how much greater a degree of freedom in the basis for discrimination is possible! Detailed recognition of particular features within a pattern is often important, contextual effects are usually relevant, illusions are common, as are perceptual constancies, and so on. An adequate and comprehensive model would have to take all these into account. In addition, human perceptual recognition is complicated by conceptual classifications of various types; by this I do not mean simply the obvious classifications such as "squares" and "circles," "plane figures" and "solid figures," and the like, but a more subtle element, manifested, for example, in the difference between recognizing two figures as being topologically equivalent on the one hand, or as similar in a Euclidean sense on the other. The example of architectural style mentioned above is another instance where conceptual factors play a dominant role.

Do not such considerations suggest that the phenomena of human pattern recognition are so intricate and various that one should despair of ever making useful contributions to their understanding, even with the aid of computer simulation? On the contrary, I shall argue that by setting some reasonable limits on what is attempted, quite a bit can be achieved.

The fact that very complex patterns can be recognized, and very subtle discriminations made, assures us that we are unlikely to be able to explain all of human pattern recognition—even at the primary detection level—at one fell swoop. However, it is useful to ask whether or not there are some general features of the process which can constrain the search for models, and also whether there may not be some special types of pattern-recognition situation which are particularly amenable to analysis in terms of structural models. In this way, one might hope to ameliorate the difficulties posed by complexity of pattern identification per se. The sensible strategy seems to be—as before—to study, as far as possible, features of the primary detection system before proceeding to the question of how other properties of human perception may be related to, or derived from, it.

An obvious first step is to study perception under highly impoverished, but well-controlled, laboratory conditions. The great mass of modern experimental work on perception falls in this category. Relatively little of it, however, is directly interpretable in terms of contour- and pattern-coding systems in the sense here developed. Another possibility is to look for very specific types of coding, the general features of which can be defined despite the complexity of normal input.

The fact that contour detection of the Hubel-and-Wiesel sort is general in the mammals so far studied suggests that similar types of detector may underlie pattern processing in the human visual system, and indeed some experimental results with humans support this view more or less directly, as will be discussed in Chapter 9. Another pointer is the fact that human vision shows various anisotropic properties. For example, it is known that visual acuity for straight contours is dependent on orientation, being best for lines oriented horizontally and vertically (Ogilvie & Taylor, 1958) and discrimination of small differences in orientation is also best in these directions (Jastrow, 1893). The relative discriminability of shapes also, under certain conditions, depends on their orientation with respect to the observer's retina (Arnoult, 1954) as well as their orientation in the environment (Rock, 1956; Rock & Heimer, 1957). Some other evidence on the importance of horizontal and vertical orientations in human vision is summarized by Taylor (1963). It seems reasonable to suppose, then, that shape recognition in humans proceeds in some fashion by the analysis of contour orientation, in which horizontal and vertical axes play a special role.

This view is generally supported by evidence of a rather different kind, namely the facts of binocular vision and stereopsis.[1] It is well known

---

[1] Stereopsis is the perception of depth based only on the slight discrepancy of the two eyes' views of a visual object. It can be produced artificially in a stereoscope. For further elaboration, see Chapter 7.

that the normal condition for fusion and stereopsis is congruence, or near-congruence, of contours in particular orientations in the visual inputs to the two eyes. In this process lack of congruity between vertical contours plays quite a different role from lack of congruity between horizontal contours (discussed in Chapter 7), which suggests very strongly that in the processing of binocular inputs different mechanisms control the coordinative analysis of horizontal and vertical disparities. This implies separate codings for them. These several sorts of evidence suggest that the separate encoding of horizontal and vertical location within the visual field may be a general property of a binocular visual system, which already constrains considerably the sorts of model it may be profitable to explore.

Some of the anistropic properties mentioned earlier (for example, better discrimination of horizontal and vertical contours than of contours in other orientations) may well be attributable in large measure to experience in the normal human environment, the relative frequency with which such judgments are made, and their importance to the person making them. However, it appears that in some degree at least fusion and stereopsis are properties of the primary detection system, so that the horizontal-vertical coding schema is at least partly built into the human visual system (the evidence for this statement is presented in Chapter 7).

Thus we find some general features of pattern recognition which suggest that horizontal and vertical directions have special functional significance. and have identified a special *type* of pattern recognition—namely binocular stereoptic vision—where these differences play a clear and major role. Stereopsis, then, appears as an obvious candidate for the model builder to try his skill on, particularly as its main properties can be—and typically are—studied in controlled situations.

Adaptation to Distortions

One might think that the ability to adapt to distortions of normal visual input should be considered as part of the third problem area, which concerns perceptual learning, motivation and set. However, there are good grounds for supposing that this type of adaptation has some special features which set it off from the general question of perceptual learning (for example, the speed with which it can occur) and it thus qualifies for separate treatment.

The extent to which a person with normal vision can adapt to optical distortions is truly amazing. Starting with Stratton's (1896, 1897) celebrated investigations of the effects of wearing a device for inverting the visual field, a long series of studies has shown that adaptation to different sorts of distortion may be quite rapid and sometimes is virtually complete. At a less rigorously studied level it is clear that most people adapt successfully to the wearing of ophthalmic lenses, which in general also produce some degree of distortion. The complexity and subtleties of a system that can recognize differences between human faces, for example, have already been referred to; the fact that recognition is usually possible without further practice when the faces are viewed through a prism or reflected in a convex mirror or similar device adds a new dimension to the problem, in addition to the fact that adaptation to the distortions can occur. Such versatility in the system might lead one to despair of ever finding a coherent model for its operation, except on an ad hoc basis for each particular type of distortion studied, or in terms too vague and general to yield useful insight, as, for instance: "The visual system displays homeostatic properties, in that its adaptation to a distorted input always tends toward reestablishment of a 'normal' visual world." This describes approximately what happens, and poses the problem, but one need scarcely belabor the point that it does not provide an adequate explanation. However, it turns out that the distortions commonly studied, and to which the visual system can adapt, may all be expressed, at least to a reasonably close approximation, in terms of just one class of mathematical transformations, called isogonal transformations. It so happens that the useful set of transformations for handling visual distortions are expressible in a quite elementary way by functions of a complex variable. Since a complex number is a vector with two independent components, and operations on complex numbers involve the separate manipulations of these components, which may be identified with horizontal and vertical locations in the visual field, we have another indication of the sort of constraint under which pattern processing occurs. The notion that such transformations play a role in visual adaptation thus is in general harmony with the conception of pattern processing suggested in the previous section. A model based on isogonal transformations is developed in Chapter 8. It is quite abstract and its elements are not identifiable with or even analogous to any known brain function. However, it handles the data reasonably well, and leads to some new—admittedly speculative—ideas about how adaptation to visual distortion may occur.

Attention, Motivation, and Experience

Several instances of the involvement of "higher-order" variables in pattern recognition have been suggested already, and further illustrations are not hard to find. Some mundane examples readily come to mind: tea- and wine-tasters, skilled hunters, athletes, and musicians all quite obviously develop their capacities for sensory discrimination and categorization (although not necessarily in vision) far beyond the level of the average person. Scientific evidence in this vein is also plentiful; almost every psychophysical experiment requires a "warm-up" period during which increases in precision of observation are usually found. As to the importance of learning and other nonvisual factors in visual perception, the work of the transactionalists (for example, Kilpatrick, 1961) and the "new look" in perception (for example, Bruner, 1957) provide a mass of findings. The relevance of these points for the structural modeler are obvious enough. The incorporation of "higher-order" variables into a structural-type model will be considered later (Chapter 10). For the moment, discussion is confined to the difficulties which the presence—or possible presence—of such factors entails. The main difficulty is clearly this: It is never possible to state unequivocally that just *this* effect or *that* process is built into a visual system and functions independently of experience, set, motivational state, or whatever. The problem of set alone is many-faceted, and can involve nonperceptual processes of several sorts, as Haber has recently argued (1966).

One can postulate a built-in primary detector system, such as the Hubel and Wiesel contour-detection system, which is present at birth and presumably provides the foundation on which the later development of pattern perception is built. But several difficulties must be faced if one wishes to define its properties and to contrast them with the properties which are contingent on perceptual experience. Neurophysiological exploration of the sort required to establish presence of such a system is clearly impossible with human neonates, and poor response indicators in the newborn seem to rule out at present the possibility of reliable behavioral evidence in the first few days of life. To attempt to infer properties of that system from behavior at, say, 6 weeks of age, is in principle no different from attempting the inference from the adult's behavior, for no one knows how rapidly perceptual learning occurs. Even if perceptual isolation of the newborn were ethically permissible, this would not help, since the unexercised system may suffer changes of one sort or another (as happens in kittens—see Chapter 4). Supposedly one might attempt to investigate the matter by using quite novel forms of display with normal adults as observers, arguing that since the organism has never encountered such displays before, its responses to them cannot be influenced by experience. The extent to which such an argument can be used depends on the definition of "effects of prior experience" one is prepared to accept. In one sense it is clear that an element of interpretation enters into the perception even of random dot patterns, since an observer has to report what he sees, and such reporting necessarily entails reference to known categories of description, even if the reference is only negative (for example, "It does not look like an *x* or a *y*"). However, if pairs of random patterns are so arranged as to yield stereopsis (see Chapter 7), it *can* be argued that the stereopsis is generated by a function of the visual system independently of experience, in the sense that no element of *interpretation* of the monocular displays in terms of familiar categories of *depth relations* is possible. That is to say, no cues of perspective, interposition, shading, and texture are present to influence judgment. A similar argument can be put forward in other cases of data-processing-like operations of the visual system, such as masking (the inhibitory interaction of two stimuli presented in rapid succession) and apparent movement. The argument is, then, not that there are no effects of experience in such cases, only that the judgments made are not influenced by interpretation or extraneous cues of *a particular type* whose effects are contingent on an observer's particular history. One must specify exactly *which* type of cues are to be excluded (in our example, nonstereoptic cues to depth) for the position to be defensible. The argument is not, and cannot be, that *no* effects of experience are present. It is altogether likely that some degree of exercise is necessary to keep the visual system functioning adequately, and it can be argued that the search for information about "perception" in a completely inexperienced or naïve visual system is meaningless (Hamlyn, 1957).

If all observers with normal vision and nonsingular visual histories report essentially the same effects in an experiment of the sort suggested, where the special interpretative element is absent, this may be taken as evidence of operation of the primary detector and processing system. In this way, one can attempt to circumvent the problem of experience, and thus "deal with" it in a negative sense. Set and motivational variables can be similarly dealt with, not by elimination, but by control and manipulation, as is done in the methodology of signal-detection theory (Green & Swets, 1966). Here the concept of judgments that are "set-free" is denied, but explicit control and assessment of the effects can be made, albeit in fairly restricted situations. Probably the notion of an entirely "set-free" judgment is as implausible as the idea of an "experience-free" perception. Certainly in our paradigm case of "pure" stereoptic depth perception an instruction to look for depth in the stereogram facilitates its appearance. But only in a case where this was a *necessary condition* of the appearance of depth would we be tempted to ascribe the whole depth effect to some higher-order process in the system.

The difficulties in attempting to investigate the unalloyed coding system in young babies have already been touched on. It might be argued that young children still are the best subjects for investigation of the system, even though some perceptual learning may have occurred in the first days and weeks of life. The point is not disputed; however, to date there have been singularly few studies of direct relevance to the coding of patterns. Interest has been concentrated more on ethological, motivational, and other collative variables (Berlyne, 1960; Spitz, 1946) than the question of pattern coding per se, which would probably have to involve training and transfer paradigms using patterns devised to test particular hypotheses about coding. Although there has been some work on pattern perception in human infants (for example, Fantz, 1967) it is relatively unanalytic and tells very little about the details of pattern-recognition processes. Perhaps the study of eye movements in infants' fixations on simple geometrical patterns (Salapatek & Kessen, 1966) is relevant, although this does not bear directly on the question of *how* patterns—or pattern elements—are coded. However, this and similar investigations by Lang (1966), Spears (1964), and others show that infants are capable of elementary pattern recognition; there seems to be here a still largely unexplored field of great potential interest.

It is worthwhile to ask whether, in a more positive vein, modeling can contribute to the understanding of experiential and motivational variables in pattern recognition. The idea that "attention" is a major factor in discrimination learning is currently much favored (for example, Lovejoy, 1965, 1966; Sutherland, 1964b; Zeaman & House, 1963). Effects of attention and experience (in general) are clearly intimately related. The difficulty with attention as a theoretical tool is that it is too readily identified with a single process at the empirical level—selective response to a particular dimension or cue, for example—and not so easily integrated into a well-specified model of discrimination learning. Perhaps it is too much to expect that such an elusive concept can be so used, but an attempt to show how it may be done is made in Chapter 10, making use of the engineer's concept of a pattern-training machine. Such a move does not come near to an explanation of all the richness and variety of the known effects, but it at least can sketch out the lines along which a satisfactory theoretical treatment may be developed.

The Phenomenological Problem

Psychologists today do not generally bother themselves unduly with questions of an epistemological nature. Inherent in the structural-model-building approach is the assumption that specification of inputs and outputs to the system can generally most usefully be done in terms of processes which have a strongly physiological flavor, even if their direct identification as physiological events is not possible. The claim that this mode of action leads to a useful framework to guide empirical investigation, and often to insight into the systems investigated, is readily defensible. However, one cannot from this infer that the phenomenological problem is meaningless or unimportant. At its simplest the problem can be stated as: Why does a square look like a square? Or, to avoid an apparent circularity: Why does a square look the way it does? The problem can be discussed from many angles, and leads to consideration of some of the niceties of the logic of psychological explanation. This discussion will be taken up in the final chapter. For the moment one may note that, so far as models for the visual system are concerned, one need only postulate a one-to-one correspondence between an "event" in the model—activity at some locus within it or a certain specified pattern of activity—and overt responses to patterns whether verbal or not. With this postulate accepted, one can make progress in the explanation of pattern recognition, but one must at the same time realize that it sidesteps some nontrivial issues.[2]

Thus, for the moment, we may claim that the phenomenological problem is not one which need inhibit our progress, since it is not the sort of problem the model-building approach can solve. Again, it must be emphasized that this is not the same as saying that the problem does not exist.

CONCLUSION

To recapitulate: It is argued that the four special problems facing the theorist who attempts to model human pattern recognition are not insuperable. By admitting the problems, but limiting our aims advisedly, we can proceed with viable analyses of pattern recognition. The phenomenological problem is set aside for the moment, and the postulate made that a one-to-one correspondence between outputs from a model and observable responses is a sufficient condition for the purposes of explaining pattern recognition as a classificatory process. The problem of complexity is dealt with, again circumscribing an area of application, first by concentrating on areas where the evidence suggests that special features of the pattern-processing system operate, and second by studying visual responses under well-controlled, but simplified, conditions of stimulation. This is done in the hope that one can thereby discover features of the primary-detection-and-processing system which may have direct relevance to the study of more complex and general situations. The difficulties posed by the well-established facts of perceptual learning are reduced—although not eliminated—by attempting to define areas of study where such effects are minimal. Admittedly the definition proceeds more on logical than empirical grounds, but this condition seems to be forced on us by the

---

[2] Incidentally, the postulate is accepted also by computer model-simulators. As far as the simulation is concerned, it is really irrelevant whether the computer's output is in the form of typed characters, graphs, punched-tape, or whatever. All that is important is that the outputs from the model should bear a one-to-one relation to the computer outputs, which is defined so that the classifications which the model makes of its inputs can be understood.

nature of the material under study. Similar arguments apply to the effects of set, special interests, and other motivational variables. To the extent that techniques are available for controlling them and/or for estimating their effects, they should not jeopardize the search for models for human pattern recognition. More positively, it should be possible to incorporate—although perhaps only in a very general way—such higher-order variables into models for human perception. This can be done if the distinction between a built-in primary-detection-and-processing (or coding-) system on the one hand, and a modifiable recognition-with-memory system on the other, is accepted. The distinction may be quite artificial, although some considerations, both logical and experimental, seem to bear it out, and it will be maintained on the grounds that it clarifies the issues and simplifies the devising of models for the visual system as pattern recognizer.

Having delineated the areas within which it seems profitable to proceed, I turn in the following three chapters to a more detailed discussion of several lines of investigation of human pattern recognition.

CHAPTER 7
Binocular Vision
and Pattern Coding

TWO EYES, BUT ONE VISUAL WORLD

Scientific interest in binocular vision has a long history, going back at least as far as Aristotle. As I argued in the last chapter, the topic of binocular vision is of particular importance to any theoretical analysis of pattern recognition, because it has some special—and surprising—properties, which need to be explained, and which themselves suggest in many cases the lines along which such explanations may be sought. Progress in understanding the facts of binocular vision has been dependent on the prior understanding of retinal image formation, the concept of visual direction, and resolution of the supposed problem of inversion of the retinal image. Several histories of these ideas are available, notably in Boring (1942), and Walls (1951a, b, c). Wheatstone's description (1838) of the stereoscope and of the fundamental role played by horizontal retinal disparities in stereopsis gave great impetus to the study of binocular vision as well as a new and powerful technique for its analysis. Again, the history is outlined by Boring (1942); Linksz (1950) gives a particularly thorough discussion of the development of the concepts of horopter, corresponding points, and visual direction, all of which required clear definition before any adequate concept of retinal disparity was possible.

As a preliminary step to the discussion of binocular vision, the main facts and concepts may briefly and in somewhat simplified form be summarized as follows:

We know that the optics of the normal eye cause a sharp image of the visual scene to be focused on the retina, and that this is the "proximal stimulus," or primary generator of visual sensation, and particularly of pattern perception. With the eye maintaining a fixed line of regard, each perceived contour or pattern element has a definite location in the visual field, or *visual direction*. It is natural to identify this visual direction with the location on the retina at which the stimulation occurs. A problem arises when the eye changes its line of regard because the retinal locus for a particular pattern element now changes, yet the position of that element in the external visual world does not change; as Rock (1966) puts it, the position with respect to the "phenomenal self" does not change. How this stability can be achieved and maintained is a very real problem to be considered in Chapter 8. But, if we stick to the definition in terms of retinal locus, the visual direction of a point will change when the eye moves.

Consider now what happens when both eyes in a normal binocular-visual system view the same scene. Initially, the lines of regard (or visual axes) will converge on some definite fixation point, as shown in Fig. 7.1. It is an established fact that the fixation point has the same visual direction for both eyes and is seen as a single point (or pattern element or feature, depending on what is being fixated). The two views are said to "fuse" into one, and form an element in the binocular-visual field (or the Cyclopean field, as Helmholtz called it). The loci stimulated on the two retinas (O_L and O_R in Fig. 7.1) are said to be *corresponding points,* in this case points at or very close to the centers of the foveas. What happens to other elements in the visual scene? Are there other positions with identical visual directions for the two eyes, and if so what are they? How can one define other corresponding points on the two retinas? The obvious move seems to be to define corresponding points in terms of retinal topography; corresponding points P_L and P_R (Fig. 7.1) are those points in the plane of the diagram which are an equal distance from their respective retinal centers, O_L and O_R. An external point, P, whose image falls on the points P_L and P_R should have, according to the concepts developed above, identical visual directions and be seen as a single point. This turns out in general to be the case—images falling on corresponding points in the two retinas have the same visual directions. However, fusion does not necessarily occur, since this depends on whether *similar pattern elements* are seen at P by the two eyes. In natural situations the elements seen will be similar because they will be the two eyes' views of the same object, but one can artifically present different elements to the two eyes, in which case there may be either *suppression* of one element by the other (only one is seen), or else an irregularly alternating suppression of first one and then the other, called *rivalry*.

The point P has a special property with respect to F, C_L, and C_R. Since the distance along the left retina, $O_L P_L$, is equal to the distance $O_R P_R$ on the right retina, the angles $O_L C_L P_L$ and $O_R C_R P_R$ are equal, which means

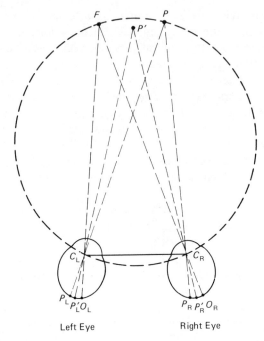

Left Eye   Right Eye

Fig. 7.1. The definition of corresponding points and their associated visual directions. C_L and C_R are the optical centers of the two eyes, F the point of fixation. O_L and O_R are the visual central points on each retina, which have the visual direction of F. P_L and P_R are corresponding points on the two retinas, with the visual direction P. F, P, C_L and C_R all lie on the so-called Vieth-Müller horopter-circle. All points which stimulate corresponding points in the two eyes lie on this circle. P' is a point off the circle, which stimulates noncorresponding points P_L' and P_R' on the retinas.

that angle FC_LP equals angle FC_RP. By an elementary theorem of Euclidean plane geometry, it follows that F, P, C_R, and C_L all lie on one circle. It follows from this that *any* point whose image falls on corresponding points on the two retinas lies on that same circle, which is called the "Vieth-Müller horopter-circle." Thus we can say that all those points which have identical visual directions for the two eyes in a given state of convergence lie on the Vieth-Müller circle, which goes through the optical centers of the two eyes and the point of fixation. It can be shown that for a different condition of convergence (say fixation on a further point, F') the same statement can be made—corresponding points (defined in terms of retinal distance) still have identical visual directions, and the relevant images lie on the (new) Vieth-Müller circle. For each state of convergence, however, there is a different Vieth-Müller circle, because it is defined in terms of the points C_L, C_R, and F.

From these considerations we can state that for all normal conditions of convergence the points having identical visual directions for the two eyes have an orderly arrangement at a nearly constant distance from the eyes, which is the distance of the point of fixation. For the central parts of the visual field (and taking into account the up-down dimension which is not represented in the figure) we can say that these points lie approximately in a plane, perpendicular to the line of regard, in which the fixation point lies.[1] This plane is called the "reference plane," or "nuclear plane," after the German *Kernebene*.

It can be shown that any point or visual feature not on the Vieth-Müller circle (or not in the reference plane, in the simplified three-dimensional case) must necessarily cast images on *non*corresponding points on the two retinas. (The proof will not be given: It depends on the fact that the angles $C_L P' C_R$ and $C_L P C_R$ cannot be equal, for if they were, P' would be on the Vieth-Müller circle, which is contrary to hypothesis. Therefore the angles $P_L' C_L O_L$ and $P_R' C_R O_R$ cannot be equal, so P_L' and P_R' cannot be corresponding points.) If P' casts images on noncorresponding points, its visual direction for the two eyes should be different—that is, it should appear in different places to the two eyes; it should give rise to *double images*. For points much nearer or farther than the reference plane this is what happens. However, for points reasonably close to the reference plane, the discrepancy between the image positions on the two retinas (the retinal disparity) is not great, and instead of two images, a single image is seen *in depth* (that is, in front of, or behind, the reference plane). Regions within which single binocular vision can be obtained are known as Panum's fusional areas. Whether the single image is seen in front of or behind the reference plane depends on the nature of the disparity, which, in natural situations, is determined by whether the point P' is nearer to or farther from the point of fixation. This single binocular image appears to have a visual direction which is a compromise between the visual directions of the two monocular images. As we shall see, this point has been much disputed.

The generation of depth impressions purely in terms of disparities between the pattern elements at the two eyes is called "stereoptic depth perception." These disparities, also called binocular parallax, are not the only cues to depth; some of the others are perspective, interposition of objects, motion parallax (relative apparent motion of near and far objects as the observer moves his head), and shadows. Pure stereoptic depth

---

[1] Strictly speaking, this should be a sector of a sphere or perhaps some more complicated surface. Nineteenth-century researchers in vision spent much time discussing and trying to measure the so-called horopter surface, discussions which we can ignore since they seem to have little direct relevance to an understanding of the nature of binocular vision beyond what has been outlined here.

perception is rare in the natural mode, but can be produced with a stereoscope, which brings two different images into corresponding parts of the two eyes, as they maintain a normal state of convergence.

Having given definitions for the most relevant terms, we can now turn to consideration of some of the facts of binocular vision and attempts which have been made to explain them.

FUSION OR SUPPRESSION?

Two schools of thought developed regarding the nature of stereopsis and depth perception, represented by the nativism of Hering and the empiricism of Helmholtz. I will not delve into the involved and frequently heated arguments over the disputed issues; however, certain residual effects can be seen in quite recent discussions of depth perception and models for stereopsis. Although there is no necessary connection between a strongly nativistic position and the suppression theory of binocular vision, that theory is sometimes defended on the grounds that a form of suppression theory is inevitable to reconcile with one another the facts[2] about visual directions discussed in the previous section, namely:

1. Considered in terms of monocular stimulation, every point on the retina has one and only one built-in, fixed visual direction.
2. Corresponding points of the two eyes (as we saw above) have identical visual directions; but in normal binocular viewing, features of the visual field which are not in the reference plane will be imaged on noncorresponding points, so must have different visual directions.
3. The binocular Cyclopean field, on the other hand, contains apparently single images near the reference plane, despite the fact that their monocular counterparts have different visual directions (fall on noncorresponding points in the two eyes).

The reason why the images near the reference plane are seen as single, according to the suppression theory, is (as the name implies) that the input from one eye effectively suppresses the input from the other. According to this account, the appearance of a single binocular image does *not* require a change in the monocular visual direction, so it can still be maintained that each and every point on the retina does have but a single visual direction which is immutable. This position is held by Asher (1953a, b) but has had many other proponents. Indeed, a suppression theory was proposed long before the relation of disparity to depth perception

---

[2] Perhaps one should say: "the *supposed* facts." As we shall see, the first of them is now questionable.

was ever known (Leonardo da Vinci is said to have entertained the notion, for instance).

To be more explicit, and to avoid a somewhat tedious discussion of empirical and ideal horopters and the complications connected therewith, consider the stereogram shown in Fig. 7.2. Assuming an appropriate state

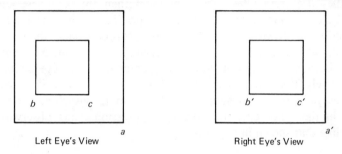

Left Eye's View   Right Eye's View

Fig. 7.2. A simple line stereogram. The two halves are viewed in a stereoscope, which superimposes the left- and right-eye views.

of fixation, so that the large squares a and a' are fused, in register, or stimulating corresponding sets of points in the two retinas, then the vertical sides of the small inner squares, bc and $b'c'$ must necessarily fall on noncorresponding points. The nativistic position, as we have seen, holds that each retinal receptor (or functional unit) signals one, and only one, visual direction, so that the vertical sides of the smaller squares *should be seen double*. But provided the horizontal disparities are not too great, a single small square is seen, and goes into depth for the observer with normal binocular vision. What happened to the different visual directions? The common answer, and the one which seems to be in harmony with the prima facie evidence, is that the small inner squares *fuse*,[3] or become one; but this fusional hypothesis is anathema to the nativist because it violates the principle of single visual directions for each point on each retina; the only alternative seems to be that one of the small squares is suppressed, so that only the other is visible.

This position seems to be tenable because suppression of one visual field by the other undoubtedly can occur, and is a normal response of

[3] This fusion, sometimes called "sensory fusion," which occurs between disparate elements in the two parts of a stereogram otherwise in register, is to be distinguished from "motor fusion," which occurs when the eyes change their vergence in order to bring the two parts of a stereogram (or other binocular display) into registry. Cyclotorsion—rotation of the eyeball about its visual axis—can also be a component of "motor fusion." By "fusion," I shall mean "sensory fusion" unless otherwise stated.

the system when nonsimilar patterns are projected to the two eyes. In particular, a sharp contour in one eye will tend to suppress a background of less clearly defined contours in the other if their orientations are different; different contours of equal prominence at the two eyes, intersecting in the Cyclopean field at an angle which is too great to be eliminated by cyclotorsion, will tend to be mutually inhibitory and rivalrous; dots or thin lines are more effective suppressors than thicker lines; and so on (Hochberg, 1964). Moving contours are particularly powerful suppressors (Grindley & Townsend, 1966). Mutual suppression is the rule, but it is usually phasic (that is, produces rivalry) and in many situations, depending both on stimulus factors and dominance, one eye suppresses more effectively than the other (Fox, 1963). Any monocularly viewed contour generally seems to suppress patterns in its visual neighborhood occurring in the other eye, the area of suppression being observable in situations like that shown in Fig. 7.3.

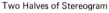

Two Halves of Stereogram   Impression of Combined View

Fig. 7.3. A pair of patterns which do not fuse when viewed in a stereoscope. The right panel gives an impression of the suppression of contours in the right eye's field of view, induced by the stronger contour in the left eye's field.

The general finding is that *any* contour viewed with one eye tends to "carry with it" a band of suppression patterns in the other eye (Kaufman, 1963). If a contour in the other eye happens to be in registry or near-registry with the original, why should one suppose that it has a special status? Should it not tend to be suppressed, just like any other? Can it not be argued that in this case the suppression is not easily detected, just because the contours *are* in near-registry? In this way, suppression begins to look like a natural explanation for the unitary appearance of the Cyclopean field, and is parsimonious in the sense that one mechanism is held to mediate both rivalry and stereopsis. However, there are some difficulties.

In the first place, the apparent position of the small square of the stereogram in Fig. 7.2 *does change* when it goes into depth. It is not the small square to the left, as in the left image, nor the small square in its position relative to the large square as in the right image that is seen, but a square further away than the reference plane and somewhere between the visual directions of the small monocular squares. Hochberg (1964), favoring a suppression model, argued at one time that eye movements may play a fundamental role in stereopsis, and postulated that each depth plane within a stereoptic array is defined by the set of vergence changes needed to bring given sets of disparities to zero. If I understand it correctly, this notion would require that, during stereoptic depth perception, the eyes scan the display in depth, in the sense that the eyes change their degree of convergence continually, in order to "assess" the amount of disparity between features in the visual display. This postulate cannot readily explain the change in visual direction for elements of a pattern seen in depth, and entails a complicated set of rules for the interaction of eye movements with suppression if the *stability* of visual direction seen in a stereogram is to be explained. There is no evidence of interaction of the sort required, and such a theory cannot explain the fact that stereopsis is obtainable from extremely brief presentations of stereopairs, and even from after-images (that is, situations where eye movements cannot play a role). It is also a well-known fact that suppression does not occur between parts of a stereopair presented only for a few milliseconds, even if they would be extremely rivalrous under normal extended viewing (for example, horizontal lines in one eye, vertical lines in the other). Furthermore the following demonstration seems to show definitely that suppression is not a *necessary* factor in "fusion" and stereopsis.

The stereopair shown in Fig. 7.4 is Panum's well-known "limiting case": Fusion of the single line *c* of the display on the right with *either a* or *b* on the left yields a strong stereoptic effect, provided the distance between *a* and *b* is not too great. A homologue in real depth is shown in Fig. 7.5A, where the suspended threads *d* and *e* are so arranged that *e* is

Left Eye's View   Right Eye's View

Fig. 7.4. The stereogram which illustrates Panum's "limiting case." When viewed in a stereoscope, *c* can fuse with either *a* or *b*, and in both instances stereodepth is seen. The right-hand line (*a*) always appears in front of the left-hand line (*b*).

superimposed on d in the right eye's view. For the right eye, this corresponds to c of Fig. 7.4. Small check-tabs are affixed to both threads at different heights, but not too far from the fixation point, so that both tabs are easily visible in both monocular displays. Under steady binocular viewing conditions both tabs are seen in both eyes; that is, two tabs are seen on the right line, and one on the left, if the line seen by the right eye is fused with line e in the left eye's view. The binocular view is shown in Fig. 7.5B. Clearly the tab marked d' is seen by the right eye, whereas e' is seen by both, and d'' by the left eye only. The appearance of d' is not as strong as e'—it is normally slightly out of focus, for one thing—and it may disappear momentarily. However, such fluctuations do not affect the impression of depth (in this situation the right-hand line appears nearer than the left) which seems to be independent of any suppression that may be occurring. A similar finding is easily verified with the stereogram of Fig. 7.5C; that is, the marker d' does not disappear when stereopsis occurs (again the right-hand line appears nearer).

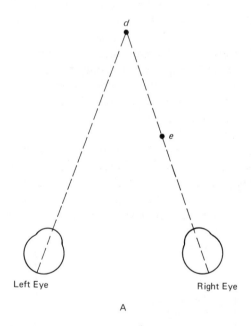

Left Eye   Right Eye

A

Fig. 7.5. (A) A real situation corresponding to Panum's limiting case. The points d and e represent suspended threads, or rods, which are so aligned that for the right eye d is behind e (that is, only a single line is seen). The left eye sees two lines. (B) The two views of the arrangement in A, with tabs attached to the lines, showing displays seen by the eyes separately and a combined view (right eye's single line fused with e). (C) The same arrangement as above, but in this case the right eye's view is fused with d. (B and C are on facing page.)

Asher (1953a, b) provides several different arguments and demonstrations in support of the suppression theory. For example, the stereopair of Fig. 7.6A is normally seen stereoptically as a circle with a black spot in depth behind the reference plane. He argues that, when check marks are added, as in 7.6B, and aligned in the stereo display, one of the patterns of 7.6C will always be seen, and never the two circles (or circle and spot) traditionally associated with this stereogram. The demonstration is quite convincing when the amount of binocular parallax is fairly large; however, it has not been established that the appearance of the display

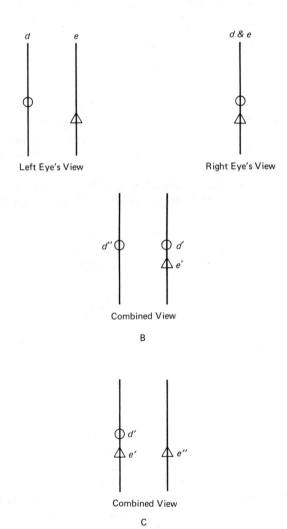

FIG. 7.5 (*Continued*)

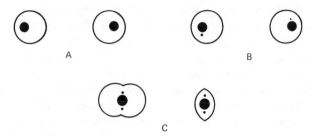

Fig. 7.6. (A) A simple line stereogram. When viewed in a stereoscope with the outer circles in register, the inner circles are seen as one circle, concentric with the outer circle and in front of the reference plane. (B) The same stereopair, but with check marks added, one to each half. (C) Two views of the combined stereopair, with check marks in place, according to Asher. This is held to demonstrate that there is no "true" fusion.

is necessarily as in 7.6C under small degrees of disparity. In this case, the "traditional" two-circle view is extremely compelling. Finding stereograms in which fusion does not occur but suppression does is not the same as proving that suppression is a *necessary* condition of stereopsis and that "fusion" is illusory.

As a further example, Asher cites Helmholtz' experiment with the stereogram of Fig. 7.7. Helmholtz realized, as had Wheatstone before

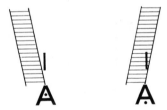

Fig. 7.7. Helmholtz' stereogram for attempting to demonstrate different visual directions for corresponding points in the two eyes.

him, that if a pair of contours in the two eyes with different visual directions can apparently change those directions so as to fuse, it should follow logically that the converse is true; two contours with the *same* visual direction in two eyes can be made, under appropriate conditions, to appear to have *different* directions. In other words, and in terms of Fig. 7.7, with the A's in register, if the shaded strip is seen as single and receding, the two I's should appear in different positions in the binocular view, despite having identical monocular visual directions (determined by the registry of the A's), *if* the fusion of the shaded strip really involves alteration of the visual directions of noncorresponding points in the two eyes. The fact that only one I is seen is taken as good evidence for the constancy of visual directions and correspondence. Failure to show any shift is taken as positive support for a suppression theory as the only reasonable alternative, and indeed rivalry and suppression between parts of this stereopair are usually very strong. Now finding one, or even several, stereo displays in which the postulated change in visual direction cannot be detected is *not* the same as proving that it cannot occur under any circumstances—a familiar weakness of negative evidence. In fact, we shall find shortly that convincing demonstrations of shifts in apparent visual direction are available, and in particular that contours with the same monocular directions can be shown to have different directions in the Cyclopean field. But the shifts can generally be detected reliably only under rather special conditions.

Although this discussion of the suppression theory of binocular vision is scarcely exhaustive, it should be sufficient to show that no incontestable evidence forces us to accept a model in which suppression is the sole mediator of single binocular vision in general, and of stereopsis in particular. This is not the same as claiming that suppression plays no part in binocular vision; it clearly does so. The fact that stereopsis can be detected in diplopic (double-image) and rivalrous displays shows that suppression can even play a role in stereoptic depth perception. The point to be established is that it is not the only mechanism, and probably not the most important one. The issue was raised at length because if suppression could be shown to be the mediator, or at least the dominant factor, in stereopsis, this would rule out the search for more complex—and perhaps more interesting—models. Further search for operations and processors of disparate binocular inputs would be redundant, since the suppression theory asserts, essentially, that both monocular inputs cannot be simultaneously effective in generating the Cyclopean field. In other words, it asserts that binocular inputs compete for a single channel, but do not interact within the channel. This closes the door on what seems to be a promising field for research into central factors in the visual system.[4] In this sense, a strong motive for discounting the suppression theory exists. One hopes, however, that the evidence has been presented without bias.

THE ARGUMENT FROM ANATOMY

It was suggested earlier that one of the chief attractions of a suppression theory is its consistency with the nativistic view that visual direction and

---

[4] It is generally accepted that binocular processing must be largely central, because of the anatomical arrangements and physiological properties of the eyes and their central connections. See further discussion below.

correspondence is a "wired-in," fixed property of the normal visual system. This position (but without discussion of the suppression theory) is most ably and forcefully defended by Walls (1951a, b, c). That defense stands as a vain monument to scientific orthodoxy, however, since both behavioral and neurophysiological evidence have since come to light to invalidate many of his arguments and most of his conclusions. His main argument, of course, stems from the anatomically close mapping of retinal points onto lateral-geniculate and subsequently cortical loci. Discussing the work of Polyak, le Gros Clark, and others, he states:

> Such work has abundantly confirmed the picture first drawn by Gordon Holmes from studies of individuals with traumatic cortical lesions and correspondingly-localized scotomata in their visual fields: Every topographic locus in the retina is projected to a very particular point in Area 17, . . . *Area 17 is thus a strict isomorph, a veritable anatomic map of the retina itself.*

And again:

> . . . an Area 17 cell . . . informs only of direction with reference to the intrinsic map in which it forms one point, and hence gives direction within visual space which is the segment of real space imaged at the moment on the retina . . . The direction of any spatial point relative to the direction of the spatial point fixated . . . is an oculocentric direction whose cortical sign is the excitation of a particular Area 17 ganglion cell (Walls, 1951b, pp. 121–122).

This is strict anatomical isomorphism, a conceptual and empirical state of knowledge that should be abandoned in view of recent work on recording from individual cortical neurons. It will be recalled that the Hubel and Wiesel "complex-field" cortical cell is activated by a contour in a specific orientation, but independently of its location within the receptive field. This does not immediately establish neurophysiologically that the visual direction for a point on the retina can change, but it demonstrates that the strict one-to-one correspondence between locus of retinal stimulation and cortical response (and hence visual direction), which is so strongly suggested by the earlier anatomical evidence, is invalid. It establishes that a certain cortical response *could have been occasioned* by a particular sort of contour in any one of several different retinal positions. "Cortical output" is thus not tied inevitably to a strictly localized retinal input, and this undermines what seems to be the nativists' principal a priori ground for espousing a suppression theory of binocular vision. I shall show presently that the single-unit results suggest quite a different arrangement for an innate binocular processing system.[5]

---

[5] Since this was written a variety of evidence in support of a true physiological fusional system has come to light. The most relevant findings are presented later in the chapter.

DEMONSTRATION OF SHIFT IN VISUAL DIRECTION

To return now to the perceptual evidence on changes in visual direction, Fig. 7.7 shows a stereogram with which Helmholtz was unable to demonstrate a shift which should be expected if fusion with stereopsis really entails changes in visual direction from the monocular to the binocular state. Various other attempts of the same sort have been equally unsuccessful (summarized by Linschoten, 1956). It can be argued, however, that the conditions for observing the shift must be favorable for it to be detected, and the conditions are anything but favorable in the stereogram of Fig. 7.7. The shaded strips are not the easiest type of stimulus to fuse; the type of disparity will tend to induce cyclotorsion; the backgrounds of the I's are different and this may promote rivalry; the two I's themselves are powerful stimuli to their own fusion (whether sensory or motor), and this creates instability of the stereoview, since there are other conflicting fusional stimuli present. Linschoten (1956) searching for more optimal conditions, presents the stereogram shown in Fig. 7.8, and under the

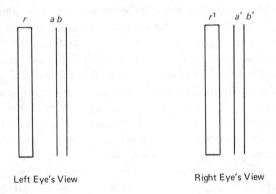

Left Eye's View   Right Eye's View

Fig. 7.8. Linschoten's stereogram, with which he succeeded in demonstrating a difference in visual direction for corresponding sets of points in the two eyes.

appropriate viewing conditions it does indeed lead to a detectable shift from monocular to binocular visual directions. In this stereogram, the rectangles are brought into register, and the right edge of the combined rectangle rr' fixated. The two pairs of parallels, ab and $a'b'$, are so drawn that the distance ra equals $r'b'$. Therefore, when r and r' are in register, the lines a and b' fall on corresponding sets of points in the two eyes and should combine with each other, if the constancy-of-visual-direction hypothesis holds. Strictly speaking, if no suppression occurs, the binocular view should then consist of the rectangle and three parallel lines to its right, a', $b'a$ (combined), and b, in that order. What is *seen* by the normal binocular observer is the rectangle in the reference plane and *one* pair of parallel lines standing out from that plane, and nearer to the observer, as would be predicted from the normal operation of binocular parallax. This is prima facie evidence that a shift in visual direction has occurred, since a seems to be fused with a', b with b', and therefore the monocularly identical directions a and b' are now seen in two *different* directions, aa' and bb'. The argument that first appearances are deceptive, and that in fact at least one of the parallels is being suppressed, can be refuted, most easily by placing checkmarks near each of the monocular lines—these checkmarks do not disappear on fusion. I have also found that where the display is presented under brief illumination (when no suppression occurs), stereopsis can still be observed. The point can be further substantiated by coloring the two halves of the stereogram differently (but not too differently). The colors tend to be rivalrous when the parts of the stereogram combine, but the rivalry occurs on the contours *which remain in their binocular directions;* that is, aa' and bb' are stable as to position but demonstrate concurrent inputs from the two eyes in terms of color. Linschoten (1956) presents a number of variants on the basic display of Fig. 7.8, all of which demonstrate the same shift in binocular visual direction and the change from identical monocular directions in the two eyes which this entails.[6] It has been argued that Linschoten's "identical" monocular directions for a and b' are not so in fact, since they do not fall exactly on the horopter.[7] This is true, but it can easily be shown that such a slight deviation scarcely affects the argument about a change from monocular to binocular directions. Also, by arranging for a and b to be moveable with respect to the rectangle, I find that Linschoten's result is obtainable over a range of positions which certainly includes that in which the monocular directions of a and b' *are* identical. This is done by providing two independent fields for the left eye, by means of a half-silvered mirror, and displaying the lines ab on a card which can be moved horizontally relative to the rest of the stereogram on a microscope carriage. The arrangement guarantees that, at some point, a and b' will fall on corresponding points. Stereoptic depth is seen, so long as the disparities between the two sets of parallels (ab, $a'b'$) do not become too large, and the amount of stereoptic depth can be observed to change as the pair ab is moved horizontally. One may conclude from this that Linschoten succeeded in demonstrating the change in visual direc-

---

[6] It is regrettable that Linschoten's work is not available in English translation. Apart from some ingenious and important experimental work, his book contains a historical review of the field up to about 1950, of which no English equivalent exists.

[7] A somewhat disparaging review by Ogle, in which the horopter argument is raised, is probably one reason why Linschoten's work is not better known to English-speaking psychologists.

tion which had eluded Helmholtz and others. It was suggested before that such a finding can no longer be held to go against the brute facts of the physical structure and operation of the visual system, since there is no reason to think there is strict one-to-one correspondence between excitation of retinal and cortical points at the cellular level. The Linschoten stereogram does not contain the conflicting elements discussed in Helmholtz' example. With only one type of contour generating stereopsis—the vertical lines—it may be that the Linschoten stereogram taps operation of a basic stereo-fusion system that tends to be overridden in the more complicated cases. Interestingly enough, those pattern elements in Linschoten's stereogram which show the monocular-to-binocular shift are the very elements which are coded in the Hubel and Wiesel system. It seems scarcely possible that this is fortuitous, and it would be extremely interesting to know to what extent other sorts of pattern element can show the same shift. (Linschoten did not investigate this question systematically.) A definite hypothesis about how such effects might be mediated will be developed, but before doing so some other findings of direct relevance will be considered.

STEREOPSIS WITHOUT MONOCULAR PATTERN RECOGNITION

A major event in the analysis of binocular vision was Julesz' report of stereoptic responses to binocular parallax in computer-generated patterns of dots (Julesz, 1960). A stereopair of the type studied is shown in Fig. 7.9; each side consists of a matrix of squares (called "dots")

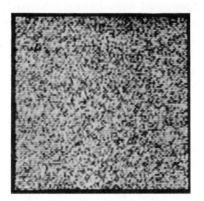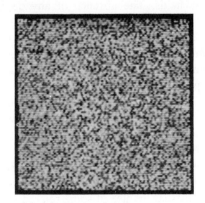

Fig. 7.9. The random-dot stereogram of Julesz. Although no contours are seen within each half of the stereopair viewed separately, when they are appropriately fused, a square whose surface has the same mottled appearance as the background stands out from the reference plane.

each assigned a brightness value at random (various quantizations of the brightness levels, from 2 to 16, have been used. The number of levels appears not to be important, so far as stereo effects are concerned). Each matrix contains some 10,000 dots, and the two are identical, except that the one on the right has a square region at its center in which the pattern is displaced uniformly to one side (the "blanks" being filled in with the original pattern-brightness values). This horizontal displacement introduces binocular parallax when the displays are combined so that their edges are in register, and the region where disparity exists stands out from the reference plane, the direction of stereopsis depending, of course, on whether the displacement in the central region is nasal or temporal. For the observer who has not previously seen the effect, depth perception may take some time to occur, often several minutes. However, there is typically very rapid "learning," and after presentation of several different stereograms of this sort, the effect is practically immediate. The initial difficulty is not surprising, since the material is unfamiliar and none of the secondary cues to depth is present. However, the real importance of the technique stems from the fact that monocular pattern recognition cannot occur, in the sense that neither half of the stereogram alone contains cues to the binocular stereoscopic pattern that emerges. Although this seems obvious in a general way, Julesz proved, in a series of ingenious experiments in which various perturbations are introduced into one or both parts of the stereogram, that monocular recognition of micropatterns is not a necessary precursor of binocular pattern perception. Rather the combining operation is shown to be one of matching-up point domains in the two fields; matching of single points is insufficient, since such a process would readily be thrown out by introducing visual "noise" into the fields. The absence of any depth cues apart from binocular disparity and the unfamiliar and "neutral" appearance of the two halves of the stereogram suggest very strongly that the system for coding this sort of information is "built into" the visual apparatus (although its operations improve with use) and is not affected by any interpretative element or special conditions of experience, in the sense previously discussed (Chapter 6). Thus, the dot stereograms seem to provide an excellent means of investigating part of the primary detection-and-processing system, and moreover of studying some of its more central features.[8] Julesz-type fields have been used in a number of subsequent investigations of binocular vision (for example, Dodwell & Engel, 1963; Hochberg & Brooks, 1962; Julesz, 1966; Julesz & Spivack, 1967; White, 1962a, b) and perhaps suggested the use of some related types of material (Kaufman, 1964a).

[8] See footnote 4.

TEMPORAL INTEGRATION OF BINOCULAR INPUTS

A rather different sort of study was reported by Efron (1957). He investigated temporal factors in the detection of depth in stereoptic displays by having his subjects observe stereograms under intermittent illumination. The displays used were "neutral" in that cues of perspective, relative size and brightness, interposition, and so forth, were not present. Each half of the stereopair consisted of three white capital letters on a uniform black background, with different degrees of disparity between corresponding letters in the two arrays. The two halves of a stereopair were viewed nonsimultaneously, as indicated in Fig. 7.10, *SI* being the

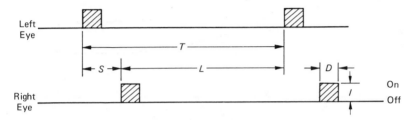

Fig. 7.10. The sequence of stimuli to the two eyes used by Efron to demonstrate temporal summation of binocular inputs. The two halves of a stereopair are presented separately, and intermittently, to the two eyes, but stereo depth is detected, provided the time intervals are not too great.

"short interval" between presentation of members of a pair, *LI* the "long interval" between pairs. The most important finding is illustrated in Fig. 7.11, namely, that stereoptic depth perception is not dependent on the simultaneous stimulation of both eyes, and that the appearance of depth under intermittent and nonsimultaneous inputs follows a lawful pattern. Practically identical results are found using Julesz-type fields, which reinforces the argument that the effects can be attributed to a "built-in" processing arrangement. It can be seen that the stereo-effect is obtained over quite long intervals, suggesting perhaps that binocular information can be extracted from the "visual image" (in Sperling's [1960] definition of that term) after external stimulation has ceased. An alternative hypothesis was developed by Engel, who postulated that each monocular pulse expands in time as it travels through the visual system. The expansion function is held to be a negative-exponential growth function, its characteristics being determined by the initial energy in the monocular pulses and by properties of the transmission lines which are physiologically plausible (Dodwell & Engel, 1963; Engel, 1962, 1964). The two monocular fields

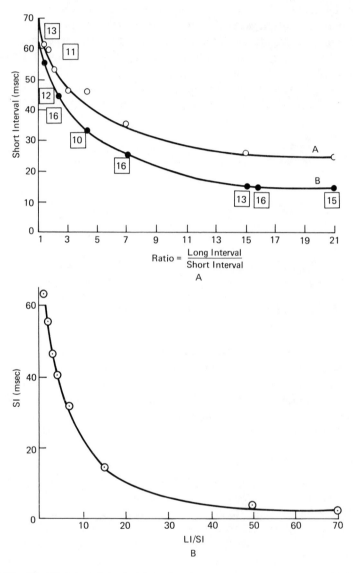

Fig. 7.11. (A) Efron's original data, showing temporal summation of binocular inputs as a function of time (two observers). Points below each curve show the durations of intrapair delays which yield stereopsis for a given *LI/SI* ratio. (B) Similar data reported by Dodwell and Engel, for stereograms consisting of Julesz fields.

are "matched up," or fused, in a coding array from which binocular signals are generated only when monocular signals are congruent, and such matching can occur only when the signals overlap temporally on the array (Fig. 7.11). Overlap can occur, even for initially nonsimultaneous monocular inputs, because of their expansion in time. The binocular signals are the inputs to a recognizer which specifically detects stereoptic properties arising from combination of the two monocular inputs. Temporal integration both within and between nonsimultaneous presentations of a stereopair shows good agreement with the transmission postulate. Such findings seem contrary to the hypothesis of a purely suppressive mechanism for stereopsis, and particularly to one in which eye movements play an important role, since the presentation time for the individual parts of the stereopair can be so short and the interval between them so long. Specifically, the two halves of a stereopair can be presented for a few milliseconds each, either simultaneously or separated by a few milliseconds, and depth is clearly seen. This time-order is far too short for deliberate eye movements to play a part in the genesis of stereopsis, and other evidence suggests that suppression is ineffective in this time range also. The long interval between the two halves of a stereopair can be as much as 300 msec, and it seems unlikely that suppressive mechanisms would be effective at this range. Eye movements have not been recorded during intermittent binocular stimulation of the sort described, but their vagaries even under steady fixation are sufficiently great to suggest that stereoptic information is extracted *despite* eye movements rather than because of them (see Chapter 9). Both temporally and spatially, the system is one which appears to work by means of some type of statistical smoothing or averaging operation.

COMBINATION OF MONOCULAR INPUTS INTO A BINOCULAR OUTPUT

To explain how matching might occur, Engel proposed a structural model for the binocular coding process which is shown in Fig. 7.12. Essentially the same notion of a "projection-fusion" array has been put forward by several authors (Boring, 1933; Charnwood, 1951; Linksz, 1950; Rønne, 1956, proposed a rather similar model); indeed, the structural arrangement suggested seems to be the natural one for conjoining the separate monocular inputs in a simple way so as to bring them into registry, even when their initial visual directions are noncorresponding. The process of conjoining, or correlating, the two monocular inputs to an array such as that shown in Fig. 7.12 is only crudely sketched, however, and little is said about the generation of binocular signals at the array (in the earlier models this problem was not even considered). Although

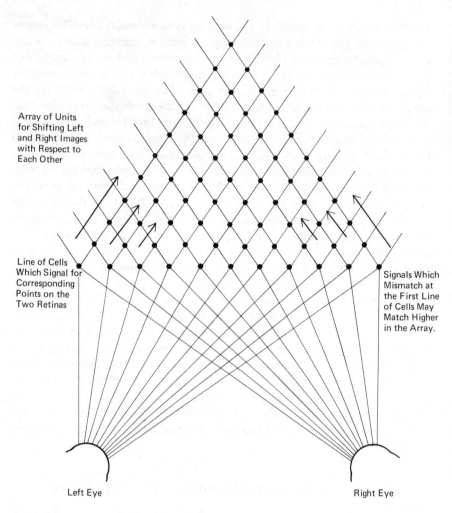

Array of Units
for Shifting Left
and Right Images
with Respect to
Each Other

Line of Cells
Which Signal for
Corresponding
Points on the
Two Retinas

Signals Which
Mismatch at
the First Line
of Cells May
Match Higher
in the Array.

Left Eye

Right Eye

Fig. 7.12. The "projection fusion" array suggested by Engel to account for stereoptic depth-perception and temporal summation.

some arguments have been expressed against any sort of fusional model (Kaufman, 1964b), it seems reasonable to consider more explicitly and carefully how the process of matching might occur and to what extent the operations of the array, and hence its outputs, might be specified in the light of other information we have about binocular visual systems. Kaufman's objections stem mainly from the fact that stereoptic depth is not generated *only* by disparities between otherwise congruent sets of contours. More thorough specification of the matching-and-combining operation can make this argument lose much of its force, as we shall see.

Practically every theorist who has proposed models for the binocular system admits explicitly that the proposals are too simple and account for no more than some of the data. Although the proposals to be made here are similarly incomplete, and lack firm empirical support in some respects, they go further than previous models in proposing specific forms for the coding of stereoptic information about contours, and particularly in suggesting how noncongruent inputs may be processed. In making use of recent neurophysiological findings in binocular processing they also attempt to give a firmer biological foundation to the process than is usual.

THE DIFFERENCE-FIELD OPERATOR

Julesz demonstrated that, at least for his type of display, stereoptic information is extracted from a fused binocular field in such a way that point domains of limited size, rather than individual points, are matched. He proposed a simple model which introduces the concept of a *difference field*. Formally, one may write $g_k(x, y) = L(x, y) * R(x + k, y)$, where k is a number identifying a given horizontal shift, and $*$ is an as yet unspecified operation. The set of g_k functions, over the range of k, is called the *analogue binocular field*, and it is on this field that depth processing occurs. If $*$ is identified with subtraction, a particularly simple representation of the system can be made, in terms of difference fields, D_k. Imagine that two identical random dot patterns are superimposed on each other in such a way that the brightness values of the points combine subtractively (which might be illustrated, for example, by superimposition of positive and negative transparencies of the same field). Clearly the result will be a uniform featureless field, which may be termed D_0. If a horizontal shift of one unit (dot) to the right is introduced, to produce D_1, the effect will be to reintroduce a pattern of dots again, with randomly distributed brightness values, and this will be true for all values of D_k except D_0. Consider, however, the stereopair of Fig. 7.9. Here, there are clearly *two* difference fields, but only two, which are not random over their whole extent, and these are D_0 and D_4 (because the horizontal shift in the central square is four dots) which are illustrated in Fig. 7.13. It is not difficult to see, then, that generating the D_k is a means of detecting any sort of horizontal parallax shifts between similar domains in random dot fields. Forming the D_ks is equivalent to shifting the two original fields laterally with respect to one another, step by step, and performing the subtraction on each pair of superimposed points each time. Returning now to the model of Fig. 7.12, it is clear that its function is precisely to shift monocular fields step-by-step with respect to each other and to evaluate the combined fields at each stage. It may thus be thought of as a possible instrumentation of the difference-field generator. There are difficulties, however, in attempting to specify the operator $*$ more

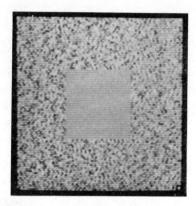 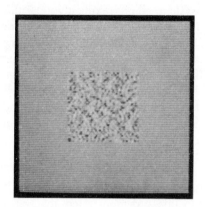

Fig. 7.13. An example of Julesz' "differencing" operation on a random-dct stereogram. D_0 is the difference field obtained by subtracting the brightness values of points in the right-hand member of the stereogram of Fig. 7.9 from the corresponding values in the left-hand member. D_4 is the difference field obtained when the same operation is performed after shifting the right-hand member four spaces to the right. It "detects" the uniform disparity shift in the central square.

fully. It seems certain that the simple operation of subtraction is wrong,[9] since it only works sensibly for Julesz-type fields. Also the specification for the generation of binocular signals must include some statement about the output of the analogue binocular field in Julesz' sense. It seems clear that a great deal of this output must be discarded (only a few of the D_ks yield useful information), and it is reasonable to suppose that this is one place where suppression plays a role. The point is made explicitly, although in a converse form, for the model of Fig. 7.12; only "matches" are signaled to the recognizer, implying suppression of mismatches. But we are still left with the problem of defining what constitutes a "match."

Complete specification of the matching operation presents very serious difficulties, since even for congruent monocular fields it is certainly non-linear so far as brightness and contrast summation are concerned, and this summation seems to depend both on the types and amount of contour in the two fields.[10] Further difficulties concern binocular mixing of color (see, for example, Treisman, 1962). As a first step, an attempt will be made to specify the matching operation for contours only, neglecting the questions of brightness, contrast and color.

[9] As Julesz explicitly recognized.
[10] See, for example, McLachlan, 1962. Engel (1969) has proposed an in-genious application of the autocorrelation function which accounts for the complex relationships between monocular and binocular brightnesses. As it presently stands, Engel's autocorrelation model accounts for brightness mixing, but not for the ex-traction of depth information, the problem we are here tackling.

It seems rather probable that binocular-pattern matching may be of more than one kind and may occur at more than one level in the system. While matching of point domains for patterns of small dots can be achieved by a difference-field operator, this would not work for macroscopic patterns, nor for contours generally. A subtractive-type operator is acceptable for Julesz fields since in nearly all cases the D_ks are essentially similar and random, and can therefore be suppressed without loss. Singular fields occur only where there is point-domain matching, so that recognition of stereoscopic depth can be defined as being equivalent to the detection of nonrandom domains in the D_ks. However, this would clearly not work for the more usual type of stereogram, such as that shown in Fig. 7.2. Here every D_k will have nonrandom features, and depth recognition must require the detection of a particular *type* of similarity in the two halves. Very probably this entails matching of contours having similar configurations and contrasts, although there is doubt as to whether this can be the complete operation, since contour is not the only available cue for stereoptic depth (Kaufman, 1964a, b). That particular problem will be taken up later. The next immediate step is to consider what form a contour-matching system might take, and to suggest a model—essentially an elaboration of the "projection-fusion" model—which makes use of the organizational properties of mammalian contour-coding systems discovered by means of single-unit electrophysiological recording. In this sense the vagueness of the projection-fusion account of binocular combination can be remedied, although the process of putting together the two separate inputs to the Cyclopean field turns out to be anything but simple.

A MODEL FOR COMBINATION OF MONOCULAR INPUTS

It will be recalled that Hubel and Wiesel (1962) found a very specific cytoarchitectural arrangement for neurons in area 17 of the cat's visual cortex, which appears also in other mammals so far studied. Neurons within a column normal to the cortical surface generally all have retinal receptive fields that have the same orientation, and there is a tendency for similar receptive field *types* to be grouped together within a column. Moreover, all the receptive fields for such a column tend to be within the same part of the retina, and display a great deal of overlap. Figure 7.14 shows the arrangement. One may well ask what the function of this apparently high degree of redundancy is. It seems unlikely that it serves simply to combat internal "noise" in the system, since the signal-to-noise ratio for any one unit appears to be high anyway when its receptive field is adequately stimulated, and in general the sharpening of contour signals seems to be mediated by more distal lateral-inhibitory processes (see Chapter 3). It appears very probable that the overlapping receptive-

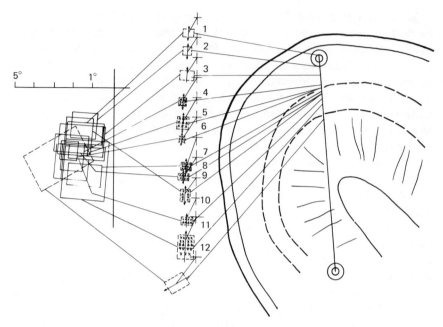

Fig. 7.14. An electrode track through the apical and mesial segments of the post-lateral gyrus of the visual striate cortex of cat. Receptive field types are shown in the column of sketches in the left center of the diagram, referred in each case to the *area centralis* of the eye (crosses). On the left are shown the superpositions of the fields on the retina. All receptive fields (with the exception of the last) are of the same type, and code for the same type of contour, a horizontal line (from Hubel & Wiesel, 1962).

field structure is part of the built-in depth detection system, particularly as a great majority of the cells within a column are binocularly driven, the two "driving" fields always being in similar areas of the two retinas and of the same type (with respect to orientation, on/off characteristics, and so forth). More recently Barlow, Blakemore and Pettigrew (1967) have shown that in the cat, binocularly driven cells of the type discovered by Hubel and Wiesel do indeed function as depth detectors, in the following sense. They found that the receptive fields for a binocularly driven cortical cell do not always fall in exactly corresponding points in the two eyes. There is variation in the amount of disparity in the positioning of the optimal stimuli at the two eyes for different cortical units, and the differences in disparities tend to be much larger in the horizontal than in the vertical dimension. This means that once the eyes are fixated on a particular point, units with a given degree of disparity in their receptive field positions will be optimally fired by contour elements at a particular distance. For instance, units whose receptive fields *are* in corresponding parts of the two retinas will be most strongly fired by pattern features on the Vieth-Müller circle; the larger the disparity for a given pair of fields, the further from the Vieth-Müller circle must the stimulating element be to give a strong output. Units were discovered for the detection of features both nearer to and farther from the eyes than the Vieth-Müller circle. We thus have good evidence for depth detection as one of the functions of the primary contour-coding system,[11] but may well inquire how these are organized into a system for the recognition of pattern-in-depth.

Consider the highly schematic arrangement shown in Fig. 7.15, which consists of labeled points on the receptor surfaces $A_1, \ldots, A_n$, and $A_1', \ldots, A_n'$, which represent simple receptive fields in the two eyes.[12]

---

[11] For additional information on the depth detection function, see Nikara, Bishop, and Pettigrew (1968) and Pettigrew, Nikara and Bishop (1968a, b).

[12] The neurophysiological terms are used, since this part of the model amounts essentially to a number of suggestions about how already-identified neurophysiological contour-detecting units might be organized into a depth processing system. Needless to say, most of the anatomical and other complications have been ignored, since the model only includes those elements and processes assumed to be directly involved in depth detection.

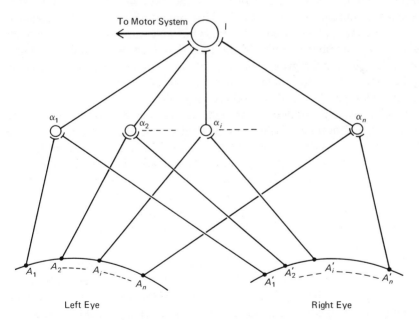

Fig. 7.15. A suggested arrangement for "locking" the eyes at a particular state of convergence. A_1A_1', A_2A_2' . . . A_nA_n' are similar retinal-receptive fields in corresponding parts of the two eyes, $\alpha_1 \ldots \alpha_n$ their cortical detectors. Outputs from the α units are summed at I, which has inhibitory connections to the system controlling eye movements, so that when similar features are detected at the two eyes, the system locks, and processing for stereoptic depth can start.

The row of units α_1 . . . α_n represents a set of cells (not necessarily all in the same column) that are activated by the fields. This set signals to a higher unit, I, which has connections to the oculomotor vergence system. Such units have not been identified physiologically but their postulated functions are not inconsistent with the known types. Units such as I have inhibitory connections to the motor system, so that when they are activated, they "lock" the two eyes at a specific vergence. The units $A_1, \ldots, A_n, A_1', \ldots, A_n'$ are assumed to represent corresponding points in the two eyes, so that this system has the function of bringing two monocular fields into registry in terms of congruent pattern elements in the two eyes. It is not necessary to assume that I and its inputs are a subsystem in which all the detector elements (field types) are the same, say for vertical contours, but if this were so a number of similar subsystems would be held to operate in parallel for different pattern features.

If the eyes are not correctly converged (that is, do not bring sets of pattern elements in the two eyes into registry), the oculomotor system will "hunt" until one or more of the I-systems inhibits it, which will occur when some pattern elements are congruent for the two eyes at that vergence state. If a number of pattern elements are in register, the output from the Is will be strong, and the eyes are "locked" into that vergence condition (motor fusion). This operation also sets the distance of the reference plane from the eyes. One may suppose there would be quite a large number of units of the type described, with similar arrangements for signaling registry (or lack of it) between congruent elements in the monocular visual fields. Where the visual display patterns contain no binocular parallax and are otherwise similar, a single "best" solution is possible. Where parallax is present, several possible states of registry can occur, and normally fusion would stabilize when some optimum degree of registry were obtained, depending on such factors as contour length, degree of contrast, and perhaps other Gestalt-like factors. Thus control would entail some statistical evaluation of the relative outputs of a set of Is, perhaps of several different sorts. In situations where no set of elements in the two patterns can be brought into register, no stable motor fusion is to be expected, and in such conditions it is in fact found that "hunting," and piecemeal suppression of parts of the two fields occurs as the search process progresses. Evidently this can be explained in terms of the I-system, since different I-systems will signal different patterns in the same part of the Cyclopean field, but the full exposition of this point depends on an hypothesis about input to the Cyclopean field to be developed later.

It is readily apparent that the model of Fig. 7.15 is a simplified version of a possible system for bringing two monocular displays into registry and keeping them there, but its principle seems to be viable. The question of greatest interest is: Given registry and fusion of major elements in the patterns in the two displays, how are disparate—but otherwise similar—pattern elements processed to yield depth information?

Here one may recall the fact that cells with similar receptive field types tend to be grouped within a column. One may assume that this arrangement facilitates the detection of binocular parallax in the following manner: Fig. 7.16 shows part of the postulated organization for such a group, with only a few of the field and associated units shown, for simplicity's sake. Each receptive field is labelled $a_1, \ldots, a_n$ and $a_1', \ldots, a_n'$ for corresponding fields in the two retinas. The fields shown may all be thought of as simple, and lying within a circumscribed area which constitutes a "binocular processing unit" (b.p.u.). Given that a set such as A_i, A_i' in Fig. 7.15 is in register, and the system locked, the inputs to the group of units $a_{11}, \ldots, a_{1n}, a_{21}, \ldots, a_{2n}$, and so forth, are evaluated. The purpose of the a_{ij}s is, specifically, to detect congruence of contours in the two eyes. The fields a_i are shown as having inputs to several higher units, although no such multiple representation is known to occur; but this is merely a simplifying device, since one could equally well show a series of closely overlapping fields for the a_is, and for the a_j's a less closely overlapping set. The resulting system would have the desired property, which is that a feature in the position a_1 is evaluated with respect to features over a rather wider region, $a_1', \ldots, a_n'$, in a similar part of the other retina. Likewise for a_2 and other fields on the left. Again for simplicity's sake, it is assumed that the system has a dominant input on the left; the generalization to symmetrical system is apparent. Suppose now that the optimal pattern element (say, a vertical line is focused on a_1, and fires the set $a_{11}, \ldots, a_{1n}$ (all units with "on" center, "off" surround). If there is no corresponding input from the right, the contour is detected at position a_1 (in the direction corresponding to the monocular visual direction of a_1) and at the same depth as the reference plane. However, if there is a vertical contour in the region $a_1', \ldots, a_n'$ it will fire "on" for one of the units associated with these fields, and "off" for others, for they are so disposed (being packed close together and overlapping) that the "on" center of one field must lie in the "off" surround of its neighbors (recall that all the receptive fields $a_1, \ldots, a_n, a_1', \ldots, a_n'$ are of the same type). In this case only *one* of the set $a_{11}, \ldots, a_{1n}$ will be strongly activated, the remainder tending to be inhibited by the mutually antagonistic responses for "on" and "off" portions of receptive fields for a single unit, even when the fields are in different eyes (see Chapter 3, p. 60). So, for example, if a_1 is "on," and a_3' is "on," the unit a_{13} will fire; but at the same time a_2' and a_4' (and perhaps some others) will give "off" responses, so a_{12} and a_{14} will give no response, and perhaps some other units in the a_{ij} set will give only "off" responses. The unit in the set a_{ij} with the greatest output therefore signals depth information relative to the "lock" established by AA'; if the unit in question happens to signal for points that correspond, the depth signaled is the depth of the reference plane. Otherwise it is in front of or behind it, according to the usual rule of binocular parallax. For unambiguous signaling of depth it must be assumed that the output of a b.p.u. differs when all the units $a_{11}, \ldots, a_{1n}$ are firing from its output when only one of this set fires, or alternatively that different outputs are activated under these two conditions. The latter assumption is perhaps more plausible, since it makes the preservation of depth information in the system more definite. That is to say, strong firing of one of $a_{11}, \ldots, a_{1n}$ entails a binocular match for the two eyes at some depth relative to the reference plane. Firing of all (or most) of the $a_{11}, \ldots, a_{1n}$ at about the same level implies no binocular match. It is suggested that the apparent visual direction will be a compromise between the visual directions of a_1 and whichever of $a_1', \ldots, a_n'$ is activated. Charnwood (1950) claims that apparent visual direction for a fused contour changes as the relative inputs (brightnesses) at the two eyes change, so that the direction should perhaps be thought of as an evaluation over the whole of $a_{11}, \ldots, a_{1n}$; the more similar the outputs of the set, the more strongly will a_1 determine binocular visual direction, and the more dissimilar (the stronger the input from the right), the more will $a_1', \ldots, a_n'$ determine it. We thus have an analogue, in terms of the output of the b.p.u., of the depth of pattern elements relative to the reference plane, and also a suggestion for the process by which change from monocular to binocular visual directions can be mediated.

At the risk of being tedious, it is again emphasized that the proposed model is oversimplified, and indicates only how one type of element in the visual fields of the two eyes is evaluated, namely small segments of vertical contour. However, it is claimed that other contour elements in the visual fields can be processed in the same way to the extent that they exhibit horizontal parallax. A large number of such local binocular-processing units is assumed to exist for different parts of the visual fields. Within a column it is assumed that units such as the one in Fig. 7.16 will operate as soon as specific convergence has been established by AA', as shown in Fig. 7.15. As we have seen, the corresponding points on the two retinas (and their visual directions) maintain their relationship for all conditions of vergence, so that the same b.p.u.'s can operate in different states of vergence. The b.p.u.'s may be thought of as stacked within columns, and interspersed with the $\alpha, \ldots, \gamma$ units of the "locking" system. Local stereoptic depth processing of this type is consistent with what we know of Panum's circumscribed fusional areas. The asymmetrical overlap of receptive fields shown in Fig. 7.16 has not been demonstrated nor has the sort of proposed evaluation over a group of simple fields such as $a_{11}, \ldots, a_{1n}$. These properties do not, however, seem to be

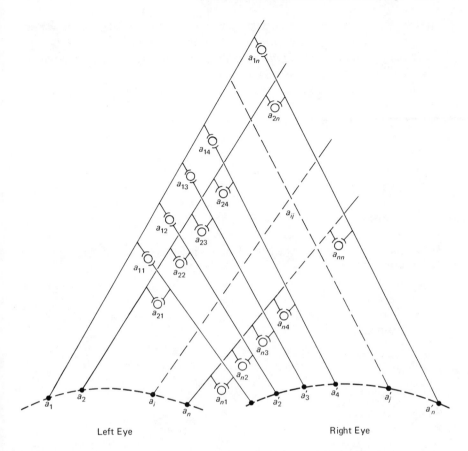

Fig. 7.16. The postulated binocular processing unit (b.p.u.). The points $\alpha_1, \ldots, \alpha_n$ and $\alpha_1', \ldots, \alpha_n'$ are similar retinal receptive fields in corresponding parts of the two eyes, $\alpha_{11}, \ldots, \alpha_{1n}$ and $\alpha_{n1}, \ldots, \alpha_{nn}$, their cortical detectors. Maximum responses from particular cortical units will be dependent on the degree of disparity between similar pattern elements imaged on the two eyes.

implausible in terms of what is known of the cytoarchitecture of the visual cortex. The operation of large numbers of local binocular processing elements of the type proposed, working in parallel and in conjunction with the "locking" system for bringing binocular displays into registry, gives the "matching" operation in detail, and can explain nearly all of the elementary properties of stereoptic depth perception, namely:

1. The mediation of constant corresponding visual directions in the two eyes under different vergence conditions, and the fact that stereoptic depth processing only occurs when a certain degree of registry between monocular fields has been achieved.
2. The establishment of a reference plane, and Panum's fusional areas,

the small areas within which "phenomenal fusion" can occur—these are determined by the retinal extension of each b.p.u. The fusional areas are limited in *depth* as well as lateral extent, and this can be taken as a further function of the "locking" system, which controls the operation of b.p.u.'s.

3. Depth processing (stereopsis) *only* occurs for the "appropriate" visual directions (fusional areas).

4. Appearance of depth is principally a function of binocular parallax between *similar contour elements*.

5. Stereoptic depth is never "absolute," but always in relation to the reference plane (established by "locking" the system).

6. Apparent visual direction can change with stereoptic fusion.

7. Suppression of "mismatching" contour information occurs within the active fusional areas (see, however, later discussion).

8. Linschoten's finding, that two identical monocular visual directions can appear different in the fused binocular field *provided* each has an appropriate contour with which to fuse within its fusional area in the opposite visual field, is accounted for (Fig. 7.8).

9. Similarly the model allows for change of fused binocular visual direction with unequal inputs (brightness) to the two eyes (Charnwood).

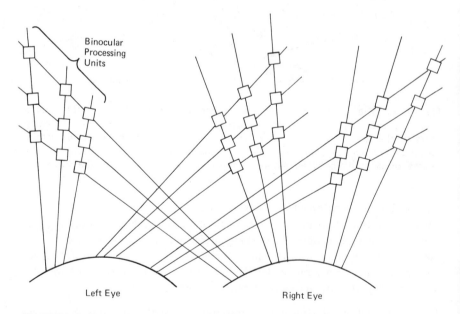

Fig. 7.17. A suggested arrangement of b.p.u.'s (Fig. 7.16) into a projection-fusion array of the sort shown in Fig. 7.12. Each b.p.u. now corresponds to an intersecting pair of transmission lines from the retinal output. Only three groups of b.p.u.'s are shown, but in fact large numbers must operate simultaneously.

It might be said that the model merely demonstrates a system which is consistent with the elementary facts without providing new predictions whose confirmation or otherwise would establish its usefulness. Against this position it can be argued that, while no predictions are made, the model does establish a physiologically plausible basis for fusion and suppression effects. The sense in which it can be viewed as an extension of the "projection-fusion" model is made clear in Fig. 7.17. Comparing this with Fig. 7.12, one sees that in the present model the elements of the projection array, and its input elements, are simply more explicitly defined, and their relationships more clearly elaborated. The present model entails a much higher degree of articulation and spatial information processing at different points within the array. Each b.p.u. corresponds to a segment of the array, and for the processing of different pattern features, or for similar features in different parts of the visual field, a large number of b.p.u.'s would have to be operating in parallel. The b.p.u.'s may be thought of as pattern-element processors, or parts of the "primary detection" system. Discussion of the relations between larger parts of the inputs to the two eyes (pattern processing, as opposed to pattern-element processing) follows.

PATTERN ELEMENTS AND BINOCULAR PATTERN DETECTION

The system may give some insight into the basic processing of contour information, but it is important to emphasize that it deals only with the most elementary sort of stereoptic depth detection on contours. Having achieved this, one must look at other phenomena and consider how the system might be modified and further elaborated to deal with more complex types of data. Right at the start, it is clear that a system with contour receptive field inputs cannot deal with the point-domain matching of random-dot fields of the Julesz type. This presents a real problem since random-dot stimuli would not provide adequate or strong stimulation to the normal receptive field unit. However it has already been suggested that stereoptic processing can occur at several levels in the visual system, and it is quite possible that a more elementary form of depth detection occurs *prior* to the elaboration of contour information, given an appropriate stimulus input. Thus depth processing might occur both on the output from lateral geniculate units (for point domains) and on the output from cortical units (for contours). The relations between the two sorts of process are completely unexplored, but investigation here might prove illuminating.[13]

---

[13] As an example, random-dot fields are powerful masking agents when applied to contoured patterns in the normal monocular-masking paradigm. What happens when stereoptic depth is introduced into the stimuli?

The most serious deficiency of the contour-fusion model proposed is that it cannot deal with binocular inputs that are noncongruent, that is, which do not comprise adequate stimuli to the *same* type of receptive field. Thus suppose that a vertical line at a_1 (Fig. 7.16) occurs at the same time as a horizontal line (or some other pattern) across a_1', . . . , a_n'. One would predict that, for this b.p.u., the output of a_1 would dominate, and any small output from a_1', . . . , a_n' would be suppressed. However, there clearly are detectors for contours in *many* orientations within a given receptor area, and the phenomena of the Cyclopean field suggest that there must be interaction between detectors for *different* contour orientations; for instance, if horizontal lines are projected to one eye, vertical to the other, the suppression occurs between horizontal and vertical lines, which typically are rivalrous and dominate at different instances and perhaps in different parts of the Cyclopean field at the same time. This indicates rather clearly that there is interaction at some stage between the outputs of *different* detector systems, but the model so far set up deals only with interaction between detectors of similar features at the two eyes, the sort of interaction strongly indicated by the neurophysiological evidence on single unit behavior. [These two points reinforce the earlier claim (Chapter 4) that present neurophysiological evidence only tells us about the initial stages of pattern recognition, and leaves much to be accomplished by other techniques.] The phenomena of binocular vision indicate interaction of unlike detectors: Can we be more specific about the matter? The simplest way to proceed seems to be to suppose that the outputs from b.p.u.'s themselves are the inputs to the Cyclopean field, or—perhaps more appropriately—to a binocular depth-detection system, or recognizer, D_B. One need not be "phenomenalistic" about this in the sense of thinking of a "field" just like the visual Cyclopean field; the main requirement is to specify processes in the recognizer in such a way that its outputs are in one-to-one correspondence with the reported percepts.

Consider again the model of binocular processing of Fig. 7.16. Its outputs specify depth properties with respect to a particular sort of pattern element. The "locking" system specifies overall registry, but b.p.u.'s for all sorts of pattern element (contours in all directions) within the specified fusional areas will function. The outputs from the b.p.u.'s then "compete" for "positions" within D_B. As a first approximation one may imagine that D_B has a fairly large number of "positions" or addresses, which together "cover" the Cyclopean field. The crudity of the notion stems from one's inability to state anything about the relations and connective features that hold between the positions. However, one assumes that some of the positions are preempted by the initial "fusional" features of the binocular array that lock the system, and thus determine the areas within which stereoptic processing is feasible. The filling of the rest of the positions—completion of a sort of mosaic of the Cyclopean field—is then determined by the strongest of the outputs of b.p.u.'s corresponding to the different positions. "Strongest" is a vague term to use, but will suffice. Clearly the majority of the active b.p.u.'s will have weak outputs, since the number of different pattern elements that can occur within each small area of retina is limited. Although many units will be activated by *any* contour, adequate stimulation will occur in only a few. Where a receptive field is adequately stimulated there will be a strong output from the associated b.p.u., particularly if there is a congruent element in the related field-set of the other eye, in which case it will capture the relevant position. Should there be a different pattern element in the corresponding part of the other eye, it will activate a different b.p.u. (but for the same visual direction) and the two will compete for a single position. Dominance of one and suppression of the other will occur, or else perhaps rivalry between the two. Because of the receptive field properties of the b.p.u. inputs, any output that captures a position in D_B will "carry with it" a band of local suppression; but this is not the same as the suppression induced by competing b.p.u. outputs—or not necessarily the same. The

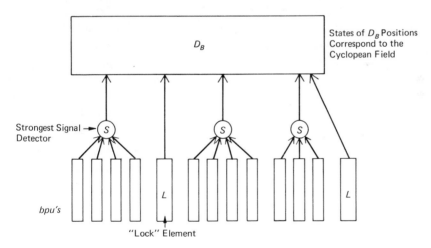

Fig. 7.18. A suggested arrangement for inputs from the fusion-projection array to the binocular Cyclopean-field analogue. Inputs compete for "positions" (visual directions) in the field, the strongest output tending to inhibit others.

extended model is shown schematically in Fig. 7.18. It bears some resemblance to Hochberg's ideas on suppression (Hochberg, 1964; see also p. 152) since different elements now "compete" for representation in D_B, which is the model's representation of the Cyclopean field. There is a basic difference, however, in that the processing for stereoptic depth is held to occur *prior* to input to D_B, so that the recognizer itself does not code depth on the basis of separate monocular inputs. Suppressive mechanisms operate at two separate levels, and subserve two different functions—pattern element detection at the b.p.u. level, and selection of inputs to D_B at a higher level. The advantage claimed for the model is that it accounts both for fusion and suppression in stereoptic depth-detection, and assigns particular functions to each. By separating out the operations of coding and recognizing depth information, a systematic account of stereoptic depth detection emerges which is consistent with neurophysiological evidence, as far as this goes, which assigns reasonable "loads" to each part of the system by specifying its computing function, and which seems to be consistent with the normal observer's reports of binocular phenomena when observing line stereograms and similar displays.

THE NATURE OF STEREOPTIC DEPTH DETECTION

There are problems still to be resolved, however. Kaufman (1964b) argues against the whole idea of fusion as a basis for explaining stereoptic depth perception, on the ground that it is too restrictive a concept. By means of a series of interesting experiments, he claims to show that a more plausible basis for depth coding would be the occurrence of correlated stimuli in the two parts of a stereogram, which are out-of-phase with respect to some reference system. For example, the stereogram of Fig. 7.19 consists of an inner 4×4 array of identical capital letters

```
qwe r H J K L Pmn b r a        a s d f g H J K L Po i u y
po i uXZASDz x c v m           mn b r c XZASD f h h j
p l mnYU l OPqwe r q           qwe r t YU l OP l k j h
z x c v G FDSAq s d f l        l k j h p G FDSA l we r
```

Fig. 7.19. One of Kaufman's stereograms. The central arrays of capital letters fuse and appear at a different depth from the rest of the lowercase letter arrays. The capital letters in the two halves are identical, the lowercase letters different.

in each half, embedded in a larger field of lowercase letters which are chosen independently for each half. The rows of lowercase letters are out of phase with respect to the inner array in the sense that four such letters occur on the left and five on the right of each row in the left half of the stereogram, and vice versa on the right. When the inner arrays are brought into registry, they are seen in depth behind the rivalrous binocular outer field. Depth is only detected when some parts of the two arrays fuse adequately, to "lock" the system, so that a "reference frame" can be set up; but it seems that to talk of fusion of the nonsimilar lowercase letters is inadequate, if not absurd, since they obviously do not fuse phenomenally, and in fact they generally display rivalry, as might be expected. Such demonstrations seem to cast doubt on the viability—or at least the generality—of a theory in which fusion plays a central role in stereoptic depth perception, yet to talk of correlation of out-of-phase patterns does not in itself solve the problem either.

A closer look at the suggested contour-matching and fusional model of this chapter shows that it can in fact deal quite nicely with situations of this sort. Indeed it can explain what the correlation of out-of-phase patterns consists in, and also why depth is detected in the presence of rivalry and suppression.

First of all, a certain degree of registry is a *necessary* condition in order for any form of binocular depth processing to occur. This is achieved by the "locking" system (acting on the inner arrays of capital letters of Fig. 7.19 for example), which preempts certain positions in D_B. Processing then occurs on the noncongruent lowercase letters. No b.p.u.'s—or very few—will be adequately stimulated, so that outputs will be variable and rivalrous, so that there are no stable inputs to D_B for these positions. Nevertheless, the *average* outputs of the relevant sets of b.p.u.'s are evaluated, and since the lowercase pattern elements as a whole are out-of-phase with respect to the fused inner array, the average output for the set of b.p.u.'s for that degree of disparity (phase-lag) will tend to capture input channels to D_B. Thus fusion does not have to mean complete phenomenal fusion, and detection of phase-lags in correlated patterns is explained in terms of an average output over a set of fluctuating signals.

The term "fusion" is not too descriptive of the matching operation in general. At the b.p.u. level perhaps one should rather talk of interaction of contour elements in the detector system, which only yield true fusion when a match is achieved for a pair of elements at a given retinal disparity. Nevertheless, this is basically a fusional type of system, since even when inadequately stimulated, the b.p.u. output is determined by combining receptive field outputs for both eyes simultaneously. Thus the original crude notion of matching on the "projection-fusion" array can be considerably refined by taking into account what is now known about contour coding at the neurophysiological level.

The notion that coding for stereoptic depth can be achieved with fluctuating signals is supported by the fact that it can be detected in the presence of rivalry, as in the stereogram of Fig. 7.19, and is shown even more clearly in an unpublished demonstration reported by B. W. White. Julesz-type stereograms are viewed in rapid sequence by means of a cine projector. Each stereogram contains the same type and amount of binocular parallax, but the brightness values within each succeeding stereogram are chosen independently, so that the surfaces in the successive combined views are seen as collections of continuously moving independent points, a sort of Brownian movement. Yet the detection of stereoptic depth is not affected by this, and is seen clearly and steadily. Such findings, and the temporal integration discussed earlier, attest to the versatility and subtlety of the binocular depth coding system—or systems. The basic operations seem to be statistical in nature, since spatial and temporal integration are both possible—fluctuations in space and time do not affect stereoptic depth perception (the data from eye-movement experiments support this point very strongly, see Chapter 9). The essential operation is probably one of correlation. Yet to say this is to state the problem, not to solve it. The model proposed in this chapter is an attempt to make some moves in the direction of a solution, keeping the operations as simple as possible at each stage, and relying heavily on the hints at the sort of system to look for that are available from neurophysiology. Perhaps its main weakness is that too little is said about the exact form of evaluation of noncongruent inputs, and of spatial integration in general. It may be that the best way to tackle the matter would be by computer simulation, using various schemes for combining information from two separate sets of local property detectors; the idea seems to contain no difficulties in principle. Be that as it may, simulation might turn up some unexpected properties, which would be an advantage, if they suggested some new experiments in binocular vision. No obvious new predictions stem from the model, a state of affairs scarcely to be justified on the grounds that all there is to know about binocular vision is already known. On the other hand, it seems to be more than an ad hoc collection of isolated hypotheses to account for an equal number of isolated facts.

One can claim modest success for the model, on the following grounds:

1. It accounts for the elementary facts of stereoptic depth perception listed earlier.
2. It reconciles the fact of phenomenal binocular fusion, and the changes in visual directions which this implies, with neurophysiological findings on contour processing and physiological fusion.
3. It accounts for both fusion and suppression in binocular vision, and assigns roles to them both which seem to be in accord with experimental evidence.
4. It takes account of the criticisms of the concept of fusion advanced by Kaufman, and suggests the sort of basis on which general correlative functions may operate.
5. It recognizes the statistical nature of the evaluation of visual inputs.
6. It assigns no special role to eye movements once the system has been "locked."

Although no predictions are made, it seems likely that further insight into the binocular processing system is most likely to come from investigations in which the interactions of particular types of simple pattern element are studied, investigations of time-integrating properties, the relations between these and movement detection (as in stereoptic movement in depth, and the Pulfrich phenomenon) and from study of the introduction of perturbations or visual noise, as in masking and similar paradigms.

CHAPTER 8

Adaptation
of the Visual System
to Optically Distorted
Patterned Inputs

THE NATURE OF THE EVIDENCE

In Chapter 6 the rather surprising findings concerning man's capacity to adapt successfully to radical distortions of his normal visual environment were touched on briefly, and the area was identified as one in which structural modeling might have fruitful application.[1] An optically produced distortion of normal visual input may be defined as any change in visual directions, produced by a device which alters the paths in which light rays travel as they enter the eye. The devices commonly used are lenses, prisms, and mirrors, which produce regular and predictable distortions (sometimes called "rearrangement") as opposed to irregular, fluctuating, and unpredictable changes (called "disarrangement"). The reason for studying rearrangements is that it is possible to adapt to them, whereas—not surprisingly—it is not possible to adapt to disarrangements, so far as is known. The process of adaptation is not simple, as we shall see, but basically it is a process of coming to *discount* the distortion. The wearer of a distorting device comes to behave as if his vision were undistorted, which can be held to mean several different things, a point to be discussed later. The early empirical work in the field was aimed at

[1] Various interesting chromatic adaptations have been reported, but here they will be ignored, since our concern is with pattern vision and contour discrimination.

description of the experience of such changes and at investigating some conditions which would facilitate—or interfere with—adaptation. A detailed review, up to about 1960, is given by Smith and Smith (1962). Recently, several explanatory models (including the Smiths' own) have been proposed, and experimental investigation has tended to address the question of which type of explanation is most adequate, and in some cases to test specific predictions from a particular model. Much of the recent work is discussed by Harris (1965), Howard and Templeton (1966), and Rock (1966).

The basic facts of adaptation to optically produced distortions of vision are as follows:

1. Whole-field distortions produced by lenses, prisms and mirrors are adapted to, at least partially, by most normal human observers.
2. Virtually complete adaptation can occur, even to "radical" distortions such as inversion of the field, in the sense that in time the observer is able to coordinate his movements with the distorted visual input, and apparently to behave normally in the distorted visual environment.
3. There are numbers of cases where complete *phenomenal* adaptation has been reported, even to "radical" distortions. That is, the observer reports that his visual world *appears to be normal,* and this is evidently not necessarily the same condition as the coordinative adaptation described in item 2.
4. Some degree of adaptation can occur quite rapidly, if the distortion is a "mild" one such as displacement of the visual field to one side by a few degrees.
5. Typically, however, adaptations are partial, and established gradually. For example, if visual directions are displaced $x°$ to the right, the subject adjusts as if the displacement were $cx°$, $c < 1$. But this partial adaptation tends to be *consistent,* that is, the observer does not fluctuate between $0°$ and $x°$ of adaptation.
6. Most devices which produce "static" distortions (changes of apparent visual direction for points in the visual field with the head and eyes being held still) also produce "dynamic" or movement distortions when the head moves. These also can be adapted to in both ways (items 2 and 3).
7. On removal of the distorting medium a reverse distortion appears, and is equal and opposite to the adaptation to the initial distortion.
8. The reversed distortion itself dissipates with time, until "normality" is restored.
9. Adaptation occurs to a variety of distortions which are continuous spatial functions of the normal input; where, however, a sudden break in the distorted visual field is introduced, poor adaptation occurs in the neighborhood of the discontinuity.

These seem to be the basic facts, although some of them, as we shall see, have been disputed quite hotly. The sorts of distortion that have been studied, and indeed the sorts of adaptation that have been measured, have tended to change somewhat with time. Whereas in the earlier investigations, such as those of Stratton (1896, 1897), Ewert (1930) and Kohler (1964),[2] "radical" distortions such as inversion were studied over comparatively long time periods, lasting days and sometimes even weeks at a time, the recent tendency has been to study "mild" distortions for shorter time periods, often measured only in minutes. J. G. Taylor's investigations (1962) fall somewhere between the two. The reasons for this change of interest and emphasis are not hard to find; rather rapid (although incomplete) adaptation can be obtained and measured when the distortion is mild, and can thus be manipulated under well-controlled laboratory conditions. It also happens that the milder distortions are more amenable to quantitative assessment. By a "mild" distortion, I mean one which preserves the spatial ordering of points of the normal visual field, but introduces changes in the distance function (as in magnification) and/or a translation. "Radical" distortions, on the other hand, entail changes— usually a reversal—in the spatial ordering of points. As yet, no sharp distinction is drawn; some distortions seem to fall somewhere between the two (for example, rotation—see, however, later discussion, p. 176).

Experiments with wedge prisms[3] have dominated investigations in this field for some years, and provide many examples of controlled studies with quantitative assessment of adaptation (see, for example, Howard & Templeton, 1966, Ch. 15; Rock, 1966). The main optical-geometric distortion produced by a wedge prism is a general displacement of the apparent visual directions toward the apex (although the displacement is not uniform) with a regular dilation of the field toward the base, and contraction toward the apex. This produces an apparent curvature of lines which are seen as straight in the normal visual field. Curvature is greatest for lines parallel to the base of the prism (see Fig. 8.1). Amount of adaptation is typically measured by determining how great the reverse curvature distortion is (when the adapting prism is removed) by "neutralizing" it with a "weaker" prism of opposite type (that is, opposite to the reversed aftereffect), or by estimating changes in hand-eye or other coordination caused by the displacement distortion. By such means it can readily be shown that even a few minutes' experience of the distorted visual world may be enough to produce measurable adaptation, if the conditions are otherwise appropriate.

[2] Originally published in 1951.
[3] A wedge prism is a "thin" prism, that is, one with an acute apex, typically not more than 20°.

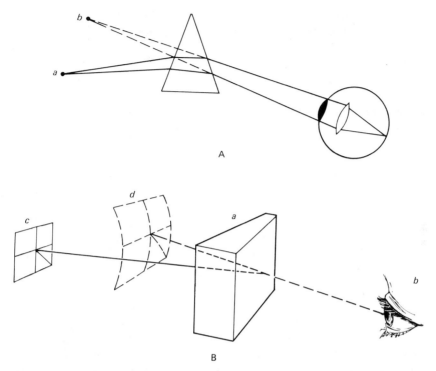

Fig. 8.1. (A) Schematic view of how light rays are bent by a wedge prism, away from its apex. The *apparent* position of the point *a* is at *b*, deviated from its true direction and closer to the eye. (B) An approximate representation of the effect of viewing a pattern through a wedge prism. Displacement and curvature effects are shown. There are also chromatic effects, which are not shown. All lines with vertical components have colored fringes if the borders of the pattern are black/white, and are viewed in white light.

SOME EXPLANATORY CONCEPTS

Several different types of explanation have been offered to account for adaptations to distorted visual input. First, there have been explanations based on the concept of conditioning particular movements (of limbs, head, eyes, and so forth) to particular visual events. On this view, adaptation consists essentially of reconditioning a set of familiar movements to novel sets of visual signals. Second, it has been maintained that adaptation occurs because of changes in the *felt positions* of parts of the body, whether viewed through the distorting medium or not. Third, adaptation has been explained as a process in which the disturbed correlation between visual and proprioceptive information is "recalibrated," or as one might

say, the distorted visual input is remapped onto the undistorted proprioceptive schema. A number of different models have been put forward, but
these three seem to be the basic themes on which variations have been
proposed.

J. G. Taylor (1962) is the main proponent of the first type of explanation. Basing his model on Hullian-type principles of learning, he attempts
to show that *all* perception involves the conditioning of movements and
movement sequences to particular classes of visual events. Strictly speaking, one should say that movements are initially conditioned to "optical-
physiological events" in the neonate, since perception is held only to occur
when the conditioning of movements to such events has already progressed
to some extent. Adaptation to artificially produced distortion, then, is
held to be simply the reconditioning of particular movements to the transformed classes of visual input. To take a simple example: Suppose that
a person wears a device which makes objects appear 10° to the right
of their normal visual directions (the head and eyes remaining still). An
object which is actually 10° to the left of the "straight ahead" position
will now *appear* to be straight ahead, and in reaching for it the naïve
observer will reach straight ahead. He will see his error (literally), and
be surprised at the visual position of his hand (apparently 10° to the
right of straight ahead). Seeing the error also shows how it may be cor-
rected, and after a few attempts the reaching movements start to "adapt,"
and errors in attempting to touch the object start to become smaller.
In Taylor's view the original reaching for objects seen straight ahead
came about through the conditioning of arm movements to visual signals
having the given visual direction. Adaptation to the "new" visual direction
is held to involve the same type of conditioning, except that the "old"
habit has to be extinguished simultaneously. A model based on conditioning laws seems to be too simple to account for the data. For example,
it is not too plausible to suppose that adaptations are really reconditioned
sensorimotor relations which can break the habits of a lifetime in a matter
of minutes, and with very few "trials." Also, such a theory has difficulty
in explaining how gradual and partial adaptation occur, as when a prism
producing a visual displacement, θ, yields partial adaptation of $\frac{1}{2}\theta$ (measured after the adaptation session). The partial adaptation $\frac{1}{2}\theta$ is—para-
doxically—correct and complete, so far as it goes, and is not an uneasy
state of conflict between adaptations 0 and θ, as would be predicted on
Hullian principles. Some more powerful and general transformation of
the visuo-proprioceptive relations seems to be involved. Similar objections
apply to the recently revived motor-outflow theory of adaptation (Festinger, Burnham, Ono, & Bamber, 1967).

A number of writers have proposed the second view, that most of
the adaptation phenomena can be explained in terms of alterations in

the felt positions of limbs and of other parts of the body, which have been viewed through the distorting medium, or of felt position of the head and eyes with respect to the rest of the body. Some of the descriptions of the earlier workers, particularly of Stratton and Kohler, have been quoted in support of this position, although neither of those authors themselves believed that this was the correct and complete explanation of their findings. Taylor also denied that changed proprioceptive perception alone explains adaptation. These three—Stratton, Kohler, and Taylor—are the three writers who have carried out the most extensive long-range studies of adaptation to distorting devices in a free environment, and it would seem strange that all three should be wrong, particularly since they all served as subjects in their own investigations. Nonetheless, some of the recent experimental evidence suggests quite strongly that alterations in proprioception can account for a great deal. For instance, in terms of our previous example, if the observer learns to reach 10° to the left of the point at which (in terms of the predistortion visual field) he sees an object, he will be adapted to the distortion in the sense that he has coordinated vision with reaching. If the adaptation were a purely visual phenomenon, one would expect the altered reaching behavior to occur for movements initiated by visual stimuli, but not for movements initiated in other ways. If one asked the subject to point to a nonvisible sound source one would expect him to do so correctly. But it can be shown that, in pointing to the sound source, the adapted subject makes the same sort of movement as he would to a visual object—he points off to the side. The simplest way to explain this is to say that in adapting to the changed visual condition there is a change in the felt position of the hand and arm, so that when the subject is actually reaching straight ahead, he senses his hand as reaching off to the side. The same discrepancy would then turn up in attempting to point to nonvisual targets. Harris (1965) in particular has argued that adaptation to visual distortion can be explained in this way, and marshalls quite an array of evidence, both old and new, to support the position. In particular, his own experiments on pointing to nonvisual targets after adaptation to a visual distortion are held to be strong evidence for it (Harris, 1963). Similar findings have been reported by others, such as Hamilton (1964) and Pick, Hay, and Pabst (1963). However, it has been found that, although the shift in reaching for visible targets does generalize to nonvisible targets, the generalization is not complete and that no shift is found for relocating a remembered (preadaptation) position of the adapted arm (Efstathiou, Bauer, Greene, & Held, 1967). In both cases a proprioceptive model would predict complete shifts, as great as for visible targets. Thus, it seems that some more general coordinative operations must occur between visual and proprioceptive inputs, or that additional constraints apply for nonvisible targets. Other arguments against a purely proprioceptive-change model will be developed later.

The third view, that adaptation to distorted visual input is brought about by a correlative—or recorrelative—system, has been championed by Held (1961) (see Fig. 8.2). The idea was based on von Holst's model

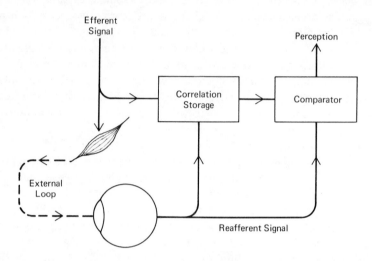

Fig. 8.2. Held's proposed model for the correlation and recorrelation of efferent signals with visual (reafferent) signals from the eye (after Held, 1961 as reprinted in 1962).

for the "stabilization" of the visual world in which an organism moves (von Holst, 1954). In von Holst's model, when an efferent signal is sent to the oculomotor system, a "copy" of that signal (called the *Efferenz-kopie*) is fed to a system that compares it with visual signals from the eyes (called reafferent signals) in such a way as to discount the visual changes which are purely a result of the eyes' having moved. If the reafferent signals do not bear the expected relation to the efferent signal, movement is seen. If, on the other hand, the reafferent signals "match" the *Efferenzkopie* the visual changes are discounted and movement is not seen. Clearly enough, any alteration in the normal relations between efferent and reafferent signals will upset the proper operation of such a system. One way of producing an alteration is to distort visual input. Von Holst seems to have thought of his feedback system as essentially fixed and probably innate (his primary evidence came from studies of lower organisms, where fixity of function is likely), but if it were modifiable under changes in the form of sensory input, it might provide the basis for adaptation of the sort we are considering. This is what Held proposed.

Held's addition of a correlation storage system to the original model intro- duces a memory component, so that the model can deal with long-term adaptive recorrelations between efferent signals and distorted sensory in- puts. Although the model has not figured prominently in Held's recent reports, the idea of changes in sensorimotor coordination via a reafferent feedback loop is still much in evidence (see, for example, Held, 1965, 1967). Held and his associates have produced many reports which demon- strate the importance of reafferent stimulation, although self-produced proprioceptive stimulation can no longer be held to be a necessary condition for any sort of adaptation to occur (Rock, 1966).

The model to be presented here shares some features with Held's, al- though it differs from it in important ways. Explicit hypotheses about the transformation of visual input which occurs during adaptation are introduced and shown to be generally consistent with the experimental findings as well as with the feedback-comparator system of von Holst. It will be argued that the major component of the adaptive process is the retransformation of the distorted visual input patterns to a normal—or near-normal—form. Scant attention has been paid to the question of pattern recognition per se in other theoretical treatments of adaptation to visual distortion. The present model is intended to remedy this, and by doing so places primary emphasis on the transformation of visual input. How- ever, it will be argued that this does not exclude the possibility of con- comitant proprioceptive changes.

The difficulty of dealing with adaptation as a pattern-recognition prob- lem stems, I believe, from the vagueness with which the problem is usually stated. It is generally conceded (Hochberg, 1957) that some criterion of "structure," "orderliness," or "stability" is required to explain how adaptation occurs and why it always tends towards the reestablishment of a "normal" visual world. The traditional, and most obvious, way to explain this tendency is to base it on the primacy of tactile space, so that a stable visual world becomes a "construction" of great complexity, arising out of the interaction of visual and nonvisual cues but having always as its basis the essential stability of tactile-kinesthetic space. Tay- lor's theory may be regarded as a modern version of this position. It will be argued that the facts can be accounted for rather better by a model that is less extreme on the "environmental" question than Taylor's (that is, one that does not attribute all perceptual stability to conditioning of movements) but still can account for the orderliness of the visual world, and for the reemergence of stability despite distortions which may be imposed on the visual input. First the distortions commonly studied will be characterized as transformations of the "normal" (undistorted) visual input and subsequently it will be shown that "normal" input itself under- goes similar transformations in order to maintain the orderliness and stability of the visual world of our everyday experience. In this sense the model can account for *both* features of pattern recognition in the visual system (stability, adaptability) at least in their more important aspects.

THE CHARACTERIZATION OF OPTICAL TRANSFORMATIONS

The optical distortions commonly studied, and to which a high degree of adaptation can occur, are displacements, rotations, inversions (about a horizontal or vertical line), regular dilation and contraction over the whole field, and combinations of two or more such distortions. Dilation and/or contraction over the field produce changes in curvature unless the change in scale is constant, which yields ordinary magnification or minification. A "regular" dilation or contraction is one in which the change in scale is a continuous function of ordered position in the undistorted field, so that no sudden breaks or discontinuities are apparent.[4] These distortions can be related to "normal" visual input by a single type of transform, which is called a conformal transformation. A conformal transformation, or mapping, is expressed by the relation $\omega = f(z)$, where $z = x + iy$, a complex number. In the geometry of complex planes (see next paragraph), each point in the z plane is mapped onto one or more points in the ω plane, the mapping being defined by $f(z)$. A converse transformation, $f^{-1}(\omega) = z$, maps points in ω onto z.[5] The transforms of interest here are biuniform, so that a one-to-one relation holds in each direction, and it will be shown that the static distortions can all be expressed extremely simply as such transformations. By "normal" visual input I mean the spatial array of the "visual field" in Gibson's sense (Gibson, 1950), which may be thought of as like the plane image of a three-dimensional scene formed by a pinhole camera. The z plane, then, is such a plane image, undistorted by the optics of the eye or topography of the retina, which for the present can be neglected.

The geometrical representation of a complex number, $z_1 = x_1 + iy_1$ is shown in Fig. 8.3, and is called an "Argand diagram." The ordered pair (r_1, θ_1), could also be used to specify z_1, where $r_1 = (x_1^2 + y_1^2)^{1/2}$, $\theta_1 = \tan^{-1}(y_1/x_1)$. If z is some function $F(x, y)$, then corresponding to the locus of z in the z plane there will be a different locus, $\omega = \phi(u,v)$, in the

---

[4] A further restriction on changes of scale (expansion and contraction) will be suggested directly.

[5] The transformations of interest are, strictly speaking, *isogonal*, namely, transformations which preserve equiangular intersection, but not necessarily sense of rotation also. Conformal transformations comprise the subset of isogonal transformations that do preserve sense of rotation, although the distinction is not always made even in mathematical treatises.

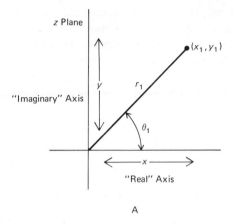

A

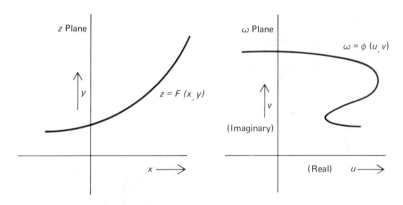

Fig. 8.3. (A) The geometrical representation of a complex number (Argand diagram). The point (x_1, y_1) defines the complex number $z_1 = x_1 + y_1$ where $(i = \sqrt{-1})$, a two-component vector, which can equally well be specified by (r_1, θ_1). (B) The relationship between complex planes z and ω is specified by some function, $\omega = f(z)$. Given points in z are mapped into points in ω. As z traces out a locus given by $z = F(x, y)$, ω traces out a corresponding locus $\omega = \phi(u, v)$. Given the relation between z and ω, the locus in the ω plane becomes $f(F[x, y])$. The coordinates in the ω plane, u and v, are in general both functions of both x and y.

ω plane, where u and v have the same interpretation in the ω plane as have x and y in the z plane, namely, $\omega = u + iv$ (Fig. 8.3B). This locus is completely specified by $\omega = f(z)$, that is by $f(F[x, y])$, and in general u and v will *each* be functions of *both* x and y. Examples are given in the following paragraph. Such conformal transformations map straight lines and smooth curves in the z plane into straight lines and/or smooth curves in the ω plane. However, in every case the important "local property" of equiangular intersection for pairs of lines (curves) is preserved. That is to say, if two lines intersect at an angle α in z, their transforms in ω will intersect at the *same* angle α. In other respects conformal transformations, even quite simple ones, can produce an enormous variety of different sorts of relationship between corresponding points in z and ω.

The simplest conformal mapping is a *translation*. Translation along

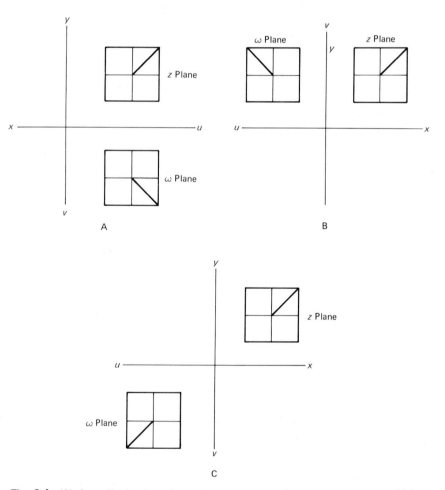

Fig. 8.4. (A) A particular transform from z to ω planes, in this case $\omega = f_1(z) = x - iy = \bar{z}$ (reflection in the "real" axis, or reversal of all values of y). (B) Reflection in the "imaginary" axis, or reversal of all values of x. Here $\omega = f_2(x, y) = -x + iy = -\bar{z}$. (C) Reflection in both axes, $\omega = f_3(x, y) = -x - iy = -z$.

the "real" (x) axis is represented by $\omega = z + A$, on the "imaginary" (y) axis by $\omega = z + iB$, and translation in general by $\omega = z + A + iB$, where A and B are real numbers. Inversion in one (or both) of the axes is attained by reversing the sign of either the real or the imaginary parts of z (or both). Figure 8.4 shows the three simple inversions, each generating a new ω plane. For convenience the z and ω planes are shown together for each pair, but this should not mislead one into thinking that the ω plane is simply an *extension* of the z plane. Reflection in the x axis is given by $f_1(z) = x - iy$ $(= \bar{z}$, the "complex conjugate" of z), reflection in the y axis is given by $f_2(z) = -x + iy$ $(= -\bar{z})$, and reflection in both axes is given by $f_3(z) = -x - iy$ $(= -z)$. More complex inversions such as inversion in a circle, can be expressed conformally (for example, inversion in the unit circle centered at the origin is given by $\omega = 1/\bar{z}$), but they do not appear to correspond to any of the distortions so far studied, or which are readily producible by optical devices. Rotation about the

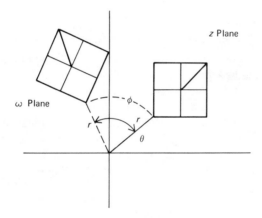

Fig. 8.5. Rotation about the origin through an angle ϕ. Here $\omega = ze^{i\phi}$. (For derivation, see footnote 6.)

origin is demonstrated in Fig. 8.5, and is most easily expressed as $\omega = ze^{i\phi}$, where ϕ is the angle of rotation.[6] Figure 8.6 is an example of the

---

[6] The transformation is seen to have this form as follows: In polar coordinates, $\omega = (r, \theta + \phi)$. Thus

$$u = r \cos (\theta + \phi) = r (\cos \theta \cos \phi - \sin \theta \sin \phi)$$
and
$$v = r \sin (\theta + \phi) = r (\sin \theta \cos \phi + \cos \theta \sin \phi)$$

substituting x for $r \cos \theta$ and y for $r \sin \theta$, some manipulation gives $u + iv = (x + iy) (\cos \phi + i \sin \phi)$. Remembering that $\cos \phi + i \sin \phi = e^{i\phi}$, the result follows.

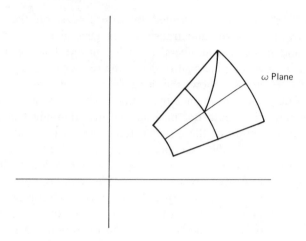

Fig. 8.6. The result of transformation by ω = antilog z (for derivation, see footnote 7). Here only the ω plane is shown.

mapping of straight lines into straight lines and curves, maintaining equiangular intersection. Only the ω plane is shown, the pattern being the transform of the pattern of Fig. 8.4 (first quadrant) by ω = antilog z. The transform z = logω maps a polar set of circles concentric with the origin and their diameters in the z plane, into a cartesian net of straight lines parallel to the x and y axes in the ω plane; the inverse transform (from z to ω) is the one given.[7] A related transform maps a rectangular system into the set of curves shown in Fig. 8.7, and many other examples of a similar nature could be given, such as transforms which produce the familiar "barrel" and "pincushion" distortions (or close approximations to them) of ordinary spherical lenses.

[7] Proof of the properties described is as follows:

$$\omega + \bar{\omega} = u + iv + (u - iv) = 2u$$

but

$$\omega + \bar{\omega} = \log (x + iy) + \log (x - iy) = \log (x^2 + y^2)$$

$$\therefore 2u = \log (x^2 + y^2)$$

and

$$u = \log (x^2 + y^2)^{1/2}$$

Hence

$$u = \text{const. entails } \sqrt{x^2 + y^2} = \text{const.}$$

$$\therefore \text{ the lines } u = \text{const. map into circles } \sqrt{x^2 + y^2} = \text{const.}$$

Similarly

$$\omega - \bar{\omega} = 2iv = \frac{\log (x^2 + iy^2)}{x^2 + y^2}$$

Putting

$$x = r \cos \theta, \qquad y = r \sin \theta$$

we have:

$$2iv = \log \frac{r^2 (\cos^2 \theta + i \sin^2 \theta)}{r^2 (\cos^2 \theta + \sin^2 \theta)} = \log (\cos^2 \theta + i \sin^2 \theta)$$

Hence the lines v = const. map into the straight lines through the origin given by θ = const.

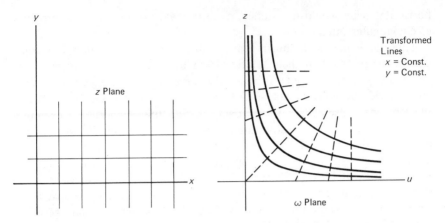

Fig. 8.7. Another common type of conformal transformation.

A conformal transformation may consist of a sequence of simpler components, each one of which is itself a conformal transformation (for example, a translation plus a rotation). The shape shown in Fig. 8.8 is produced from the original (Fig. 8.4) by the successive application of a logarithmic

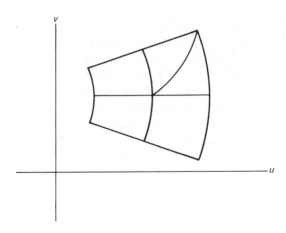

Fig. 8.8. The original shape of Fig. 8.4 remapped by a logarithmic transformation followed by rotation and translation.

transformation, a rotation, and a translation. It gives a fair approximation of the appearance of the original pattern as viewed through a wedge prism, although the representation would be improved by some degree of differential lateral compression. Incidentally, simple reduction of the horizontal scale would not suffice, as this would not preserve the property of equiangular intersection.

Thus far it has been shown that the distorted inputs commonly studied can be represented in their "static" form by conformal mappings of the original, undistorted input. Although the representation may not be perfect, and indeed probably is not so for more complicated distortions such as the last one presented, it is surprising to find that such simple examples of a single class of transformations give a close approximation to the perceived distortions. I have not been able to find a distortion that has been studied, and to which a high degree of adaptation is possible, that is not representable in this way. This is not to say that *any* continuous distortion can be expressed conformally; for example, many simple affine transformations cannot be.[8] Also it is perfectly apparent that there are many bizarre and complicated conformal transformations which, even when they yield one-to-one mappings, cannot be considered as reasonable paradigms for visual distortions (see, for example, Kober, 1957; Koppenfels & Stallmann, 1959; Phillips, 1947). Nevertheless, the main point remains valid.

A TRANSFORMATION MODEL FOR ADAPTATION

It is postulated that the visual system makes use of conformal transformations in adapting to optical distortions. From this it follows that the further restriction on scale-change distortions mentioned earlier (footnote 4), is that they should be expressible as conformal mappings. The appeal of this postulate lies in the fact that only very simple conformal transformations are needed to describe the distortions. At first blush it may seem rather far-fetched, but it will be argued shortly that even *without* introduction of artificial distortions, the visual system must operate some such transformations in its normal activities. Additional strong evidence in favor of the postulate will emerge when adaptation to movement distortions is discussed.

Suppose that the visual system contains a "true" representation of the visual field (in the sense previously described) in some suitably coded form. Introduction of a distorting medium such as a lens or prism in front of the eye now transforms the input by some $f(z)$, where z represents

[8] This point is worth emphasizing since the concept of conformal mapping is probably unfamiliar and one needs to grasp the limits it entails. Having once been rebuked publicly for proposing a fanciful theory, it transpired in subsequent conversation that the critic thought conformal mapping could, among other things, transform a square into a circle—this, from a "mathematically sophisticated" psychologist!

the normal input. There will in general be some immediately obvious visual distortions (such as curvature) as well as disruption of sensorimotor coordination. It is proposed that the system operates in such a way as to find the inverse transformation, $f^{-1}(\omega)$, and apply it to the distorted input $[f^{-1}(\omega) = z]$ thereby restoring the normal visual representation and hence also sensorimotor coordination. Although active movement and concomitant reafferent stimulation may not be *necessary* conditions of adaptation in all conditions, they certainly seem in many cases to be important factors in bringing it about. The structural model of Fig. 8.9 is suggested

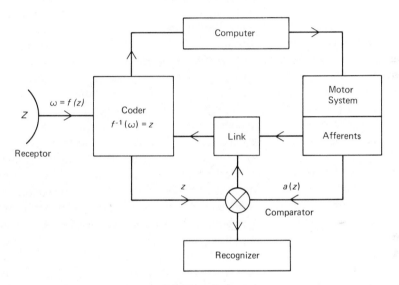

Fig. 8.9. A model for the adapting visuomotor system.

to account for the process; its similarity to the model of Fig. 8.2 scarcely needs elaboration, but there are also some important differences. When the normal input z reaches the coder, this "veridical" representation of the visual field passes to the computer which controls motor output. This in turn produces reafferent stimulation $a(z)$ which is matched with the coder's output by the comparator. If the two agree, events in the visual field are recognized, and the link is not activated. However, when the input to the coder is $f(z) = \omega$, visual and proprioceptive information do not match, the link is activated, and its function is to cause the coder to apply some $\phi(\omega)$ to the visual input, so as to reduce the mismatch. If the coder attains $\phi = f^{-1}(\omega)$, then visual and proprioceptive information again agree, stable recognition occurs, the link is shut off, and $f^{-1}(\omega)$ continues to be applied until further mismatches occur in the comparator.

The operation of the model is rather straightforward, but several points should be clarified. It could be argued that separation of computer and recognizer is unnecessary—and unlikely to be correct. One would clearly expect them to interact, and the separation is merely a convenience to show that activation of the motor system is at least partially under immediate visual control, even when the system is in an unstable condition. The comparison of visual with afferent information, control of graded movements via proprioceptive and visual feedback and recognition of the congruence between them, on the other hand, involves an additional sequence of operations. Anomalous "recognition" will occur when there are discrepancies in the visual and motor inputs to the comparator, and this seems to accord with the often-reported peculiarities of both visual and proprioceptive perception when distorting spectacles are worn. One might ask whether the action of the link is simply to cause random changes in the $\phi(\omega)$ applied by the coder, or whether some use is made of information in the discrepancy that is present. The latter seems to be the correct alternative, since changes occur quite rapidly and are nearly always in the direction of reducing the visual-proprioceptive discrepancy adaptively. In the simplest case of a horizontal displacement the discrepancy is constant, and to reduce it to zero the coder must find some $\omega = z + A$, where A is the desired change in visual direction on the abscissa. This seems to be done by a series of successive approximations, as the findings on gradual and partial adaptation show. The occurrence of an opposite distortion on removal of the distorting medium, the extent of which depends on the amount of adaptation to the original distortion, is a natural consequence of the operation of such a system.

It can be argued that, since proprioceptive adaptation occurs in some situations, the model should incorporate this feature. It can be done only in a general way, since no ready representation of the "body schema" like the two-dimensional description of a visual field is available.[9] In fact the representation would have to be extremely complicated before one even attempted to account for the coding of adaptive changes. One can suggest that the mismatches detected by the comparator will determine whether visual or proprioceptive changes occur to reduce the discrepancies, on the basis of a sort of "law of least effort." The clearest evidence for a proprioceptive explanation comes from situations where the head is clamped by a bite board, and a single limb is viewed through the distorting prism (Harris, 1965). Both visual and related proprioceptive input are highly restricted. In fact the only mismatches occur for movements of a single limb; there is little a priori reason to expect adaptation, except in connection with that limb. The easiest way to achieve the recorre-

---

[9] This point is discussed further in Chapter 11.

lation is by a proprioceptive change, that is, a change in the felt position of the limb. The evidence for proprioceptive changes is not nearly so clear in other situations, for instance when the head is free to move. It will be shown later that it is logically impossible to account for all adaptations in terms of proprioceptive changes alone. This is not the same as denying that such changes can, and do, occur, only we are not as yet in a position to develop precise hypotheses about how they are coded and mediated. The acknowledgement that they play a role complicates any account we may wish to give of adaptation, but does not force one to abandon a model based principally on visual coding and adaptations thereof. Some evidence from long-term studies (Hay & Pick, 1966) suggests that changes in proprioception tend to be temporary, in contrast to changes in visual adaptation. This is in harmony with the "law of least effort" suggested above. (See also the further discussion in Chapter 11.)

The fact that adaptations occur gradually and often are incomplete is well known. Pick, Hay, and Pabst (1963) reported that adaptation to different aspects of a distortion (for example, displacement and curvature when a wedge prism is the distorting device) generally occurs at different rates, and may reach different degrees of completeness over an extended period of use. This is consistent with the point made earlier, that a conformal transformation may comprise several separate transformations; it would not be too surprising if the components of the total transformation were to adapt at different rates. Indeed this is to be expected, since the different components generally differ in complexity. To be explicit on this issue, translation can be expressed as addition/subtraction of the same constants for each (x, y), rotation and magnification by multiplication by constant factors. All these may conveniently be expressed as matrix operations of addition and multiplication, the transform matrix containing only constants. The constants which reduce visual and afferent stimulation mismatches to zero would then be found by a process of successive approximation as already suggested. Simple inversions, on the other hand, involve changes of sign (for example, $-\bar{z} = -x + iy$) for which a step-functional operator seems more probable (Ashby, 1952). However, these processes do not themselves depend on sampling *particular* values of x and y. That is, if the transformation is $\omega = -\bar{z}$, it can be attained by matrix multiplication, the transform matrix again containing only constants. On the other hand, when a more complicated transformation such as $\omega = \log z$ is required, the transformation operator itself involves the values of the argument, x and y. To add to the complications, not only may the specific values of x and y enter into the transformation, but other sorts of information may also be required. In the usual case of wearing distorting spectacles, in which the eyes are free to move with respect to the distorting device, a very complex relationship between proprioceptive and visual factors is entailed, as Kohler realized; it implies that information about eye position also occurs in the transform operator. In transformations which require more complicated computations such as finding $\frac{1}{2}$ log $(x^2 + y^2)$ step-functional processes are again implied, rather than gradual approximations, and the reported evidence seems to bear this out (Kohler, 1964; Taylor, 1962).

The distinction between "mild" and "radical" distortions suggested earlier may now be more definitely characterized as the distinction between distortions which can be reduced by successive approximation of constants in an additive or multiplicative operator and those which cannot.[10]

FURTHER EVIDENCE FOR A CONFORMAL-TRANSFORMATION MODEL

For a system to operate by conformal transformations of its input, measures on two mutually perpendicular axes must be preserved independently. This certainly happens in a visual system in which stereopsis occurs, since—as has already been discussed—vertical and horizontal disparities play fundamentally different roles in such a system. One might think that the notion of a conformal model is supported by neurophysiological findings such as Hubel and Wiesel's on the "complex field" cortical units, which are selectors of information about straight lines in the *visual field*. Complex fields may cover a large proportion of the total visual field (up to 30° in the cat) which implies a large possible distortion in curvature (via the optics of the eye and curvature of the retina) in passing from one part of the field to another. This sort of evidence gives no real support to the model, since it could be explained by a fixed set of connections built into the visual system (albeit a rather complicated set). Although image formation through a powerful lens can be expressed approximately as a conformal mapping, as can the mapping from a plane surface to a hemisphere (in this case exactly; Coxeter, 1961), this may be irrelevant, since a built-in "correction" system in terms of the functional organization of receptive fields appears more probable. However, there is other more convincing evidence that the visual system operates with conformal transformations in the absence of external distorting media. When the eyes converge asymmetrically, particularly if the point of fixation is above or below the line of normal regard, the images at the two eyes are of different sizes and suffer different amounts of rotation (through cyclotorsion), and yet the images fuse perfectly without introducing

---

[10] Thus rotations of less than 90° are classified as "mild," the operator being

$$\begin{vmatrix} \cos \phi & \sin \phi \\ \sin \phi & -\cos \phi \end{vmatrix}$$

where ϕ is the angle of rotation (constant).

anomalous stereoptic effects. The reduction of the two images to a normal form may be considered as a pair of conformal transformations applied separately to the inputs to the two eyes. This is certainly not a trivial point, since the unreduced image differences can be very large with respect to the known limits of normal stereo acuity.[11]

ADAPTATION TO MOVEMENT DISTORTIONS

Perhaps the most telling piece of evidence in favor of the conformal transformation model is found when one considers the question of adaptation to *movement* distortion. In normal circumstances the visual world[12] appears stable as the head and eyes move, which may be explained on von Holst's principle (see also Gregory & Zangwill, 1963). The visual field, of course, may be said to flow uniformly and without distortion in a direction opposite to that of a uniform head or eye movement (with respect to the visual world). If a wedge prism or similar distorting device is worn, the visual world no longer appears stable under head movements and various changes occur in the visual field so that the pattern of "visual flow" is destroyed. It is no longer uniform, and the extent of distortion may depend in a precise way on position within the field. And yet, in time, the observer adapts to his condition, even when—as in the case of left-right reversal—the visual flow is in the opposite direction, and at twice the speed, of the normal flow that accompanies head movement. Further complications are introduced by the fact that for most distortions the pattern of flow is a function of eye position and movement, as well as of head movement.

A close parallel can be drawn between the relation of "visual flow" under distortions and "visual flow" under normal conditions, on the one hand, and the manner in which engineers study hydraulic flow patterns, on the other. The passage of a homogeneous fluid through any but the simplest of environments gives rise to a complicated flow pattern. The analysis of such patterns is greatly facilitated by the fact that, under certain restrictions, a flow pattern can be conformally mapped into a parallel rectilinear uniform flow pattern. The condition that must be met is that the flow pattern should be irrotational (nonturbulent), which in turn is a necessary and sufficient condition for the pattern to be representable by an analytic function of a complex variable (see Vallentine, 1959, pp. 139–147). This condition is embodied in the Cauchy-Riemann equations, which specify invariant "local properties" of the flow pattern, which are

---

[11] It is perhaps surprising that there has been no investigation of binocular effects after separate adaptation of the two eyes. One might expect to gain considerable insight into both systems (adaptational, binocular) by such means.

[12] "Visual world" is again used in Gibson's (1950) sense.

closely related to the local property of equiangular intersection for static mappings discussed earlier. The condition is also sufficient to ensure that "reduction" of the flow pattern to uniform rectilinear parallel motion is possible by means of a conformal transformation.

The parallel is more than a loose analogy; the restoration of "uniform visual flow" in the visual field can be attained by an appropriate conformal mapping, *which is the same mapping* that corrects the static distortions, as might be expected. A simple example will make this clear. In a left-right inversion, the distortion is represented by $\omega = -\bar{z}$, so that the sign of every value of x is reversed.[13] What of the flow pattern? The flow velocity is twice as fast as it should be, and in the wrong direction, since du/dt and all higher derivatives with respect to time have the "wrong" sign (whereas the head "signals the expectation" dx/dt, the visual system records $-[dx/dt]$). The fact that $du/dt = -(dx/dt)$ is already entailed by the static transformation. Head movement, which introduces the flow pattern, yields *additional* information about the transformation to be applied to correct for distortion that, far from conflicting with that from the static display, actually supplements it.

The example given entails an adjustment which is constant over the whole visual field. Clearly there will be cases in which the movement distortion is a function of position within the visual field, and in such cases the transformation to be applied will not be so simple. But here also the situation is precisely analogous to that which obtains for static displays; restoration of the "veridical" visual field can be attained by the appropriate conformal transformation, even though in some cases the transforming operations are more complicated than in others. The appearance of an opposite movement distortion on removal of the distorting medium is well documented. This again fits naturally into the proposed model. The fact that both static and dynamic distortions, and the adaptations thereto, fit the same transformation paradigm appears to be strong evidence that the visual system does make use of a conformal mapping analogue in its adaptation to optically produced distortions.

MOVEMENT ADAPTATION AND OTHER EXPLANATORY MODELS

The observation of reversed-movement distortion, to the extent that adaptation had occurred, cannot well be explained in terms of a conditioning model. The argument against such an explanation is the same as

---

[13] If the center of the visual field is taken as the origin of the transformation, it does not entail an additional translation, as Fig. 8.4 might suggest.

in the case of static distortions: Gradual and partial effects and reverse-adaptation effects are paradoxical on this account and the "reconditioning" process is too rapid to be plausible. Even less can adaptation to movement distortion be accounted for by a proprioceptive model. Consider first the argument that adaptation to *static* curvature distortions can be explained by a scanning process, in which the eye scans a curved contour but is *felt* to be moving rectilinearly. This does not seem to be possible, since generally the curvature varies in different parts of the field (directions of view through a prism, for example), and scanning a contour in one part entails movements of contours *across other parts of the retina,* which are inconsistent with the movements which would be observed without the distortion. Thus the "correct proprioceptive adaptation" for, let us say, a vertical line in the center of the (distorted) field cannot simultaneously be the correct state of adaptation with regard to other parts of the field which are viewed peripherally. Even though the felt movements of the eye change appropriately for different directions of regard through the prism, the felt movements will not be appropriate for more than a small part of the whole visual field at any one time. For a proprioceptive explanation of adaptation to curvature to be at all plausible, therefore, one would have to postulate that information about contour and contour deformation is discarded from all but the most central part of the retina. If one presents the argument in terms of movement adaptation and "visual flow" it becomes even more compelling. Suppose that the eye moves uniformly from left to right, the visual field being distorted by a wedge prism; points on the horizontal bisector of the field (the line of scan) move at different rates as the eye moves. For any one point on the retina, the characteristics of this movement change continuously, and the changes in movement parameters for different retinally defined points are also functions of the eye's position with respect to the prism. Thus *both* the points on the retina which are stimulated during movement *and* the eye's position with respect to the prism at that time must be taken into account, and again both position on the retina and position of the eye relative to the prism affect the movement parameters. For argument's sake, let us suppose that there is a change in perceived motion of the eye such that, for a small foveal area, motion of the visual field relative to the eye "appears normal" (and is therefore discounted). Although the eye accelerates and decelerates in a complicated way as its direction of regard changes with respect to the prism, its apparent motion is uniform. That motion of the eye which reduces foveal visual movement to normality must *necessarily* further alter the flow of other parts of the visual field, in some cases decreasing the distortion, but in others actually *increasing* it. Since the parameters of visual movement are functions both of retinal points stimulated and of eye position (and velocity) relative to the prism, there can by definition be *no* set of eye movements that simultaneously reduces the visual flow in all parts of the field to normality. The eye cannot move with several different velocities at the same time, so no matter what the real or felt movement is, it cannot accommodate to the distortion in all parts of the field at once. Even in the much simpler case of left-right inversion, where the flow across the field appears to be more or less uniform although reversed from the normal, it is difficult to imagine changes in felt eye position and movement which could account for adaptation. On the other hand, if the adaptation consists of a general transformation of the visual input, such puzzles do not arise. Indeed it is difficult to think of anything but a general transformation over all the inputs that would be powerful enough to handle such situations.

WHY PROPRIOCEPTION?

One wonders what the special attractions of a proprioceptive model may be, since the position has been vigorously defended at various times. Is it possible to argue that the stability of the visual world is, essentially, guaranteed by the fixedness of visual directions for points on the retina? This would be a reversal of the traditional argument about the primacy of tactile space (see p. 165), a reversal clearly demonstrated in Harris's concluding remarks (Harris, 1965). Since our visual world is ordinarily so stable and orderly, and since proprioceptive adaptation certainly can occur in situations other than those involving distortions of visual input, there is something quite appealing about the notion that visual adaptation is only *apparent* and is mediated by change in the felt positions of parts of the body—changes of which one is normally not aware. If one espouses such a view one can avoid the difficulties about changes in visual direction discussed in the previous chapter, since by definition a purely visual adaptation, or one with a visual component, must involve changes in the visual directions associated with particular retinal loci. Thus one might argue that the proprioceptive theorist's position is like that of the suppression theorist vis-à-vis binocular vision. Enough seems to be known about the detailed structure and function of the visual system to indicate that changes in visual direction are inherently unlikely; on the other hand, much less is known about the processing of proprioceptive information, to the extent that one may feel more comfortable about assigning adaptive changes to that modality rather than to vision. In this way the stability of the visual world, and the reemergence of stability following distortions of input, can be accounted for by postulating a "built-in" stabilized system which is thrown out of gear by distorted visual input, but which adapts by changes in the felt position of limbs, and so forth. By this account, "visual adaptation" would be only apparent, since the thing that matters is the coordination of movements with visual control. We have seen, however, that the proprioceptive position is untenable as a general explanation for the phenomena under discussion and also that there is no reason to hold to the belief in the inherent immutability of visual directions any more. To stick one final spanner in the proprioceptive model's works, one may point out that there are several types of visual movement aftereffects which are adaptational phenomena and clearly do not have a proprioceptive explanation. I have in mind the "waterfall" and "spiral" aftereffects and related phenomena. These make nonsense of the idea of fixed visual directions for retinal (and cortical) loci during pattern processing. It seems to me that some recent theorists have been misled by concentrating on too restricted a range of evidence; this is particularly true of the emphasis on studying wedge prism distortions. There is much to be said for a model which can subsume these studies as special cases under a broader explanatory schema.

PARALLEL PROCESSING

The transformation model has been presented in such a way that the input is transformed *in toto* by the coder. This is a simplification of the real situation, since there is a deal of evidence—again coming mainly from descriptions by the earlier investigators—to show that at least in some situations (mainly those involving radical distortions) the transformations occur in a more piecemeal fashion. For example, Kohler quotes cases where some parts of the visual field will adapt before others or where the adapted field will suddenly "destabilize" in one area and not others. Taylor also describes such situations, frequently correlated with differences in the ways in which visual input is used to control behavior; the part-field adaptations appear to be fairly permanent in these cases. The question of the relations between adaptive states in different parts of the visual field has not been subjected to detailed experimental investigation, but it seems quite plausible to suppose that separate operators may be formed for different parts of the field, so that a great deal of processing goes on in parallel. The outputs from such processing units—reminiscent of the b.p.u.'s postulated in the previous chapter—would then proceed to a recognizer which "covers" the whole field, "smoothing" the articulated inputs into a coherent representation of the visual field. In most cases the operators would all have approximately the same task—for instance to apply constant increments to the coordinates of a displaced visual field—so that the adaptation would proceed apparently as a uniform transformation over the whole field. In other cases—as for example when adaptation of the immediate lower-frontal field becomes important for control of locomotion—a subset of the processing units would proceed to accomplish this, and would adapt more rapidly than units concerned with the upper part of the visual field. It is not unlikely that the rest of the units would fail to adapt completely if their respective visual and proprioceptive inputs were never activated, or that they would adapt only to the extent required for "smoothing" in the recognizer's representation of the visual field. Such special adaptations, and their effects on the rest of the field, seem worthy of much more detailed study than they have as yet received.

Kohler explains his anomalous partial effects or "situation-specific" effects—such as the sudden rereversal of a familiar object, or the appearance of atypical features as a result of additional (for example, gravitational) cues—as being due to the attempt to reconcile the general adaptive state with some particularly familiar or otherwise powerful determinant of the normal visual world. Such local perturbations are consistent with the notion of parallel processing, but too little is known about the time-course of such anomalies, or their possible effects on the rest of the field, for one to be able to infer anything specific about the relations between parallel processors from them.

SOME POSSIBLE OBJECTIONS TO THE MODEL

One possible objection to the conformal mapping model is that it postulates a particular form of transformation without presenting any strong evidence that this, and only this, is the sole type of transformation required. In the simpler cases (such as translation and rotation) the postulation seems unnecessary, since these are simple linear transformations. Perhaps a simpler *general* set of transformations than those chosen would do the job. It is of course entirely possible that some other characterization of the transformations could be found. However, no such alternative has ever been suggested. Conformal transformations are in general powerful nonlinear systems (and some of the distortions are clearly nonlinear) that have just the two attributes which seem to be required: a strong local constraint on the characteristics of neighboring points and intersecting contours, together with great flexibility in the overall mapping of one plane onto another. The point that both simple and complex transformations fit the paradigm is again emphasized, as well as the fact that both the static and movement distortion situations can be accounted for.

The more telling criticism is that the actual distortions produced by some media are not exactly describable in terms of conformal mappings.

This is true, as can be ascertained by looking through a strong wedge or, for example, at the photographs of patterns taken through a wedge prism presented in Kohler's monograph (1964). The evidence consists in the fact that right angles are not preserved, as they must be in a conformal transformation. Two lines of argument that are complementary to each other can be taken against the criticism.

First, it is clear that there are several sorts of adaptive process which occur in the visual system that are different from the processes here described. One of these is the set of operations which give rise to various constancies, including shape constancy. It is conceivable that this process acts locally on the distorted visual input in the direction of restoring contour and angle characteristics to their undistorted form—a suggestion that is not too ingenuous in view of the known "regression to the real object" which occurs in the normal visual world. Some purely visual adaptations such as those discovered by Gibson (1937) might act in the same way. A model to account for such processes has been proposed by Andrews (1964), based on the idea that the visual system maintains certain statistical features of the visual field invariant, by a process of local rescaling of the metric of visual space. In an ingenious experiment, Mikaelian and Held (1964) have shown that two different sorts of adaptation can indeed be distinguished experimentally, one of the Gibson-Andrews type (visual rescaling) which is not dependent on self-produced movements, and another which is. The latter, as would be expected on the present hypothesis, tends to produce much larger adaptive changes than the former, which also seems to operate on a much shorter time scale. It must be admitted that there is no positive demonstration that such purely visual changes (that is, adaptive rescaling on the basis of visual input alone) must necessarily change a distorted visual input in the direction of making it more nearly a conformal mapping of the undistorted input, but this seems to be the most probable direction of change. (See Andrews, 1964, for a detailed discussion of the sorts of invariance which changes in the visual metric are held to mediate.) It is also clear that visual rescaling (essentially local) alone will not account for the sensorimotor recorrelations and gross phenomenal changes which the present model attempts to explain.

Second (to return to the defense of the conformal model), it is not as yet established that complete adaptation to distortions which are clearly nonconformal can occur. The requisite experiments have not been done. It may be tentatively suggested that adaptation is only possible to the extent that the distortion (modified, perhaps, by local rescaling) is expressible conformally. This is, of course, entirely speculative. Much more elaborate quantitative experiments on the detailed course and extent of adaptation than have yet been attempted would be needed in order for it to be offered as a definite hypothesis.

TWO STAGES OF ADAPTATION

It was stated earlier that two apparently different stages of adaptation are known to occur, the first a sort of "practical" adaptation which solves the problem of controlling behavior in a visually-distorted environment, the second a "phenomenal" or "pictorial" adaptation, in which the distorted visual world actually comes to *appear* undistorted. The reports of this event are too frequent and too definite to be dismissed lightly as mere failure to notice the distortion. Kohler in particular emphasizes the fact that his adapted subjects often could not detect anomalies in the visual world even if they were particularly asked to pay attention to a feature that was known to be distorted by the devices they were wearing. In the proposed model this difference could perhaps be accounted for by suggesting—bearing in mind the finding that proprioceptive adaptation tends to be less stable than visual (Hay & Pick, 1966)—that adaptation in the second, pictorial, sense only occurs when an overall transformation $f^{-1}(\omega)$ has been found for visual input, such that input to the recognizer is again normal and involves no transformation on $a(z)$ to achieve matching at the comparator. In other cases, where $\phi(\omega)$ is changing, or different functions are being applied to different parts of the field, or where $a(z)$ is changing, adaptation in the first sense only can occur. Thus a particular "integrative" function is possible at the recognizer if, rather than one comparator, there is a considerable number operating in parallel, as is implied by the suggestion that different parts of the visual field are coded by parallel visual processors. This again is a suggestion which cannot be put forward at all strongly in view of the lack of detailed experimental evidence of the sort that would be required to confirm it.

SOME PREDICTIONS

Can any definite predictions be made from the conformal model? The first and obvious one is that complete adaptation to distortions which deviate radically from a conformal mapping of the normal visual field will not be possible. This has to be qualified, in view of the discussion of nonconformal features of distortions already discussed, so that the prediction cannot be exact—"radically" is not precise enough to circumscribe the class of nonconformal distortions which the prediction should identify. If the limits of rescaling of the purely visual metric were known, the prediction could be made more confidently. At all events, if the model is on the right lines, one should expect not to find adaptation to distortions such as a large change in scale on one axis only, or where a considerable shear is introduced which distorts all the angles at which contours intersect.

Similarly, one should not expect adaptation to movement distortions where "turbulent flow" occurs—the sort of noncontinuous flow one can observe in the neighborhood of bubble faults on looking through thick plate glass, for example.

Another prediction is that adaptation to a certain size of distortion will facilitate adaptation to a similar but more powerful distortion of the same type but not to distortions which are of different types. For instance, one would predict that full or partial adaptation to a rotation ϕ_1 of the visual field would facilitate adaptation to a rotation ϕ_2 but should not show positive transfer to situations where other types of distortion, such as a translation, are introduced. One might even expect interference in this case. On the other hand, adaptation to a simple distortion (for example, translation) which is a *component* of a more complex distortion (for example, prismatic) should facilitate the latter. It may also be predicted that successive adaptations to the same sort of distortion should occur more rapidly on successive occasions (as indeed seems to happen) but that this facilitation will again be relatively specific to the type of distortion. It may be expected that adaptation in general, as well as the two types of facilitation mentioned, will be more rapid, the simpler the distortion is in terms of its conformal description. Also it appears likely that successive adaptations should require proportionately less afferent information to reach completion. According to most conceptions of how adaptation occurs, successively applied *opposite* distortions (displacement to the right vs. to the left, for example) should interfere with each other and give strong negative transfer. However, according to this model, successive opposite distortions of the same type should interfere only weakly, and perhaps even show positive transfer. At the least they should interfere with each other less than successive adaptations of different types. This prediction follows from the notion of visual adaptations as functions of overall transformations of the input by a specifiable operator.

In view of the argument about the natural occurrence of transformations when the eyes are asymmetrically converged (p. 176) it must be expected that different transformations can be imposed separately on the two eyes. Although there have been reports of interocular transfer of adaptation, the matter appears not to have been studied in detail—as, for example, by attempting simultaneous complete adaptation of each eye separately (alternately) to a different distortion. It would be of great interest to know how such simultaneous adaptation, if it can be achieved, would affect other pattern processing systems, for example in binocular vision. Given a system in which primary binocular interaction occurs at a fairly low level of pattern processing (as in the cat—compare the Hubel & Wiesel data—and probably most other mammals too), it should by such means be possible to gain some ideas about the level at which adaptation to optical distortion occurs. Incidentally, the study of different adaptive states for the two eyes could well throw further light on the role proprioception plays in adaptation.

Thus the model generates some interesting new consequences, even if most of them cannot be dignified with the name of strict predictions. These also lay the model open to the possibility of empirical falsification, which is as it should be. It would be too much to hope that such a model could be right in all particulars or that it could serve to explain successfully all the features of adaptation to distorting optical media. In pointing out the form which adaptation probably takes, it may, however, yield further insight into the process.

CHAPTER 9
Some Further Characteristics of Human Visual Pattern Recognition

THE ROLE OF EYE MOVEMENTS

A great deal of attention has been paid in recent years to the role which eye movements play in visual perception and to their relationships to pattern recognition in particular. It has of course been known for a long time that the eyes are not static in the normal state; Helmholtz remarked over 100 years ago on "wandering of the gaze" even during fixation, but the exact description of their minute movements was dependent on the development of sensitive recording methods, which has happened only fairly recently. Ratliff and Riggs (1950) reported on a reliable system for eye movement recording in which collimated light is reflected from a tiny mirror attached to a contact lens. The reflected beam is focused onto a strip of moving film, which provides a permanent record. They found, using this method, that eye movements during fixation are complex and have at least three readily distinguishable features: high-frequency tremor (physiological nystagmus) in the range of 30–70 cycles/sec of low amplitude (15–20 sec of arc); slow drifts which may last over 10 sec and have an amplitude of 5 min arc or more; and saccades, or very rapid flicks, which occur at irregular intervals and vary greatly in amplitude (the mean being close to 6 min of arc). Figure 9.1 summarizes these effects graphically.

It is remarkable that these comparatively large eye movements do not affect the apparent stability of the visual world. Cornsweet (1956) has shown that only the saccades are under visual control and serve to realign the eye on its fixation point; the greater the fixation error, the higher is the probability of a saccade, which is usually in the appropriate direction. Stability of the visual field under saccade movement can be explained on von Holst's reafference principle, by supposing that a visual signal for "off target" simultaneously activates the appropriate motor-control

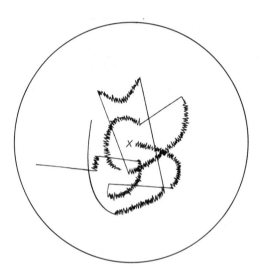

Fig. 9.1. An impression of the three main sorts of "involuntary" eye movements; slow drift, on which is superimposed a fine tremor (physiological nystagmus), and *saccades,* or rapid "flicks." The lines shown can be thought of as the track of a steady spot of light on the retina as the eye moves.

and efferent centers. But this can hardly be true of the fine tremor and drift components, which appear to be caused by imperfect muscle balance and are not under direct visual control.

It has been suggested that the function of the high-frequency tremor may be to improve visual acuity by increasing the numbers of retinal receptors stimulated by details in the visual field, such as fine contours. As we shall see in discussing the effects of image stabilization later in the chapter, the facts contradict this notion; but tremor does have a definite function of a different sort in detail vision. The fact that visual stability is maintained *despite* tremor and drift suggests rather strongly that there is some statistical averaging, or smoothing, of the coded visual input over time.

EYE MOVEMENTS AND BINOCULAR VISION

Even more remarkable than the monocular smoothing effects is the fact that these sorts of eye movement do not seem to affect stereoscopic depth perception in any obvious way. In several experiments the role of eye movements in binocular vision has been analyzed. Krauskopf, Cornsweet, and Riggs (1960) found that eye movements during binocular fixation are fundamentally similar to those during monocular fixation, and that the movements of the two eyes are, with one important exception, independent.[1] The exception is again saccadic movement. Figure 9.2, taken

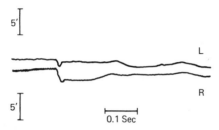

Fig. 9.2. A sample record of eye movement recordings made simultaneously for the two eyes, demonstrating that the movements are essentially independent of each other, except for the yoked *saccade*.

from the original paper, shows a normal binocular record. The single saccade shown is typical; practically all such movements occurred simultaneously for the two eyes, and in the same direction, so that although the movements are tightly yoked in this regard, the saccade is not *directly* a means of correcting vergence errors (if it were, one would expect some of the saccades to be in opposite directions for the two eyes). To quote from the original report:

> These facts imply that a central coupling mechanism must be included in any model proposed to account for the maintenance of binocular fixation. On the other hand . . . the dependence of saccade occurrence, direction, and magnitude upon eye position are not attenuated during binocular fixation. These facts can be incorporated into a model for the maintenance of binocular fixation which does not require that the eyes respond directly to vergence errors.
>
> According to this model the monocular response functions . . . determine the occurrence, magnitude, and direction of the saccades for each eye during binocular fixation as well as during monocular fixation. In

---

[1] The recordings were made with a double contact-lens-with-mirror system of the type already described for monocular recording.

addition to this response of the separate eyes to their deviations from the on-target position, there is a central mechanism such that when a saccade is triggered in one eye in response to its deviation from the on-target position, the other eye will show in general a smaller saccade in the same direction. Since the probability of occurrence of a saccade increases with the deviation of the eye from the on-target position, the eye with the greater deviation will more often trigger the saccade. This would result, on the average, in a reduction of vergence error without the vergence component of the saccades being directly determined by the vergence error before the saccade (Krauskopf, Cornsweet, & Riggs, 1960, p. 577).

The nonsaccadic eye movements are uncorrelated with each other, and the saccades are not direct vergence-adjustors, so it seems highly unlikely that eye movements themselves play an important role in the genesis of stereoptic depth, although this has sometimes been suggested (see Chapter 7). While I can find no reports of eye movement recordings during observation of stereograms, as opposed to real binocular targets, it is most improbable that eye movements during fixation are different in the two cases, as long as the stereograms are nonrivalrous, that is, they contain stable stereoscopic features. Krauskopf et al. also report on the average vergence errors during steady binocular fixation. The standard deviation of convergence for two experienced binocular observers exceeded 2 min of arc for sample durations of 60 sec, and was well over 1 min of arc for one observer over a sample duration of only 2 sec. Considering the fact that stereoscopic acuity has been variously reported at between 2 and 5 *sec* of arc for experienced observers, it seems clear that some sort of statistical operator must extract information about stereoptic depth from the "noisy" analogue of the binocular field implied by the inaccuracies of fixation. Stereoptic depth is perceived in spite of—not because of—eye movements.

There is, of course, the important fact that initial fusion (motor fusion) in binocular vision is achieved by rotation of the eyeballs in opposite directions. This has been investigated by a number of people, some of the earlier workers claiming that the vergence movements of the eyes are extremely inaccurate. However, Riggs and Niehl (1960) point out that this erroneous conclusion is accounted for by the poor techniques previously used. Riggs and Niehl themselves (1960) used a double contact-lens-with-mirror system, and were able to show rather accurate vergence changes, as the binocular target's position was changed from far to near and vice versa. Figure 9.3 shows the record for an exceptionally steady observer. Yoked saccades (A and C) and a very small amount of drift can be seen, but the resolution is not good enough to show the high-frequency tremor. B and D are control monocular conditions in which it can be seen that the rapid saccade-like change in monocular fixation

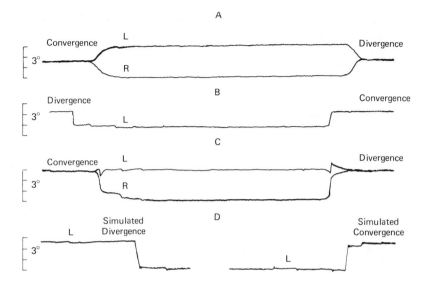

Fig. 9.3. Samples of eye movement recordings made during monocular and binocular fixation at different distances.

is different from the relatively slower fusional movements in A. Record C shows that, for asymmetrical convergence, in which one eye is already correctly aligned, the fusional system still imposes some "unwanted" movement. The record demonstrates clearly enough that the fusional movements are not controlled in the same way as vergence adjustments after fusion, as described previously, and appear also to be under a different guidance system than the more rapid, saccade-like movements in monocular changes in fixation. The achievement of correct registry appears to be the only specific function of eye movements in binocular vision.

EFFECTS OF IMAGE STABILIZATION

Helmholtz supposed that one function of eye movements was to prevent retinal fatigue by subjecting any one part of the retina to alternating strong and weak stimulation. It has also been suggested (for example, Andersen & Weymouth, 1923) that small eye movements serve to increase acuity by increasing the number of retinal units stimulated and thereby providing extra data on which a "mean retinal local sign" can be based, or as we should say today, by increasing the signal-to-noise ratio for the set of stimulated units.

Precise investigation of the function of small high-frequency eye movements in visual acuity—and in pattern vision generally—was only possible after a technique had been devised for controlling them. This was done independently by Ditchburn and Ginsborg (1952) and by Riggs, Ratliff, Cornsweet, and Cornsweet (1953). The technique is well-known and needs no detailed description here. It depends on the fact that a system can be constructed to compensate for the movements of the eye. A tightly fitting contact lens, on which a small mirror is mounted, is worn by the observer. A beam of light containing the viewing target is reflected from the mirror onto a screen, so that the target's motion on the screen follows the eye movements. The target is viewed through an optical system which precisely cancels the target movements with respect to the eye. That is to say, there is no motion of the image relative to the eye. The system is flexible in the sense that by changing the characteristics of the optical system from eye to screen, any fraction of the normal retinal-image motion can be obtained, including fractions greater than unity. However, most attention has been devoted to the special case where the retinal image is stabilized.[2]

The general findings are again too well-known to need detailed exposition: The stabilized image is at first seen clearly, but after a comparatively short time starts to fade. The manner and speed of disappearance have been variously estimated and described by different authors, but it appears from Barlow's work (1963) that the better the stabilization, the more rapid and abrupt is the fade-out, a point which is supported by the rapid disappearance of various entoptic images. Image regeneration can be obtained by several means, including destabilization, imposed fluctuations in brightness, and other forms of sensory input, such as a different input to the "unstabilized" eye.

A somewhat surprising finding is that visual acuity is better than normal for a stabilized target in the short time before it disappears (Riggs et al., 1953) which refutes the notion that physiological nystagmus increases the eye's sensitivity for fine detail. Further evidence against this view is reported by Keesey (1960), who found that there are no consistent effects of eye movements on acuity. The well-known improvement in monocular acuity with increasing exposure duration (typically between .01 and 1.0 sec) has been interpreted as favoring the eye movement sensitivity notion, since an increased effect of eye movement is possible under longer exposures. Keesey showed, however, that increase in acuity with increased exposure is very similar for stabilized and nonstabilized images, which means that it is not the eye movements themselves that improve acuity. A similar result for stereoscopic acuity is reported by Shortess

---

[2] Stabilization can also be attained by attaching the target to the eye directly. This has been done by Ditchburn and Pritchard (1956) and by Yarbus (1957). The target is carried on a lightweight stalk attached to the contact lens.

and Krauskopf (1961). Thus, while eye movements are clearly necessary to maintain pattern detail in the visual image, they do not apparently contribute to increasing the sharpness of detail detection.

Barlow (1963), using a Yarbus-type lens, which suffers very little slippage when properly fitted, found that image disappearance was fairly abrupt, in contrast to some of the earlier reports. Regeneration was never complete, the regenerated image lacking the detail and contrast of the original and being textureless and shadowy in quality. Fluctuations in the image finally cease, leaving a sort of "fog or gray sky with ill-defined dark and light clouds in it corresponding to the black and white parts of the original image" (p. 63). This state, once achieved, seems to persist for as long as the conditions are held unchanged. The evidence supports Barlow's hypothesis that there are two different systems for signaling information about visual stimulation to the brain, a rapidly adapting channel signaling changes of illumination over small regions relative to the overall average, and a second, slowly adapting (or perhaps nonadapting) channel, which signals for larger areas of the retina in terms of general illumination and without contour detail. The former carries pattern information in the sense in which the concept has been used in this book. It is worth noting that many of the cortical contour-detecting units described earlier (Chapter 3) are selectively activated by moving contours; however, the complete cessation of activity that one might expect in view of the stabilized image findings has only been observed for hypercomplex units.[3]

CHARACTERISTICS OF IMAGE REGENERATION

While it may be true that the spontaneous image-regeneration found in many experiments on stabilized images can be explained in terms of incomplete stabilization, whether through lens slippage or for some other reason,[4] some of the most interesting phenomena have been discovered by studying what the characteristics of the regenerated image are. In this regard the peripheral stimulus to regeneration (if any) is not important, since the effects are almost certainly nonretinal in origin. What they indicate, basically, is how the visual system attempts to recognize patterns in, or "make something of," a highly impoverished input that nevertheless contains some information about patterns. An important study of this sort was reported by Pritchard, Heron, and Hebb (1960), who used a

[3] The electrophysiological evidence bearing on explanations of stabilized image phenomena has been summarized by Heckenmueller (1965).

[4] The eye is not a rigid body, and there is a variety of mechanical factors which might cause enough distortions to it to destabilize the image, even with a "perfect" stabilization procedure.

wide variety of stabilized targets mounted on a stalk on the contact lens and viewed at optical infinity. A number of characteristics of the fading and regeneration process were observed. On first presentation, the time to initial fading was a function of target complexity, the simpler targets fading most rapidly. The greater resistance to fading of a complex target cannot be explained in terms of random threshold fluctuations in different parts of the field, it is claimed, since such fluctuations would entail random fading and regeneration of different parts of a target. It was found, however, that fading and regeneration were distinctly nonrandom in several regards. In the first place, a "meaningful" target, such as a face, appeared to remain in view longer than a nonmeaningful shape of about the same complexity, and the partial fading of meaningful targets and symbols tended to be determined by which parts were meaningfully connected together. Straight lines tended to fade as units, and if a part faded, this tended to occur at a point where the one line intersected with another. Straight lines within a figure such as a triangle or square generally faded independently, except that parallels had a tendency to fade and regenerate in concert, and horizontal lines were more dominant than others. A pattern which consisted of rounded contours was generally less "active" than one with jagged corners and more likely to act as a whole. Gestalt-like tendencies to completion were sometimes observed, as well as "field-effects" in which the presence of a pattern in one part of the field modified activity in a neighboring part. A pattern consisting of "random squiggles" tended to regenerate in such a way as to form more coherent patterns of one sort or another, and so on.

Pritchard, Heron, and Hebb interpret their findings as supporting the notion of formation of "good *Gestalten*" as well as—at least partially—Hebb's concept of cell assembly activity. Although no tendency was found for corners to act as units as would be predicted from the original cell assembly model, the predominant tendency of straight lines to fade and reappear as units is remarkable in view of the subsequent findings on mammalian contour-coding systems (Chapter 3). It seems clear enough that effects of this sort cannot be explained in terms of a purely retinal-adaptive system, as indeed the authors themselves argue. However, one should remember that the authors were their own subjects in this investigation, and the results were not quantified. Without in any way suggesting deliberate bending of the observations to fit a preconceived hypothesis, some caution is necessary in accepting these reports as being typical for the average observer, since manipulation of perceptual reports by set or expectancy can certainly occur and probably does, unsuspectedly and unintentionally, in many cases (Dodwell & Gendreau, 1969). McKinney (1960) has shown explicitly that verbal reports of image regeneration can be strongly influenced by an observer's prior set, or expectations of what will be seen.

More recently Evans (1965) has reported rather similar experiments to those of Pritchard et al., using experimentally naïve observers and quantifying his results. Happily his findings agree in general with theirs, although there are differences of detail, and the range of targets observed was far more limited. Specifically, Evans was able to show that "structured" target disappearances are much more frequent than any other sort, "random" and "unitary" disappearances accounting for only about 25 percent of the total. The meaning of "structured" fading is illustrated in Fig. 9.4. By far the most common "structured" fading for the pattern

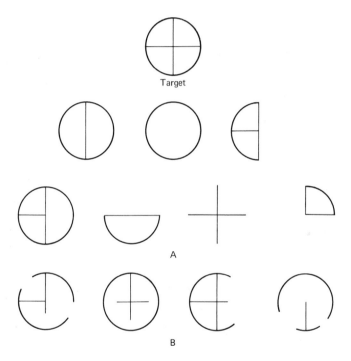

Fig. 9.4. Examples of (A) "structured" and (B) "unstructured" regenerations of the image shown at the top of the figure, in the experiment of Evans.

in Fig. 9.4 was the disappearance of the horizontal or vertical bar. In agreement with the Gestalt notion of "good-figure" dominance, it was found that ellipses have a much greater tendency to disappear than circles, and unitary fading and regeneration is relatively more common for circles than for less "good" patterns. The earlier finding that "jagged" figures tend to fade more readily than figures with smoothly rounded contours was confirmed, both by studying disappearances of the letters *S* and *Z* and, to avoid a possible criticism about relative familiarity, by observing the same phenomenon with "nonsense" figures.

Evans also argues against an interpretation of his results in terms of purely retinal processes, and, while admitting that lens slippage may have played a part in causing image regeneration, points out that the special features of regenerated images can scarcely be explained thereby. If the point needs further emphasis, one may note that similar "structured" fading can be observed with long-lasting afterimages (Bennet-Clark & Evans, 1963) where the question of image slippage with respect to the retina does not arise. A very recent study by McKinnon, Forde, and Piggins (1969) shows, moreover, that the characteristics of fading and regeneration are highly similar in the two situations.

The evidence that the nonrandomness of regenerated images is to be explained by processes occurring more centrally than at the retina is mostly presumptive, but nonetheless rather persuasive in terms of what is known of the physiological activities of the retina and of higher centers. The process of "figure forming," or one might even suggest of "figure construction" in Bartlett's (1932) tradition, is not unlike similar processes which occur when other inadequate—highly impoverished and/or conflicting—sensory input is provided to the visual system. One is reminded of the curious partial adaptations to visual distortions described in Chapter 8 and even more of the findings described in Chapter 7 on rivalrous perceptions in binocular vision, in which temporary dominance of parts of one visual field or the other are common. In these cases also it is unusual to find *really* random components of the inputs entering the visual field. Far more commonly it appears that one pattern, or a distinct part of one pattern, will appear or dominate at one instant, to be replaced (in the binocular case) perhaps by a new configuration from the other eye's view, but again in terms of the whole pattern or some particular segments of it. The characteristics of the process have never been fully described or carefully investigated, but it would certainly be of interest to know how closely it can be compared with the image-regeneration phenomena in stabilized viewing. The fact that the same sort of partial effect occurs in rather diverse situations is at least suggestive of a common process. Also the fact that the size of field over which the part-processing occurs can vary—and depends greatly on the stimulating patterns' characteristics—indicates a very flexible system in which not just local properties in the primary detector sense are involved. Rather one is reminded forcefully of the pattern-assembly routines described by Grimsdale, Sumner, Tunis, and Kilburn (Chapter 5) and by Clowes for their computer models. Our ideas about how pattern forming might be incorporated into models for the visual system are still rather primitive, and whether the processes themselves can be more fully characterized and manipulated experimentally remains to be seen. A possible move in this direction is Kolers' (1968) recent work on reading transformed text, but there is actually very little empirical work that seems to be relevant to the question.

The idea of *constructing* or actively assembling perceptual "wholes" has recently received some impetus from Neisser's work (1967) which claims descent from Bartlett's earlier views (1932) about memory and cognition. Theoretical and empirical investigations along these lines should prove to be particularly rewarding for visual perception, since we now have rather good evidence from neurophysiology for some of the sorts of element which presumably go into such constructions (see Chapter 3).

EVIDENCE FOR HUMAN RETINAL RECEPTIVE FIELD ORGANIZATION

Although it seems fair to assume that the human visual system will have similar receptive field properties to those found in other mammals, it is also important to look explicitly for evidence of such properties. Several investigators have done this, and—not surprisingly—the best evidence comes from experiments which look at very restricted forms of visual input or at rather special conditions of stimulation.

One of the earliest experiments of this genre is also one of the most straightforward: Campbell and Kulikowski (1966) studied the visibility of a grating made up of alternating dark and light bars (actually, a sinusoidal grating) as a function of the presence and relative orientation of a second, similar grating which was somewhat brighter, called "the mask."[5] Their results showed very clearly that the greatest interference occurs when both gratings are in the same orientation and falls off rapidly as the angle between them increases. For instance the masking effect was halved for a mask tilted 12° from the vertical when the test grating was itself vertically oriented. This demonstrates a contour interaction which depends primarily on the relative orientations of the two sets of contours and suggests that it is mediated by detectors for lines in specific orientations. Campbell and Kulikowski were able to show that their result cannot be explained as a purely optical effect, but must depend on a property of the visual nervous system. They relate this psychophysical evidence on orientational "tuning" to the neurophysiological findings of Hubel and Wiesel, which is scarcely surprising, since the latter provided the motivation for their experiment; nonetheless, it is satisfactory to find that the fit between the two sorts of evidence is good.

Westheimer (1967) has demonstrated spatial interactions (inhibition and facilitation) in the human foveal retina by studying thresholds for the detection of a small flashing light spot in the presence of a steady

---

[5] It should be noted that the masking grating was continuously present, so that this is *not* the type of masking paradigm described later in the chapter.

circular adapting field. The findings are compatible with ideas of receptive field organization, since the effect of the adapting field depends very much on its size. As the illuminated field is increased in diameter the adaptation state is first raised, but beyond a critical diameter it is lowered. The critical diameter is about 5 min of arc for the fovea. Such findings are suggestive, but they are not as strong evidence in favor of a particular form of receptive field organization as those described in the previous paragraph, since as yet they tell nothing about contour orientation specificity in the adaptation phenomena. Another possibility is that these adaptational changes are purely retinal, in which case orientational "tuning" should probably not be expected (see Chapter 3). Westheimer states that the adaptation is probably retinal, since binocular interactions are not found. Interestingly enough one form of orientation-specific chromatic adaptation has been found by McCullough (1965), which seems to be explainable only in terms of "colored edge" detectors, and thus to support the notion of orientation-specific receptive field organization in the human visual system.

Perhaps the most extensive and ingenious attempt to find and interpret evidence for detectors of the Hubel and Wiesel type in humans is that of Andrews (1967a, b). He showed that the observation of small, very briefly flashed line-segments results in rather unreliable perceptions. On repeated presentation a segment would appear to change its orientation, to rotate, to be thicker on some occasions than others, and so on. From repeated observations of the same set of segments under constant stimulus conditions, various characteristics of the detection performance were determined. Assuming that the statistical variation in response to a given stimulus condition could be interpreted in terms of the characteristics of the output of a population of detector units, Andrews makes the following points:

1. Most such units are binocular, and their selectivity for orientation is best when "tuned" near the horizontal and vertical directions.
2. Units integrate their outputs by a process of mutual inhibition, which takes a fraction of a second to develop.

The evidence for the second statement is that increasing the exposure duration reduces very quickly the variation in perception which is characteristic of the short-duration exposures. In the second paper (1967b) the question of spatial integration is taken up, and Andrews uses his data to estimate the probable extent of foveal receptive fields (about 9 min of arc). While the arguments of both papers are too detailed to enter into here, Andrews makes out a good case for a hierarchical arrangement with primary detector units at the lowest level, whose outputs are subjected to statistical evaluation at higher levels, where special operations of combination for the outputs of different types of unit also occur. His line of argument is very much in the same spirit as that which I have given in earlier chapters, particularly in Chapter 7, although it is couched much more in terms of the details of integration of specific features (for example, of short line segments into a longer line) rather than the "construction" of *Gestalten*.[6]

IMAGE FORMATION AND NOISE IN THE VISUAL SYSTEM

Andrews' conception of statistical evaluation over a set of fluctuating inputs leads us back to a question about the stabilized image work which merits further emphasis, although it was touched on earlier; this is the relationship of eye movements to acuity. On the one hand, one might expect the visual system to make use of physiological nystagmus to improve its power to detect fine visual detail, but this seems not to be the case. On the other hand, it seems curious that contour detection should be largely eliminated by retinal stabilization which, in the short run, improves acuity slightly. Clearly enough the form of coding for contour information that occurs in mammalian visual systems has developed in such a way as to cancel out the effects of physiological nystagmus, and presumably does so by a time-integration technique. In this sense the nystagmus produces what amounts to unwanted noise in the coding system. The remarkable fact is that the system can extract information in spite of it, which is particularly clearly shown by the fineness of stereoscopic acuity as compared with the average error of binocular fixation and its variation over time.

Another considerable factor which must add to visual noise is the formation and persistence of afterimages. These, it is generally agreed, result from photochemical changes in the visual pigments (Brindley, 1960). Because of the long recovery phase for photopigments, even in the cones, there must be a serious response lag which can interfere with the fast-responding contour-coding system. Yet, surprisingly, afterimages do not obviously interfere with the perception of a changing visual scene. Why are they not more persistent and ubiquitous? Even a couple of seconds' fixation in moderate illumination on a scene containing borders of high contrast will produce afterimages under appropriate viewing conditions. Daw (1962) investigated the phenomenon of afterimage regeneration and discovered what seems to be, essentially, a mechanism which tends actively to suppress afterimages except under one special circumstance. In his

---

[6] Not surprisingly, research aimed at demonstrating specific coding properties is rapidly becoming a hot topic. Since this chapter was written, a number of relevant papers have appeared, and to keep up to date with this growing point of new knowledge would require almost monthly revisions of material.

experiments an observer viewed a richly contoured primary scene (in color) for 12 seconds, followed by a secondary scene containing the same contours, but in black and white and with different contrast relations. Afterimages are present in the form of apparent colors in the hueless secondary scene, so long as the same relative point of fixation is maintained for the two scenes. However, as soon as the point of fixation is changed, the afterimages disappear, but can be regenerated by returning to the original fixation condition. Disappearance and regeneration can be achieved several times, each succeeding afterimage becoming fainter. In a further study it was found that the amount of afterimage that can be observed is a function of the strength and amount of contour in the subsequent scene. Looking at a plain surface as the second field of view the observer sees an afterimage which is less stable and colorful than that observed in the original secondary (black-and-white) scene, but more than is apparent in looking at some other softly contoured surface. Thus, although the retina may suffer quite long-term effects from prior stimulation, in most cases this will not constitute useful information and there is effective suppression by current contour stimulation, unless the first and second contour displays happen to match in some way. The reappearance of the afterimage in Daw's situation is analogous to an effect described by Kahneman, in which the threshold for the detection of a colored surface is contingent on the presence or absence of appropriate contours in the preexposure field (Kahneman, 1965). The "filling in" of a shape already in the field is achieved more rapidly than the perception of the shape with its colored surface *ab initio*. Thus there is both a facilitating and a suppressing system. Little enough is known about the relation between surface perception and contour detection, or shape recognition, and there seems to be scope for further investigation in this area.

TEMPORAL FACTORS IN CONTOUR FORMATION

The time-course of contour formation and detection has been widely studied in experiments on visual masking. In a masking paradigm two brief visual displays are exposed one after the other, and interference effects are found if the delay between the two is small. Backward masking in particular has received a lot of attention (Raab, 1963; Kahneman, 1968). The backward masking paradigm, in which a later stimulus (the mask) interferes with an earlier one (the probe) is of special interest, since it should afford a means of assessing "contour-processing time" or "perceptual-storage time." Under appropriate conditions the mask may completely "erase" the probe, although the erasure process is probably different from the inhibitory system described by Daw. A number of studies of this sort have been interpreted as evidence for a short-term visual-storage mechanism (a representative group is reprinted in Haber, 1969). One might hope, then, that such studies would lead to useful insight into the contour-coding and "pattern-forming" properties of the visual system, particularly since the types of contour in mask and probe, and their relative positions in the visual field, are effective determinants of the masking function (Kolers, 1962; Werner, 1937).

There are some methodological problems, however, and changes in design and procedure can yield highly conflicting results (for example, Eriksen & Hoffman, 1963; Eriksen & Collins, 1964; Eriksen & Lappin, 1964; Weisstein & Haber, 1965). It seems that two quite different sorts of backward masking can occur; one in which *luminance summation* is the effective agent, and one in which there is genuine inhibitory interaction between two contour-forming processes. Kahneman (1967) has recently reviewed the evidence, and concludes that the two types of masking can be distinguished primarily in terms of their different time courses. When a blank white mask is used, a linear, backward-masking function is typically obtained, in which masking is greatest when mask and probe coincide, and declines steadily as the probe-mask interval increases (Eriksen & Collins, 1964). The explanation of this phenomenon may be that mask and probe luminances effectively summate, so that the contrast relations in the probe are reduced, and it thus becomes less detectable.[7] This sort of masking is effective over only quite short time intervals, typically up to 40 msec or so. Masking of a contoured probe by a mask which also contains contours, on the other hand, has been found over much longer time intervals, and the greatest masking effect may be found when the mask and probe are nonsimultaneous, so that a *U*-shaped masking function is obtained (Averbach & Corriel, 1961; Weisstein & Haber, 1965). These findings are usually interpreted as evidence that information in the probe has to be "read out" from iconic (immediate visual) memory into a short-term store, and it is this process which the mask interrupts (Neisser, 1967). Nearly all this work has been done with letters and numbers in the probe display. There is evidence that the read-out system is a directional-scanning process for the normal literate adult, which suggests that the highly overlearned skill of reading letters and words is a major factor (Bryden, 1960; Mewhort, Merikle, & Bryden, 1969). Fascinating and important as this work is, the complications of directional scanning create difficulties if one wants to infer anything about the basic processes of contour and pattern formation; one can argue that to find out about these processes, much more systematic studies of particular types of simple contour interaction in masking are required. [Compare

---

[7] For other possibilities, see Dodwell and Standing (1970).

the work of Andrews and others described earlier.] Thus, while the masking work suggests a valuable avenue for exploration of contour formation and interaction processes, it throws little direct light as yet on the sorts of problem with which we are here concerned. The relations of pattern coding to higher-level linguistic and cognitive skills is discussed later, in Chapter 11.

FIGURAL AFTEREFFECTS

A figural aftereffect (*FAE*) is the distorted perception of a contour or pattern when it is viewed in a part of the visual field which previously contained other, similar contours or patterns. They were first extensively investigated by Köhler and Wallach (1944). The typical *FAE* is a repulsion between contours which occupy adjacent positions in the initial and subsequent displays, and *FAE*s have usually been interpreted as evidence of a fatigue-like physiological process (satiation, in Köhler and Wallach's own terms). Their findings excited a good deal of interest, for they seemed to demonstrate readily obtainable perceptual effects which are a direct result of physiological contour-formation processes. A number of interesting theories have been proposed (for example, Köhler & Wallach, 1944; Osgood & Heyer, 1952; Deutsch, 1964; Ganz, 1966) and a vast amount of experimental work generated. However, nearly all the early studies are suspect because of defective methodology[8] (Gaze & Dodwell, 1965), and this is unfortunate from the present point of view, since many of those studies concerned effects on patterned stimuli which should be of importance for a theoretical treatment of pattern coding. There is little doubt that the *FAE* is a genuine phenomenon, and some technically competent studies have been carried out in recent years. However, almost none of these has addressed specifically the problem of what *FAE*s can tell us about pattern coding as such.[9] The recent theoretical preference has been to explain *FAE*s as being occasioned by lateral inhibition (Deutsch, 1964; Ganz, 1966). But lateral inhibition itself, while it may be a mechanism for the "sharpening" of contours and also may explain some interactions between neighboring regions of stimulation, can scarcely be the sole basis for a pattern coding system. The boot should be on the other foot; only when we know, or infer, something about the pattern-

[8] For example, in many cases the observers knew what sorts of *FAE* report were expected and this can certainly influence reports of *FAE;* quite often elementary control conditions have not been instituted, and so on. There are very considerable differences and inconsistencies in the reported properties of *FAE*s, which can probably be attributed to such factors.

[9] A start in this direction is a paper by Dodwell and Gendreau (1969).

coding system can we say anything useful about what lateral-inhibitory effects can be expected in the *FAE* situation. In fact, in view of the Hubel-and-Wiesel findings, one could predict at an elementary level that the main strong interactions observable as *FAEs* should be between contours that are parallel to each other, or nearly so. This follows from the fact that, at least at the simple receptive-field level, there is no interaction between cortical units for contours in different orientations, and the response of an individual unit is highly selective for its preferred orientation. At least one may suggest, on the basis of this argument, that one might hope to analyze some receptive-field-type characteristics in the human visual system, that is, to throw some light on elementary contour and pattern coding, by study of *FAE* with appropriately contoured stimuli. If, on the other hand, lateral inhibition is thought of as a purely retinal phenomenon, perhaps related to afterimage formation and local adaptation, no directional effects in contour interactions should be expected. Ganz is not entirely clear on the point. He seems to think of lateral inhibition in his model as a peripheral process, and yet makes the identification with the Hubel-and-Wiesel "higher-order" phenomenon specifically (Ganz, 1966, p. 137). The level at which inhibition is supposed to work in the generation of *FAE* needs careful consideration. As Daw's work shows, afterimages are themselves evidently subject to peculiar laws of direct inhibition whose relationship to contour coding per se may be very complex.

Much recent work on *FAEs* has in fact been concerned with interactions between single pairs of parallel contours, and it would be of great interest if different processes could be found in other situations involving nonparallel lines and more complicated patterns. One might even hope to throw some light on the relation between possible peripheral and central factors in the generation of *FAE*; the early theoretical predilection was for explanations in terms of central processes, and more recently for peripheral factors. Knowing as we do that contour-coding processes involving inhibition go on at several levels in the visual system, it might not be too much to expect to separate out some of their different properties insofar as these may be reflected in *FAEs*.

VISUAL ILLUSIONS

Several writers have pointed out that at least some of the so-called *FAEs* can be observed as simultaneous illusions (Ganz, 1966; Logan, 1960). That is to say, they do not require the steady fixation of an inspection figure prior to the presentation of a test figure in which the effect is to be observed; in some cases the effect is obtained when inspection and test figures are presented together. This suggests quite strongly that the *FAE* is not, or not just, a result of physiological satiation or fatigue, but may be an immediate effect produced by the contour-coding process itself. It has been pointed out by Wallace (1966a) and again by Ganz (1966) that many of the well-known optical illusions, such as those of Hering and Zöllner, seem to involve the principle that two intersecting contours are seen as intersecting at an angle slightly greater than the "true" angle. In a pattern where the effect is repeated many times, this can lead to an apparent bending of straight lines and nonveridical length judgments. (See also Bouma & Andriessen, 1968.) The disruption of apparent angles of intersection is readily imagined as resulting from mutual inhibition between a pair of simple receptive-field systems. One might then argue that *FAE*s and simultaneous illusions are both instances of distortions arising from "competition" between sets of units in the primary coding process. It is not certain that one can explain all the classical visual illusions on this principle; nevertheless, its explanatory power is considerable (Wallace, 1966a). In some degree, then, the classical visual illusions may yield evidence about contour coding. Other variables affect the situation, including probably shape and size constancy (Gregory, 1966) so that an unambiguous interpretation becomes difficult. In fact the attempt to explain classical illusions is a good example of the difficulties of finding a single model to account for even a fairly small and well-identified aspect of human pattern recognition. While Gregory's ingenious model of inappropriate constancy scaling is successful in many respects, it cannot explain some rather striking features of the illusions (Wallace, 1966a,b; Hotopf, 1966; Zanforlin, 1967; Fisher, 1968; Wallace & Crampin, 1969). It seems probable that two different levels of processing are involved (at least)—the basic level of contour coding, or the primary detection system as I have called it, and a higher process, perhaps of the figure-forming or pattern-assembly type, at which level subtle processes which are generated by the subject's past experience of the world are involved. Whether the contributions of these different systems can be teased out or not remains to be seen.

   This quick survey of some recent discoveries and lines of research in human pattern perception illustrates, one hopes, some characteristic directions in which psychological investigation of the visual system as pattern recognizer is moving. Clearly there are many questions that are unanswered and many difficult problems to solve. The evidence has been presented in ways which bring out its significance for structural models, and in particular the multistage nature of the processes has been empha-sized. Some important lines of perceptual research have been ignored, but deliberately so, in an effort to focus on those issues and findings most relevant to our present purpose.

CHAPTER 10
Structural Models and "Higher-Order" Factors in Perception

CODING AND PERCEPTUAL LEARNING: CONFLICTING POINTS OF VIEW

In the preceding chapters I have emphasized the fact that adequate theoretical treatment of pattern recognition, particularly at the human level, requires that we postulate a multistage system, starting with a primary detector process (reception and coding). It is at this level that structural modeling has enjoyed most success. A model that goes no further than this, however, is incomplete. Recognition as a distinct process must be dealt with (see Chapter 2), and still the questions of learning, set, and attention remain. Such other factors, not primarily concerned with elementary property detection and recognition, I call "higher-order" factors, and the difficulties they pose for theoretical treatments of perception have already been touched on in earlier chapters. In this chapter I shall examine the relations between theoretical work on higher-order factors in perception and the sort of structural modeling here advocated, first by showing how other theoretical treatments relate to this one, and second by considering to what extent our approach can be extended to deal with these variables.

Notice that the concept of several stages of pattern processing in human vision is not a general feature of perceptual theories. Two notable and influential general theories of perception—and I call them theories because they attempt to explain the general nature of perception, not just to model some of its aspects—have been propounded by Gibson (1950) and Taylor

(1962), respectively. Neither one embodies more than a single stage of processing, at least within the meaning of the phrase as it is used here. The two theories are very different from each other, yet both purport to explain essentially the same range of evidence. One might say that whereas Gibson's theory is couched almost exclusively in terms of a primary reception-and-coding system, Taylor's deals entirely with higher-order variables and ignores the question of detection and coding. While a strategy of seeking compromise is not necessarily scientifically ideal, I shall argue that these two approaches are both too extreme and, in the sense implied, are too simple to be correct; either one if held rigidly is inconsistent with the evidence and seems to lead to absurdity or paradox if pushed to its logical limits.

Gibson's basic position (Gibson, 1950) is too well known to need extensive redescription: It is that classical psychophysics and perceptual theory viewed the visual system as fundamentally too simple an entity, one which could detect elementary features, simple contours, changes in intensity and extension in its input, but which did not detect or analyze a variety of stimulus attributes inherently available in that input. This notion of the basically meager information-processing capacity of the visual system per se then leads naturally to the Berkeleyan conclusion that a great deal of the visually perceived world has its origin in nonvisual events, or at least in happenings which are not exclusively visual, such as the coordination of proprioceptively and visually sensed motions of the observer's own body. The "perceived world" is thus a largely nonvisual "construction" out of a variety of simple elements. Gibson, on the contrary, seeks in the purely optical stimulus-array sufficient richness and variety to account visually for a great deal more than is accounted for on traditional lines; hence his "global psychophysics." One can grant this point readily enough: It is evident that complex stimulus attributes such as texture, perspective, movement and disparity gradients exist, and there is evidence that they are effective as purely visual cues for the normal observer. So the richness of visual cues and the elaborateness of visual information processing are greater than one had supposed. From this it does not necessarily follow that *everything* about visual perception can be explained in terms of such processing; and yet this seems to be the position that Gibson maintains. Basically the same position is redrawn with some changes of emphasis in his more recent book (Gibson, 1966).

The reason for holding such a view, despite the apparently impressive amount of evidence to the contrary (see below) is perhaps as follows: It seems paradoxical to maintain, as many philosophers and psychologists have done, that what *appears* to be a purely visual experience (as, for example, the experience of visual depth) should in fact be based on (should be a contingent outcome of) a set of events and experiences which are in part, at least—and perhaps in large measure—nonvisual. One must be careful to characterize clearly the claim that is made here. On the one hand, the argument might be taken to mean that nonvisual cues are the sole basis for a visual experience, which is surely a paradoxical claim. On the other hand, the argument might be taken to mean that the *interpretation* of a visual cue, or set of visual cues, is only possible when they are coordinated with other, nonvisual events in the organism's sensory order. Gibson's position is equivocal here; he points to a number of features of visual input which logically are capable of analysis as properties of the visual world (rather than the visual field). Empirically he shows, too, that such features are—or at least can be—effective cues to visual discrimination. But he does not show that the analysis of such features is *always necessary* or *ever sufficient* in itself to account for the veridical perception of the visual world.

Gibson thus claims too much for his "global psychophysics." If complicated properties of the optical array were both necessary *and sufficient* conditions in themselves for veridical perception, it would follow that nonvisual properties of the environment are *irrelevant* to visual perception. One could thus dispose not only of the apparently absurd argument that visual discriminations can be based on nonvisual features of the environment, but also of the argument that visual cues are interpreted in conjunction with nonvisual events in constructing (learning) a stable perceptual world. It seems to me that these two arguments are not separated in Gibson's thesis. It also seems clear that we should reject the first argument, but not the second. We should reject the first argument because it *would* be paradoxical to maintain that visual discrimination (for instance, of depth) can be independent of features in the visual input. We should not reject the second argument, however, since no good reason for doing so has been proposed (by Gibson or anyone else) and there is a great deal of evidence to show not only that perceptual learning occurs, but also that one of its important properties is that intermodal coordination develops as a basis for interactions between the organism and a stable perceptual world. A more subtle question, however, is concerned with the development of visual discrimination per se. In the celebrated controversy between the Gibsons and Postman about the nature of perceptual learning (Gibson & Gibson, 1955; Postman, 1955), the question was posed in terms of differentiation vs. enrichment: Are progressively finer visual discriminations possible simply because the organism comes to detect ever-finer distinctions in its visual input, or is it necessary that *responses* be attached to different discriminations to establish their separation? In one sense the answer seems to be trivially obvious; the only evidence we ever have of differential discrimination is that different responses (be they only verbal) are made, or can be made, to different visual features, so that response attachment is a necessary condition. On the other hand, since the attachment of a response to a discrimination implies, apparently, that the discrimination has already been made (otherwise what is the response "attached" to?) one can argue that the response itself is not an essential feature of the learning of a discrimination. It seems to me that, in so far as the *capacity* to discriminate between different visual cues is "built in" to an organism, in terms of a primary detection system, the "attachment" of responses is a secondary and contingent matter. What is important, however, is the question of attention, set, or in general the *means* by which an organism comes to make (or make use of) new discriminations. This, it may be argued, is the primary nonvisual factor in discrimination learning, which is manipulable by response reinforcement, and so forth; we shall return to the point later in Chapter 11.

Gibson's position that the visual input contains potentially all the information which is necessary and sufficient for the veridical perception of the visual world should not be taken as equivalent to the statement that organisms *in fact* use only this information. The latter statement seems to be patently false—witness the evidence of the transactionalists (Kilpatrick, 1961) and "new look" (Bruner, 1957) school of perceptual theory, as well as an older empirical tradition (for example, Bartlett, 1932) and recent experimental work on perceptual development (for example, Held & Hein, 1963). The Gibsonian view amounts to claiming that all of the visual system's behavior can be understood in terms of visual detection and analysis, and, moreover, if I understand the view correctly, that this detection and analysis is all potentially available in the neonate, in the sense that the vicissitudes of experience are not decisive in the elaboration of sets of perceptual categories (that is, of the perceptual world). As such, the position is not merely strongly nativist, in the traditional sense, but leaves no room for what seems, even to common sense, to be the obvious enough and highly influential intellectual, "cognitive" component in much of human perception. Stressing as it does the potentialities for "differentiation" in the visual input at the expense of "enrichment," Gibson's position seems in danger of relegating human perception to the category of completely stimulus-bound behavior. This view is too simple and too narrow.

Taylor's "behavioral" theory of perception is as different from Gibson's theory as any dialectician could desire—he explains visual perception by just those principles which Gibson rejects as both irrelevant and wrong. The essence of the theory is that perception can only be said to occur when an organism starts to correlate recurring states of extrinsic stimulation with its own movements. From an initial blooming, buzzing confusion, order begins to arise as regularities between input states and movements (or orientations) of the organism start to occur.[1] No account is taken of any detection or analytic capacities which may be present in the organism *ab initio,* except insofar as physical energy must be transduced into visual signals in some regular fashion. The correlations of movements with sensory events are held to occur through a species of conditioning of movements to sensory inputs. This is held to lead to the comparatively rapid elaboration of a stable perceptual world since the organism comes to distinguish "equivalence classes" among sets of inputs to which the same movements are conditioned; thus "perceptual learning" is not simply a matter of piecemeal, one-by-one, conditioning of separate movements to separate sensory inputs. Rather, perceptual categories are established in terms of common responses to a range of stimulations. Taylor ignores what we have termed the primary detection system, and explains *all* of perception in terms of "higher-order" processes, principally the correlation of (conditioning of) movements to events in the sensory order. The position is as extreme as Gibson's, and I confess appears to be at least as problematic. Like Gibson's theory it is too simple, and too metaphysical, in the sense of attempting to explain such a wide and rich field of phenomena in terms of a very few basic principles.

Passing over the difficulty of understanding how the initial correlations are detected before "perception" occurs (see footnote) and the implausibility of a simple conditioning model for the association of visual inputs and movements (Chapter 8), one notices another paradoxical feature of Taylor's theory. An "equivalence class" is formed by the conditioning of the same movement (or set of movements) to a set of sensory inputs which changes over time, and perhaps in some spatial characteristics, but which nevertheless has an inherent property to which the organism responds and by so responding achieves a stable perceptual world. The paradoxical point is this: How can the organism recognize the members of an "equivalence class" or the properties which render members of a class "equivalent" if the process of recognition (perception) is itself defined as the *formation* of such equivalences? At least some prior process of detection is implied, without which no basis for the conditioning itself can be present. The theory can perhaps be applied to adaptation to perceptual change, given an initial perceptual world (set of perceptual categories) which is stable, and this is the main use to which the theory *is* put (Taylor & Papert, 1956; Taylor, 1962). Without some clearer basis for its initial

---

[1] There is the suggestion of a ghost in the machine, if not an infinite regress, here. If the correlations occur, they must surely be *registered* within the organism to be effective, but this can only occur if the organism has some elementary detector (perceptual) system already in action.

conditions, such as a primary detector system, the theory seems to be too paradoxical to be tenable. Empirically, also, it comes up against the recently discovered facts of neonatal form discrimination (Chapter 6) and neural processing (Chapter 3). However, the main argument against the theory is a conceptual one.

CODING AND ATTENTION

The sort of theoretical position advocated in this book is, if not a compromise, at least an attempt at reconciliation between extreme nativism and empiricism. A compromise which simply asserts that both inborn and environmental factors affect perception would be empty of useful empirical content, although not tautologous. A reconciliation, on the other hand, by recognizing the positive features in the extreme positions and attempting to demonstrate their compatibility by modeling specific aspects of the visual system, can avoid their paradoxical features. At the same time some factual content can be claimed since such models are open to empirical test. Thus it is not simply a question of *whether* both nature and nurture are important, but rather of *how* inborn and experiential variables interact in the formation of a perceptual system. In this sense the present arguments can be thought of as a reformulation in up-to-date terms of something like Hebb's overall theoretical position of twenty years ago (Hebb, 1949; see also Chapter 2).

The specific models considered in previous chapters have been concerned very largely with the primary detection-and-recognition systems. Where learning and memory have entered (Chapter 2), their role has been "neutral"; selectivity has played no part beyond the filtering of specific stimulus properties implied by the coding system. It has been argued in detail elsewhere (Dodwell, 1961) that such coding or structuring is bound to be taken into account in any realistic theory of discrimination learning, and stochastic learning theorists were there taken to task for neglecting the matter of stimulus coding. Taking the argument a step further, one may enquire whether or not coding of the type described in earlier chapters is sufficiently flexible and comprehensive as a basis for discrimination-learning models. More precisely, one asks whether the filtering introduced by a coding system is sufficient in itself to explain the selectivity for stimulus attributes which certainly occurs in human adult perception and which, it is claimed, also holds for discrimination learning in animals, even at the invertebrate level. So-called attentional theories of discrimination learning have recently been widely promulgated (Lovejoy, 1965; Sutherland, 1959, 1966; Zeaman & House, 1963) and the evidence favoring a system in which variable selectivity operates in animal discrimination learning has been summarized by Mackintosh (1965). Although not without its critics (Gardner, 1966; Kendler & Kendler, 1966; Matthews, 1966) the notion of selectivity for cues in discrimination learning is supported by a fair amount of evidence for infrahuman subjects and by convincing findings with humans (for example, Haber, 1966; Egeth, 1967). The question is whether all types of selectivity can be explained in terms of such coding or filtering. Clearly this could only be so if the selective effects were fairly constant for particular types of stimulus material in different situations, since the very nature of coding, at least as a feature of a primary detection system, is that its functioning is innately programmed, and hence relatively fixed. (This fixedness of the coding effects is supported by neurophysiological evidence, but to some extent is still more in the nature of a postulate than an empirical proposition; to deny it would be to deny that the concept of coding as it has been developed here is valid. By maintaining the postulate we shall see that a plausible account of variable selectivity can still be found.) But a great deal of experimental evidence shows that selectivity can be manipulated, whether by deprivation, by selective reinforcement or punishment, or by instruction or other social agents. The means of manipulation depends, of course, in part on the phylogenetic level of the subject, but the means is contingent and not centrally important to the point, which is that changes in selectivity can be produced at many different levels under appropriate conditions.

It has been argued, particularly by Eriksen (1960), that most, if not all, of the so-called demonstrations of changes in selectivity (at least in humans) are really pseudoperceptual changes, and can readily be explained in terms of manipulations of response probabilities (see also Broadbent, 1967). One may grant the point that response probability manipulation can be an important variable, yet there are a few cases where such an explanation is clearly inadmissible (for example, Dixon, 1958; Mewhort, 1967; Worthington, 1964, 1966) and a great many others where the interpretation is questionable. It seems sensible, then, to accept the fact that perceptual selectivity can be manipulated and to ask whether the process can usefully be modeled. Obviously, flexible selectivity belongs with that complex of "higher-order" variables previously discussed in Chapter 6 which complicate the search for models in perception so greatly. We shall take selectivity as a paradigm case, indicating how it may be modeled and incorporated into the sort of scheme already presented. First, a general model for discrimination learning will be discussed, leading naturally to the incorporation of a system for manipulation of selectivity—our theoretical analogue of attention.

A MODEL FOR DISCRIMINATION LEARNING

To show how flexible selectivity may be modeled within a general discrimination learning system, the concept of a trainable pattern classifier is introduced (Nilsson, 1965), and the proposed system follows Nilsson's treatment of such classifiers quite closely. The basic model for a trainable pattern classifier is developed as follows:

The input consists of d real numbers, $x_1, \ldots, x_j, \ldots, x_d$, and one output line which responds with signal i_o, having R distinct values labeled $1, \ldots, R$, each value representing a category into which a pattern may be placed. A pattern consists of some set of x_js, each member of the set being a component of the pattern. This sort of pattern classifier is shown in Fig. 10.1 and is immediately reminiscent of the coder described in

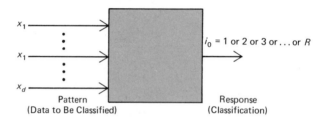

Fig. 10.1. A pattern classifier (from Nilsson, 1965).

Chapter 2. However, there are important differences to notice. The coder has fixed binary inputs, so that a pattern is defined only in terms of which inputs are activated at a given time, whereas the inputs to the pattern classifier are not so restricted. The output from the coder is defined in terms of trains of pulses varying in frequency and amplitude, but the output of the classifier is not so closely identified. The classifier is thus more abstract than the coder, and of course as presented so far is quite vague and incomplete; it is more general, the relations between input and output remain to be defined, and it is these relations that are, as we shall see, the useful features of the model for our purposes. The most important difference between the coder and classifier is that, for the latter, measures of a pattern *have already been selected and coded;* the x_j represent preprocessed or coded pattern components. They are an abstract representation of these components, and no precise transduction of original pattern elements to machine representation (x_i) is considered. For our purposes the x_i could be, for example, numbers representing a coder's output ($x_1 =$ frequency, $x_2 =$ amplitude of first pulse, $x_3 =$ relative amplitude of second pulse, and so forth) or outputs from a system such as D_M. It is assumed, then, that transduction of the original pattern information has already occurred before input to the classifier; in engineering terms, it is assumed that measurement selection and preprocessing are problems outside the scope of the classifying system itself.[2] The question now is how to define the operations of the classifier on its inputs x_i, in order to sort patterns into the outputs R.

Since each pattern is defined in terms of d real numbers, x_1, x_2, . . . , x_d, it can be thought of as a point in a d-dimensional Euclidean space, E^d, the *pattern space*. The classifier has to map points in E^d into the category numbers (outputs) 1, 2, . . . , R. To achieve such a categorization, point sets R_j in E^d which are mapped into different outputs must be separated by boundaries called *decision surfaces*. The problem is to find means of defining decision surfaces that can be embodied in the classifier. This is done by defining a set of functions $g_1(X)$, $g_2(X)$, . . . , $g_R(X)$ which are scalar, single-valued functions of X (x_1, . . . , x_d) called *discriminant functions*. These are chosen in such a way that for all X in R_k, $g_k(X) > g_j(X)$, $j = 1$, . . . , R, $j \neq k$. That is, in R_k, $g_k(X)$ has the largest value, and similarly for other R_i. The decision surface between adjoining regions R_i and R_j is then given by $g_i(X) - g_j(X) = 0$.

We thus have a straightforward account of the formal conceptual basis for a pattern classifier. Complications may arise, of course, when one attempts to specify particular discriminant functions to fulfill the conditions for different types of pattern separation. Since it is not our purpose to pursue the theory of pattern classification as such, discussion will be restricted to the simplest case of *linear machines,* which will be sufficient to illustrate the sort of modeling that is possible.

In a linear machine the discriminant functions are, as is implied by the name, linear functions of the components of X. Thus: $g_i(X) = w_{i1}x_1 + w_{i2}x_2 + . . . w_{id}x_d + w_{id+1}$ is such a linear discriminant function. Clearly the decision surfaces for such machines will be lines ($d = 2$), planes ($d = 3$) or hyperplanes ($d > 3$). A linear machine is illustrated in Fig. 10.2, where the operations implied are simple weighting and summing. It is included to reinforce the point that each pattern component (x_i) enters into each discriminant function in a different way, according to its weight, w_i ($i = 1$, . . . , d) and the different weights are assigned independently for each $g_i(X)$. Clearly the values of $g_i(X)$ can be changed by adjusting the values of the weights; that is, the positions of the decision surfaces can be so changed. Thus we have a system where the patterns and pattern components are fixed (the x_i), but the categorization can be adjusted.

---

[2] It is instructive to compare this point with the pattern-recognition systems described in Chapter 5. Clearly in those cases measurement selection and preprocessing were of the essence of the different models.

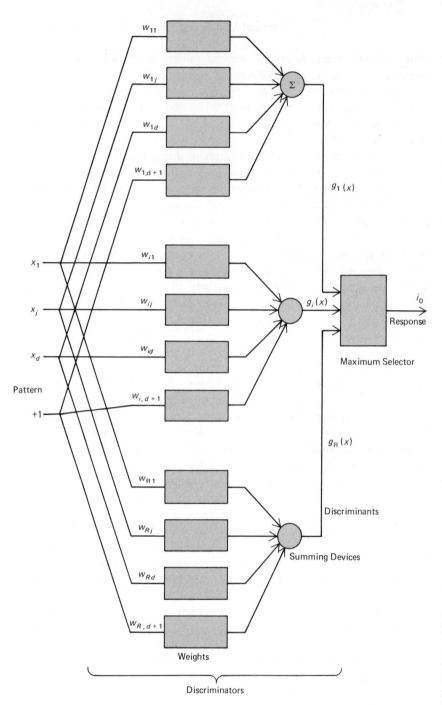

Fig. 10.2. A linear pattern classifier. Each of the inputs X (x_1, x_2, . . . , x_d) is weighted, the weighted sums evaluated. The maximum weighted sum is identified and determines the responses (from Nilsson, 1965).

Such a system is called a *pattern classifier*. It is called a *trainable* pattern classifier under the following conditions: A number of patterns is chosen, typical of those which the machine must classify, and for which the desired classification is assumed to be known. Discriminant functions are then developed by adjusting the decision parameters until the training set is adequate. Such functions are obtained by training, in the sense that rules are laid down for the adjustment of paramaters in terms of the classifier's performance at any one time. In the case of linear machines, for example, this could be done by a process of random trial-and-error adjustment of weights until acceptable categorization were attained, although this would not be the most efficient training procedure.

An alternative procedure will be described, showing intuitively how classification training may proceed.[3] Consider the discriminant function $g(X) = w_1x_1 + w_2x_2 + \ldots + w_dx_d + w_{d+1}$. Clearly the weights may be thought of as coordinates of a point in a $(d+1)$-dimensional space, or the vector W may be used to represent the set of weight values, as previously X was used to represent a pattern. This space may be called *weight space,* and can be considered the dual of the pattern space previously described. The x_is now have the function of specifying the dimensions of the to-be-discriminated patterns. A linear discriminant function of X can be written in matrix form as: $g_i(X) = W^{(i)}Y$.[4] Taking the simplest case of two-category discrimination, the discriminant function is a hyperplane which separates weight space into two regions. For any pattern Y there is a hyperplane in weight space which is the locus of all weight points for which $WY = 0$. This is called the *pattern hyperplane.* Points on one side of it yield $WY > 0$, and on the other $WY < 0$. If this pattern plane dichotomizes the categories correctly, then they are said to be linearly separable, and a value of W exists such that $g_1(X) > 0$ and $g_2(X) < 0$, that is, where $WY_1 > 0$ and $WY_2 < 0$. This value of W is called a solution weight vector, for obvious reasons. What happens when weight space is divided by a number of pattern hyperplanes corresponding to training patterns? Correct classification training can now be thought of as finding a solution weight vector which lies in the "solution region," that is, which yields the correct categorization for all training patterns. This is illustrated in Fig. 10.3, where patterns 1, 2 and 3 are all assumed

---

[3] The method is sketched in barest outline there. For an adequate treatment, and for the general statement of the logic and overall theory of the pattern classifier, the reader is referred to Nilsson (1965). The example given is a so-called nonparametric training procedure, which seems most appropriate for a form discrimination model.

[4] Where Y is an augmented pattern vector, equal to X plus an additional $(d+1)$ component, always equal to 1, which has the purpose of keeping the dimensionality right.

to belong in the same category (all provide the same response). Various procedures can be suggested for changing W in such a way as to approach the solution region. For instance supposing the response is erroneous for some pattern Y_k, that is, W is on the wrong side of the pattern hyperplane for Y_k. W is moved along a line normal to the pattern hyperplane by a fixed amount, and this is achieved by adding the vector cY_k to W. Thus the new weight vector W' is given by $W + cY_k$, c being the *correction increment*. This is the simplest of the error-correction procedures, but

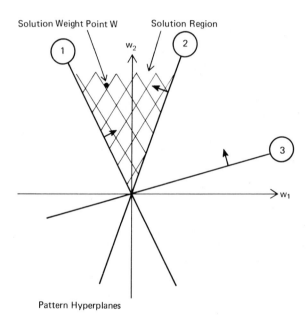

Fig. 10.3. A two-dimensional weight space with three pattern planes, which determine the "solution region."

illustrates the essential point, that adjustments are made to W, step-by-step, in such a way as to eradicate errors progressively. A graphical illustration of this error-correction training is shown in Fig. 10.4, in which the four patterns are presented sequentially: It should be noted that the movement of the weight vector is always perpendicular to the pattern hyperplane presented (the order in this example being 1, 2, 3, 4, 1). Clearly, a corrective change with respect to one pattern may lead to the introduction of error with respect to another, although eventually the solution region (if it exists) will be attained. Other methods of iterative training have been suggested, but the principles are generally similar to the one described.

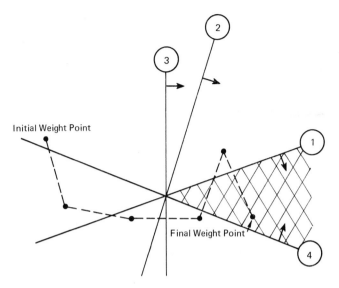

Fig. 10.4. A sequence of error-correcting moves in weight space, leading to the solution region.

PREDICTING THE LEARNING CURVE

It is clear that the trainable pattern classifier manifests behavior which we can call "discrimination learning." The question is, however: Does the consideration of this system add anything new to our concepts of discrimination learning in biological organisms? To answer this question, one must consider how well the trainable pattern classifier mirrors features of discrimination learning which are ordinarily thought to require explanation. This can only be done within limits, for reasons that will become apparent, but it is hoped nevertheless to educe some promising suggestions from the exercise.

In the first place, consider the typical backward-learning curve giving probability of correct response vs. trials, as shown in Fig. 10.5A, for the common form of two-choice discrimination-learning situation. Such curves have been obtained with many species (including rats, squirrels, monkeys, and retarded and normal children) in a variety of experimental situations and with different sorts of material. It scarcely need be said that such a curve is inconsistent with classical incremental learning models. Two popular alternatives are illustrated in Figs. 10.5B and C in terms of the "ideal" curves that they generate, namely the single-element one-trial conditioning model some mathematical learning theorists have proposed and the "dimensional-selective" model of attentional theorists such as

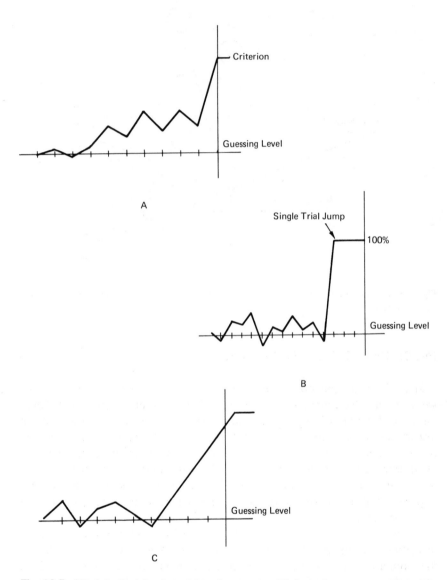

Fig. 10.5. (A) A typical backward-learning curve. (B) Learning curve predicted by one-element sampling and conditioning model. (C) Learning curve according to an attentional model.

Sutherland and Zeaman. Although both these approaches predict learning curves that are closer to the facts than the classical incremental curve, neither one fits the data very closely, even allowing for the inevitable "noise" in the measurements. The single-element conditioning model predicts that the first limb of the curve (as in Fig. 10.5B) should be flat, and at the guessing probability level, that the discontinuity should be complete, and that the second limb should be at the level of 100-percent correct responding. Clearly no one of these conditions holds very exactly, and it is difficult to see how the data can be reconciled with such a model even with the aid of ad hoc assumptions. The attentional model is more interesting, since it comes closer to the mark. However, it is impossible to say *how* close. It is claimed that discrimination is approximately at a chance level until the organism starts paying attention to the relevant dimension(s), in which case discrimination proceeds very rapidly to a high level of correctness (provided the task is not too difficult). It is not possible to state *how* rapidly the rising part of the curve should climb on the basis of the attentional model; a theoretical derivation of this rate would strengthen the case for the model. The point of greatest divergence between the theoretical and empirical curves occurs in the "presolution" period. Both models state that responding is virtually random (guessing) in the early trials, but in fact there is good reason to suppose that this is not so. We have found repeatedly in discrimination-learning experiments, mainly with rats and children, that the "presolution" rate of correct responding very frequently is somewhat above the "guessing" rate. For example, in a two-choice situation the probability of correct responding for many subjects is closer to .6 than .5, a finding which occurs with sufficient regularity to be statistically reliable. Although this fact has not been commented on in the literature, a number of reported curves bear it out (for example, Doan, 1966; Dodwell and Niemi, 1967). Consistent responding *below* the guessing rate, on the other hand, is rare. However, the presolution rate certainly varies between subjects, and cannot be estimated accurately by conventional statistical techniques. All one can be reasonably certain of is that it tends to stay at the guessing rate, or somewhat above it, for some time before the discrimination is learned. Another finding which seems to be fairly common is illustrated in Fig. 10.6 which is the record of a rat's performance in a shape-discrimination experiment. Besides the presolution level of about 60-percent correct responding, there is a marked increase in oscillation between correct and incorrect responses immediately before the rapid rise to 100-percent correct choices. It is not claimed that this is a typical record; in fact it shows the effect rather more clearly than most. Nevertheless this sort of oscillation seems to occur too frequently to be ignored as a property of discrimination learning. Unfortunately, again, it is not possible to estimate the size or reliability of the effect very well by conventional statistical techniques, nor does it occur for every subject and every type of discrimination, and it tends to be obscured in a group backward-learning curve such as that of Fig. 10.5A.

Can these features of discrimination learning be explained by taking the training pattern classifier (*TPC*) as model? In the first place, it

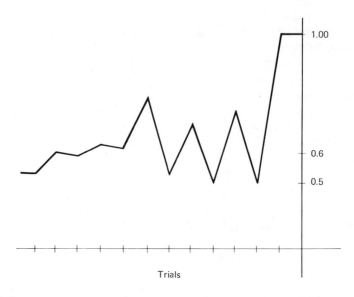

Fig. 10.6. Actual learning curve obtained (Dodwell and Niemi, 1967).

should be clear that this model would predict the general shape of the backward-learning curve. Referring back to Fig. 10.4 and the accompanying text, we see that if the original weight solution is far from the solution region, a period of trials is implied in which responses are made approximately at random, but since most adjustments result in moves toward the solution region, over a run of trials the actual probability of a correct response will be somewhat above the guessing level. However, this increase in probability of a correct response need not necessarily be monotonic, since correction in terms of one pattern may reverse a previously correct response to a different one. Also it is clear that as the solution region is approached, the probability of a correct response will rise rather rapidly, since presentation of all but a few of the training patterns implies a positive response. It should be remembered that the dimensionality of the training patterns would very likely be much higher than two, the dimensionality of Fig. 10.4, so the figure presents an oversimplified situation. Thus, in a general way, it is plausible to argue that the training pattern classifier can be taken as a model for discrimination learning, and accounts for the typical discrimination-learning curve at least as well as alternative models. Can the *TPC* account for oscillation too? Unfortunately there are too many free and indeterminate properties of the model for one to be able to answer this question with assurance. For example the correction procedure for iterative convergence on the solution region can take several forms; undoubtedly methods could be derived that would imply oscillation (see below), but this property would also be affected by pattern dimensionality, number of training patterns and "reinforcement rules," that is, rules for deciding on the size of correction increment within a given method. In order to be able to advance a particular version of the *TPC* as an empirically verifiable model for discrimination learning, it would be necessary to explore in some detail the effects of varying some of these characteristics on the resulting learning curves. In a model with so many degrees of freedom this could probably only be done by computer simulation. The relevant studies have not as yet been carried out, so far as I can determine.

Craving indulgence for the presentation of a model that lacks strong empirical support then, I shall propose some ways in which the model could be developed, and discuss their relation to other psychological concepts and findings. One hopes that this "theoretical enrichment" will further the cause of understanding processes underlying discrimination learning. On the whole, theoretical formulations in this field have been simple and parsimonious, but it is questionable whether they do justice to the data.

A MODEL FOR VARIABLE SELECTIVITY OF CUES (ATTENTION) IN DISCRIMINATION LEARNNG

The error-correction procedure described earlier is relatively crude, inflexible, and "neutral" in the sense previously defined. While it was argued that the typical discrimination-learning curve could be generated by a *TPC* using this procedure, it may be pointed out that yet another dimension of variation can be considered, which allows one to incorporate an analogue of attention (that is, variable selectivity) into the *TPC* model, and which perhaps could account straightforwardly for the oscillatory phase of the discrimination-learning curve. The usual error-correction procedures for *TPC*s involve shifting W in weight space by some fraction of its distance from the training pattern presented on a given trial, if its response to that pattern was incorrect. This means that *all* the components of the training pattern enter proportionately into the determination of W', the new weight vector. One might propose, as an analogue of attention, that when an incorrect choice is made, the system takes account of the consequences of previous weight changes in the different pattern dimensions in making its next adjustment. For example, the rule might be as follows: If a change in weight w_{ij} has been associated in the past with increased probability of correct choice on subsequent trials, then the probability of a similar change at the next incorrect trial will be greater than for weights not so associated. Weight changes which had been correlated with decreased probability of correct choice, on the other hand, would have a decreased probability of occurring. The rule could be written down in terms of conditional probabilities and formulated in such a way that a threshold condition must be reached before the probability of changing the weight at a given trial itself changes. For simplicity's sake, we may assume that there are just three probabilities that a weight will be changed, P_c, P_n, and P_w, where P_c is the probability of change in a weight whose previous changes have been associated with correct responding, P_n is for "neutral" weights, and P_w for "incorrect" ones. Thus if a nonrelevant weight change (that is, pattern dimension) has been fortuitously associated with correct responding in early trials so that P_c is reached, it will continue to be changed for a number of pattern trials, but since it is irrelevant, the conditional probability will eventually drop below the threshold required for P_c so that P_n is reinstated. The principle is very like that which determines which pattern detector matrices operate in Uhr and Vossler's pattern recognition model (Chapter 5). Its effect, in this case, will be to delay attainment of the correct solution, since changes of terms of irrelevant weights imply movements of W in weight space that are random with respect to reaching the solution region. Effects of this sort would be much enhanced if the system operated in such a way that only a few weights could change on any one trial, or on a principle of "maximum permissible shift" in weight space, whereby W can shift a limited distance on any one trial, but could be distributed over many dimensions, or concentrated on a few, depending on how many weights are "above threshold" (P_c). There would be a tendency for *fewer* weights to be "above threshold" as training progressed, assuming that few pattern dimensions are correlated with correct choice, but even so some might still be "wrongly" selected. The fewer the effective weights, the fewer the degrees of freedom for movement in weight space, and therefore the higher the variance of sample estimates of the population parameter, or true proportion of "correct" choices, in the presolution period. That is, toward the end of the presolution period unusually long runs of all-correct or all incorrect choices become more probable than before. In other words, oscillation is predicted.

It now seems that more postulates have been made for the *TPC* model than there are facts to explain. Can it then be justified, even as a speculative scheme for discriminating learning? Are not more parsimonious hypotheses adequate? The object of the exercise is to show *in principle* how selective attention may be modeled, even though precise delineation of the system and estimation of its parameters would be premature. One doubts whether a simpler system would be adequate, or even if this one can be. However, a somewhat sharper concept of attention can be defined in terms of the weighting properties of the model than is usual. Most "attention" theorists content themselves with an empirical definition of attention which limits the scope of the concept in model construction (see Chapter 6, p. 117). Differential weighting of the input on a particular dimension, and definition of a weight space within which the effects of weight changes can be described, enriches the concept, and is heuristically useful. Further hypotheses about its properties immediately suggest themselves. I believe attention theorists are on the right track, but find their formulations generally too vague. The same charge can be leveled against the modified *TPC* model, but it seems to represent a step in the right direction. The range of phenomena it can explain is not too different from the evidence adduced by attention theorists in support of their position, but it can explain a few additional phenomena. Its principal virtue, I believe, is that it suggests a means of bridging the conceptual gap between two schools of thought on discrimination learning.

WHAT IS LEARNED IN DISCRIMINATION LEARNING?

The schism goes back quite a way, at least to the continuity-noncontinuity controversy of the 1930s, and in its modern form is represented by attentional and structural theorists on the one hand and neo-Hullian and mathematical learning theorists on the other. In an earlier discussion of the issues between the two schools of thought (Dodwell, 1961) the role of attention, it was suggested, might be simply to control a hierarchy of possible discriminators, or analyzers, as proposed by Sutherland (1959). Recent evidence (summarized by Mackintosh, 1965) shows that this is too simple a hypothesis, since organisms do not always learn to discriminate just in terms of one property or another. A more correct generalizisitic seems to be that the more an organism learns about one characterisitic (or dimension) of a stimulus array, the less it learns about others that are simultaneously present, and the extent to which one or another dimension is "attended to" can to some extent, at least, be manipulated experimentally. The behavior of the modified *TPC* is in harmony with this generalization, and suggests a formal basis for it. The strength of the stochastic-type learning models lies in their prediction of discrimination-learning phenomena from simple operators or sampling-conditioning postulates; their weakness is in their failure to specify adequately what constitutes "a stimulus" in the organism's environment.[5] A pool of "equipotential" stimulus units is generally assumed, implicitly or explicitly, but without conceptual or experimental justification. The strength

[5] This is a weakness, so far as application to animal discrimination learning is concerned; specifying "the stimulus" in experiments with humans is not so problematic.

of attentional theories, on the other hand, is their ability to account for selectivity of cues and differences in the "prepotence" of different dimensions, their weakness being the lack of specification of other operations of the learning process (see, however, Zeaman and House, 1963). The *TPC* model may be held to bridge the gap, in the sense that the coding dimensionality and prepotence of stimuli can be expressed in the choice of x_is, the effects of selective manipulation of cue values in the initial choice of the w_{ij}s and rules for their modification during training. The latter also defines the actual operations of discrimination learning, which amount to the step-by-step changes in the multicomponent vector W until a solution region in weight space is attained. There is evidence that some learning processes occur in an incremental fashion, some in an "all or none" way. The *TPC* suggests how both sorts of learning may be combined in one system.

SOME PROBLEMS WITH THE *TPC* MODEL

The modified *TPC* model has been presented in a very general way, and tests of it would depend on further specification of the coding dimensions, weighting functions, and rules for changing weights. Some evaluation of the relevance of the model might be possible by computer simulation, as I have already suggested. Apart from this, further development of the model seems scarcely appropriate in our present state of knowledge about discrimination learning. Not the least of the problems here is the fact that the dimensions manipulated by the experimenter do not necessarily correspond with those which are effective for the experimental subject (Matthews, 1966). There are some other difficulties which can be raised, which merit discussion. First, the *TPC* model presented by Nilsson learns to classify a number of different patterns into two or more categories, whereas the usual behavioral situation involves only two patterns and two categories of response—apparently the sort of problem the *TPC* should solve too rapidly to be plausible as an analogue for our purposes. Such an argument, however, implicitly assumes that the pattern displayed *is* the effective pattern in toto, an assumption which one cannot make. If the "pattern" to which the organism responds is the whole of the stimulation impinging on it at a given time, this could clearly be multidimensional, including visual, proprioceptive, and probably other cues, so that the effective pattern space (and hence weight space) will be multidimensional. Many dimensions of adjustment will be available, at least in initial training, and "finding the effective dimension(s)" could entail many trials, despite the apparent simplicity of the experimenter's design. "Noise" in the system, represented by small, random fluctuations in the weight values from trial to trial, for instance, would further complicate the search for a weight solution. Operations in weight space of the sort suggested imply the formation of learning sets, and are readily seen to be close to the "error-factor" theory of Harlow (1949) in conception.

Another more substantial difficulty is this: The operations in weight space under the simple and automatic correction procedures described by Nilsson are straightforward and can be shown to converge on the solution region, but the more labile procedures introduced above to account for manipulation of selectivity are more problematic. They seem to be tailored to have just the properties which they are supposed to explain, and there is no demonstration that they necessarily lead to solution of these discrimination problems (convergence on the solution region). In other words, it may be argued that denying the neat algorithms of the normal correction procedures robs the *TPC* model of its explanatory power. This argument cannot be countered convincingly at present. It is true that the model has been too loosely formulated in its modified form to yield reasonably testable behavioral deductions. On the other hand, the postulate that discrimination learning proceeds by the selective weighting of coded stimulus properties, although merely suggestive at present, seems capable of development into a testable model if the coding of stimuli could be specified adequately. The postulate need not be vacuous, since several possible forms of selective weighting can be suggested and they should lead to different predictions about discrimination learning. We are back at a familiar problem: Further progress does not seem possible until stimulus coding is better understood, and this requires more empirical investigation.

DISCRIMINATING AND RESPONDING: DECISION PROCESSES AND THE *TPC*

A further question which requires some thought is the relationship between the *TPC* model and the earlier suggestions (Chapter 2) for a recognizer with memory, based on Uttley's conditional-probability computer. In that system, it will be recalled, two levels of stimulus equivalence, or generalization, were shown to be possible, one based on the properties of the stimulus coder itself, and one based on the contingencies of visual experience, namely that coder outputs which occur in regular temporal contiguity come to evoke the same state in the recognizer. It was suggested earlier (Dodwell, 1964) that such states—or outputs—of the recognizer might be coupled to "response generators," at which stage the operators of stochastic learning theory might function. The idea may be sharpened by proposing that the recognizer outputs are in fact the visual pattern inputs to a *TPC*, the output of the latter being the immediate response determinant.[6] In this way the coding system and a "purely perceptual" learning system (the recognizer with memory) can be integrated with a system in which decision processes are determined by responses and response-contingent events such as reinforcement and reafferent stimulation. The coupling of these two systems would further complicate the characteristics of the *TPC*, since the x_is would now no longer be fixed functions of the stimulus input, but would change with the system's perceptual history. However, it harmonizes with the notion that pattern preprocessing and measurement selection occur prior to the operation of the *TPC* itself. In the normal adult organism the inputs to the *TPC* would still be fairly constant over time, although subject to change under novel conditions of stimulation. It is clear also that the dimensionality of the discrimination problem for the *TPC* will vary as a function of prior perceptual learning, and several "levels" of pattern information from the recognizer will be fed to it simultaneously. The problem then becomes one of selecting those levels of pattern information which are relevant to a particular problem—and this is just what the *TPC* is designed to do, that is, to weight selectively the various x_is.

The sort of solution that this mixed system offers to the problem of perceptual learning, as posed by the Gibson-Postman controversy, can now be formulated. In the first place, the importance of the detectability of visual cues is in a sense fixed, since it is determined (for pattern vision) by the properties of pattern coding. The recognition of pattern *configurations,* on the other hand, is primarily a function of the recognizer (D_m) and is contingent on prior visual learning. Suppose now that a discrimination is required between two complicated but highly similar patterns. The initial response would fail to discriminate between the two, if it is based on the overall Gestalt similarities, that is, if it is based on a high-level output from D_m. This would occur in the visually experienced organism because the conjunction of many similar pattern elements has, through past association, led to the firing of a corresponding counter in D_m. Because of the "inferential" property built into the system, small variations in individual pattern elements will be ignored at this level. In the *TPC*, however, the high-level counter's output (one of the many inputs to the *TPC*) does not contribute to the solution of the problem. Its weighting will therefore tend to be reduced, but other inputs from lower-order counters in D_m, corresponding to parts of the patterns, if not to single elements, will be correlated with successful discrimination, and their weights will therefore have higher probabilities of changing appropriately.

---

[6] It should be remembered that the *TPC* has additional, nonvisual inputs as well as inputs for other visual characteristics such as brightness.

That is to say, the pattern *parts* or *elements* become the effective determinants of discrimination. In commonsense terms, this means that the organism comes to attend to smaller features of patterns if the patterns generally are similar to one another. Although discriminative features may be present in the patterns *ab initio* the problem is one of *coming to attend to* the relevant features. In this sense responding in particular ways, and response reinforcement, may be important characteristics of the discrimination-learning process. However, the actual form of the response does not seem too important, and the function of responding need not be to form *S-R* connections in any simple sense. Rather, responding—and the results of responding—can be thought of as a method of feeding back information to the system concerning what should be attended to in the visual input. Needless to say, in the cognitive organism there will be other ways of processing the weighting of various inputs too (see Chapter 11).

This formulation takes account of the fact that many visual cues are potentially present in a rich visual environment and that perceptual learning may be thought of as a process of differentiation in the sense that ever finer discriminations become possible as relevant features are attended to. Although in an obvious sense the visual input does not change, the organism's categorization of the inputs does. It takes account also of the fact that such perceptual changes mainly occur in the adult organism as a result of the posing of a discrimination problem the solution of which has some value for the organism—be it only an experimenter's approval. It does not claim, however, that all perceptual development must necessarily be of this sort.

One may place the mixed system in a wider context by noting that the importance of innate factors is fully recognized in the postulation of coding as basic to all visual pattern-recognition processes and that perceptual development can occur through stimulus contiguities which are entailed by an organism's normal commerce with its environment. The effects of deliberate training, set, and attention, are accounted for by the *TPC* characteristics, thus acknowledging the role of responding and response-contingent events in the process of perceptual learning. In a multistage system of the sort proposed, ample scope can be provided for both nature and nurture to play a part, and some particular hypotheses about their interactions can be proposed. In this sense the mixed system seems very much more plausible than the extreme, even metaphysical, systems discussed at the beginning of the chapter. A flexible, multistage system in which many sorts of processing can occur, and in which several different sorts of influence can play a role, accords well with physiological findings on several stages of processing in the visual system and does not generate the sorts of puzzle which are implied by the theories of Gibson and Taylor. Against it, one might argue that the proposed system is too flexible—flexible enough to account for anything, and hence untestable. I have argued against this charge already, and only further research will show whether it is justified. Certainly the system goes well beyond the established knowledge of experimental science, but one hopes that such a conceptual step will not be irrelevant to new empirical investigations or to the general understanding of the nature of the visual system and its development.

CHAPTER 11
Review: Structural Models and the Theory of Visual Perception

A basic theme which I have tried to develop in this book is that visual perception can only be understood if we are prepared to analyze its functions into several fairly distinct stages. To talk of visual information processing as if it were a unitary process is misleading, for it seems most unlikely that the working of the system can be based on just one sort of activity, or a single principle of categorization.

The analysis of visual functioning here advocated may be rather artificial and is necessarily an oversimplification. Probably processes of coding, pattern elaboration, and identification, and so on, are not so clearly separable in the real system. But it seems worthwhile to review the various different sorts of model which have been discussed in earlier chapters, to consider their interrelations, and to discuss the sort of theory of visual perception which this exercise suggests.

In the first place, we have the rather well-established idea of a primary detection, or coding, system. This concept had its roots in Lashley's notions about interference patterns, in Pitts and McCulloch's scheme for the analysis of sensory input, and Hebb's ideas about the cell assembly. It has played a prominent role in subsequent psychological models for shape recognition and in the work of computer scientists on pattern recognition. It also now has firm empirical support from the findings on microelectrode recording from individual units in various parts of the vertebrate visual system. Hubel and Wiesel's work on newborn kittens suggests very strongly that in cats the primary detection system is essentially built-in (Hubel and Wiesel, 1963), and it is reasonable to suppose that this is true for other mammals also. However, as I have argued in Chapter 4, it is clear that a primary detection system which is limited to the coding of specific features of patterned visual input cannot by itself yield an adequate account of pattern recognition. So far, the neurophysiological evidence on changes in coding functions is limited to cases of sensory deprivation, where the changes can be understood as being due to dysfunction of a coding stage, which is caused by neural atrophy (Wiesel and Hubel, 1965a, b), and perhaps to some cortical control of peripheral coding functions (Spinelli and Weingarten, 1966; Weingarten and Spinelli, 1966). There is as yet no direct neurophysiological finding which suggests how the features coded by the primary detectors are integrated to specify complex shapes—for example, a pattern made up of a set of contours in different orientations.

Although nothing forces us to the conclusion, it is reasonable to postulate, in the Hebbian tradition, that this further stage in pattern elaboration is a function of perceptual learning (compare Dodwell, 1970a). One can readily specify a model in which temporal and spatial contiguity are sufficient conditions for the organization of categories for a variable input, as Hebb's cell-assembly model does. The criticisms aimed at Hebb's ideas in Chapter 2 were concerned with his failure to specify adequate and economical means of generating input classes, not with the associationistic basis for further categorization. The pattern classifier with memory based on Uttley's conditional probability computer, described in the same chapter, is simply a more explicit realization of Hebb's sensory-associationistic postulate, in which categorization can be well specified. This type of model is passive, in the sense that associations are between "sensory events" or, to put it more neutrally, between coded features of visual input patterns. Borrowing from an older tradition, one could call it pure S-S learning. In one respect to call this a passive process is misleading, since the organism's scanning of its environment determines what the input sequences at the receptors will be, and this brings to mind the probable importance of eye movements (Salapatek & Kessen, 1966) at a low level of the system, and things like exploratory drive, Berlyne's "epistemic drive" (Berlyne, 1960), and Piaget's theory of the initial stages of the construction of sensorimotor schemata (Piaget, 1954) at higher stages of organization. Up to this point, perceptual learning is thought of as a function of sensory input sequences, although the sequences themselves may be more or less under the organism's control. Questions of control of responses, decision outcomes and reinforcement have not been raised, and this sort of S-S perceptual learning is not held to be dependent on specific choice responses to particular stimuli.

One may distinguish conceptually a further sort of perceptual change with experience, which may initially be called "discrimination learning," since it corresponds fairly well with the denotation which that label has in psychology. Discrimination learning is treated as a function of a modifiable "decision structure," or decision space, which is itself characterized in part by stimulus attributes (Chapter 10). The partitioning of this space into decision regions is held to be an isomorph of the generation of responses to different patterns of stimulation, and the consequences of decisions bring about modification in the partitioning. Nothing is said directly about the mechanism of reinforcement, but this seems to me to be a contingent matter so far as the development of a decision space is concerned, since different sorts of reinforcement can be effective in motivating learning. In this sense the model for discrimination learning is similar to the typical mathematical model (Estes, 1950; Restle, 1955; Trabasso & Bower, 1968), in which stimulus elements are "conditioned" to responses usually in an all-or-none fashion. It differs from them in placing far more emphasis on the characteristics of stimulus input and analysis, and indeed explains the learning of discriminative responses primarily in terms of the organism's categorization of stimulus patterns. The most important feature of the *TPC* model however, in contrast to the mathematical model, is that the categorization itself is modified as a function of learning: In this sense the model can be thought of not just as one for discrimination learning, but for perceptual learning in the traditional sense. To distinguish it from the *S-S* processes described in the previous paragraph, it may be called a model for perceptual (*S-R*) learning, to emphasize its more "active" character.

THE PROBLEMS OF PERCEPTUAL LEARNING

What light can this analysis of the processes of categorization and development shed on the issues raised by the Gibsons and Postman concerning the nature of perceptual learning (Gibson and Gibson, 1955; Postman, 1955)? The Gibson position, it will be recalled, is that the visual sense is itself a *perceptual* system, that visual information of a high order is contained in the stimulus array which impinges on an organism in its normal environment, and that the question of perceptual learning is essentially one of inquiring how the organism comes to make ever more adequate use of the stimulus information available to it. Perceptual learning, then, is concerned with differentiation—the process of detecting successfully relevant features in the stimulus field. Postman, on the other hand, argues that perceptual learning is fundamentally a question of enrichment, of attaching responses to stimulus features, of incorporating memory, imagery perhaps, and generally of synthesizing a perceptual world from its stimulus components. The two points of view seem to be mutually incompatible, but at the risk of proposing too bland a compromise I shall argue that both are probably correct. However, they are correct in a limited sense, and neither one alone does justice to the richness and variety of perceptual learning.

In the first place, Gibson is obviously correct in maintaining that a vast amount of information is present in the visual-stimulus array, a point which is clear enough once it has been made. But this is not sufficient to ensure that it is *available* to the organism without more ado, and the question of availability is surely an empirical one which cannot be answered by dialectic alone. The weight of evidence on perceptual development summarized by Hebb (1949) for example, as well as much of the more recent literature (for example, Held & Hein, 1963; Rock, 1966; Salapatek & Kessen, 1966) suggests rather strongly that active processes of construction, with motor involvement, are necessary conditions for the genesis of a normal perceptual world at least for mammals. Neurophysiological findings such as those of Hubel and Wiesel (1962) are also compatible with this position, as are the findings—at an entirely different level—of the transactionalists (Kilpatrick, 1961) and of Piaget (1951). Second, the Gibsons have demonstrated that perceptual learning *can* consist of a process of differentiation (Gibson, Gibson, Pick, & Osser, 1962). The demonstration is not sufficient, however, to prove that *all* perceptual learning is like this. It is a commonplace observation that the perceptual worlds of a child, a scientist, a poet, and a musician vary enormously; and who is to say that their differences are due only to the degree to which different sorts of people discriminate attributes of a given stimulus array to different degrees? At a commonsense level it is very difficult to believe that differentiation is the only relevant factor, that the associations, evocations, emotional responses or "meaning" of a picture, a poem or a piece of music are purely a function of stimulus information and the degree to which different aspects of this information are discerned by a painter, a poet, and a musician. To take another example, it is not self-contradictory to say that an architect and an engineer might both look at a building, and discriminate all the same features (although they might label them differently), and yet "see" two quite different things. To one it might represent an example of the intuitive use of important structural principles which anticipate a theoretical development in mechanics, to the other it might represent a fine example of early Gothic architecture (Pevsner, 1942). In a clear sense we should want to say that this difference was at least in part a function of perceptual learning. At a more formal level the same point can be made by denying that every perceptual response is entirely stimulus bound. This argument might be countered by stating that the differences just discussed have nothing to do with perception per se, but I think that this would simply be to legislate an unusual restriction on the use of the word "perception." To my mind, the element of interpretation is a necessary facet of that word's meaning, a point made more subtly, if more obscurely, by Wittgenstein (1953).

There are examples in the literature of differences in perception and perceptual categories that are clearly related to the general physical and/or social environment in which a person grows up, even at the rather low level of geometrical illusions and size constancy (Bartlett, 1932; Taylor, 1962; Segall, Campbell, & Herskovits, 1963; Gregory, 1966). Gregory, for instance, relates differences in susceptibility to the Müller-Lyer illusion in Western Europeans and Zulus to the fact that the latter live in a predominantly "circular" culture, where the opportunity to observe solid angles formed by mutually perpendicular planes, and their perspective transformations, is virtually absent. This and the failure of size constancy among jungle-dwelling tribes described by Taylor I take to be instances of variety in perceptual organization as a function primarily of *S-S* perceptual learning. It is unlikely that the differences are dependent on a history of specific responses to one or another feature of the visual environment; rather it seems plausible to argue that they are functions of nonspecific interactions with the relevant characteristics of visual stimulation. If there is such a general ecological determination of perceptual organization, it is probably related more to the processes described by Postman than to those proposed by Gibson. As I argued earlier (Chapter 2) a classifier with memory provides a logical basis for size constancy, for perceptual invariance and stability, and for the inferential properties of visual recognition which Hebb and others have emphasized. However, Postman's argument explicitly invokes the factor of response attachment, and thus is closely allied to what I have called *S-R* perceptual learning. In fact I shall maintain that there are three sorts of process, not two, and that no one of them is precisely identifiable with differentiation or enrichment in the sense of the Postman-Gibson controversy.

It was suggested in Chapter 10 that the dimensions of a decision space are determined by the outputs from a recognizer with memory (D_m), and that potentially such a space has as many dimensions for visual input as there are different classifying units within D_m.[1] The effective decision space, however, will normally have many fewer dimensions, since normally the organism responds to a class of stimuli, or a type of object, rather than to idiosyncratic features of visual input or individually coded elements

---

[1] I shall discuss the decision space in terms of its visual dimensions, but it should be remembered that these are but a subset of the possible dimensions.

of a pattern. This means that the effective inputs from D_m will normally be at some level substantially above the base, but does not exclude the possibility of differentiation—responses to more elementary properties, or finer distinctions among a class of inputs—under appropriate conditions. Such differentiation would be close to Gibsonian perceptual learning, but the process here postulated is contingent on the *prior* elaboration of D_m through nonspecific associationistic processes, in contradistinction to Gibson's ideas. The *availability* of different sorts of stimulus information is thus held to be dependent on complex processes involving the ecological background and history of the organism.

If Gibson-type perceptual learning is identified with progression downward in the hierarchy of D_m, to generate new effective dimensions of decision space, Postman-type perceptual learning can be thought of as something like the reverse process. New decision regions are created by the novel conjunction of inputs, so that new categories of perceptual objects, wider associations, and new "constructions" are generated. The dichotomy into two perceptual-learning processes can hardly be as neat and simple as this description suggests, however, since one must suppose that even in the very young organism the two types of perceptual (S-R) learning are concomitant with the elaboration of D_m by means of response-nonspecific S-S associations. Although the theoretical framework postulated is thus rather a complicated one, it seems to me to be far more realistic than the rather simplistic conceptions of either Gibson or Postman taken on their own.

Both Gibson and Postman assume a set of static initial conditions: The organism is provided with stimulation, which it codes either in a complicated (G) or simple (P) manner. Perceptual learning then is held to proceed on the basis of operations of differentiation or integration on these coded inputs. I suggest, on the contrary, that the most relevant input conditions are always changing, and that the fixed coding of the primary detection system is removed one stage from specific S-R perceptual learning by the activities within D_m. The resulting picture is complicated, but it seems to accord quite well with the properties that a general theory of perceptual development and learning should have. First, it recognizes explicitly that the study of perception is the study of perceiving organisms, and that the properties of a perceptual system are conditioned by the environment in which it develops. Second, it allows for a sort of infrastructure of perceptual categorization which will generally be shared by all organisms brought up in similar environments—in the case of humans, in similar cultures. Third, it recognizes the important role which special interests and training, attention, and other selective factors may have on perceptual development. Fourth, it makes some sense of two types of specific perceptual learning, by enrichment and by differentiation, and is open to the development of a model of cognitive decision and choice which is intimately related to a perceptual-decision space.

This last point will bear further discussion, although it is not intended to develop here such a model of cognitive functioning in any detail. The possibilities may be roughly sketched by considering what happens when, let us say, a child starts to learn about a natural science such as biology (almost any novel intellectual discipline could serve as well as an illustration). To start with, the child has a general conception of the difference between living and inanimate objects, can distinguish a variety of categories within each, can perhaps name quite a few plants and animals correctly, and so on. Some of this, but not all, will have come about through having learned specific discriminations and labels for them. Even more basically, he has developed a general conception of a stable world furnished with permanent objects whose behavior in some important respects is quite predictable. From such initial conditions, the first steps in learning about biology will no doubt involve a good deal of perceptual differentiation and labeling—learning to identify and name the parts of a flower or a skeleton, to apply such definitional terms as "invertebrate" and "deciduous"—but at the same time learning how to fit these new categories into larger perceptual and conceptual schemata. Thus, for example, learning to discriminate the various parts of a flower leads immediately to the fact that a functional or conceptual class (such as stamen, sepal) can be manifested perceptually in great variety, and this, in turn, leads to the classification into orders, genera, and species, the notions of metamorphosis and evolution, and so on. This is a constructive intellectual process, but based initially on perceptual learning. Conceptual and perceptual development are inextricably conjoined, and involve processes of both differentiation and enrichment: differentiation in the formation of finer perceptual discriminations and conceptual distinctions; enrichment in the broadening of categories by association and the creation of new inductive classifications. Although our example is a rather formal one, the line of argument can really be applied to almost any instance of the acquisition of empirical knowledge, and this is what perceptual learning, in the traditional sense, is about.

ACCOMMODATING THE SPECIALIZED MODELS

To return to our review of multistage processing, one may ask how the models for stereoptic binocular vision (Chapter 7) and for adaptation to visual distortions (Chapter 8) fit into the theoretical framework here proposed. For the model of binocular processing there is no problem, but some amplification of the role of the Cyclopean-field analogue, D_B

(Fig. 7.19) is in order. As this model is described, D_B has functions clearly similar to those of D_m (the *S-S* perceptual learning model) of Chapter 2. That is, its inputs are themselves the outputs from a primary detection system—in this case for the detection of stereoptic depth information—and its outputs are described as representing in some sense the visual field, according to which pattern characteristics are signalled for various parts of the field. The units of D_B may thus be thought of as a subset of D_m which specify a particular sort of stimulus information, other units being concerned with different aspects of patterns, including uniocular cues to depth. If the D_B units are a subset of D_m, they share the recognition-with-memory characteristics of D_m. But it must be remembered that this perceptual-learning characteristic is *not* a property of the units themselves, since each one has a fixed pattern-element signaling function, but it is a property of the *interrelations* of such units. The (fixed) coding of stereoptic depth in D_B can thus contribute to the elaboration of pattern-in-depth (which will include learned features), without being the sole necessary or sufficient condition for depth detection. In this sense D_B units may, but do not necessarily, contribute dimensions to perceptual-decision space.

The question of how the model for adaptation to distortion can be brought into the wider scheme is not quite so straightforward. Referring back to Fig. 8.9, the obvious step seems to be to identify the recognizer with D_m, since it receives (via the comparator) the coded visual input, $f^{-1}(\omega)$. This, however, involves some inconsistency in the overall scheme of things, since the *computer-motor-system-link* chain's operation invokes decision processes of the type ascribed to the *TPC* model in Chapter 10 (that is, processes "higher up" in the system, which receive inputs from D_m). It might therefore be neater to attempt to recast the coder of Fig. 8.9 so that its outputs define some of the dimensions of decision space. Another puzzle, at least at first sight, is that adaptation to purely visual distortion involves adjustments in several modalities (Hay and Pick, 1966) which indicates that perceptual-decision space is the seat of change, rather than the visual-input side alone (the coder or D_m). Indeed this fact indicates a real deficiency in the model of Fig. 8.9, since there most adaptation is considered to be in the visual mode. A modification to the model which takes these points into account can be suggested; the modified version is shown in Fig. 11.1, using the ideas developed in Chapter 10.

The general idea is that changes in visual coding are still made, basically, at the initial coding stage, but that information about visual-motor lack of coordination is also relayed to the weighting functions of decision space. In this way one can preserve the conceptually tidy notion of direct recoding of visual input within the primary detection system, which would reestablish the "normal" visual input to D_m when the correct transformation is formed, together with immediate means for adaptation of the sensori-

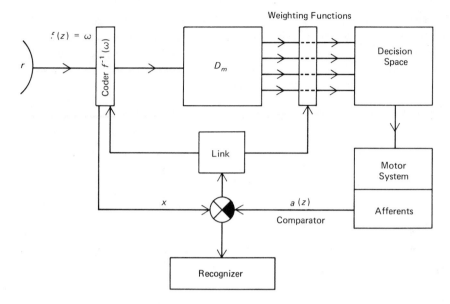

Fig. 11.1. Model for adaptation to distortions of visual input elaborated from model of Fig. 8.9.

motor coordination system via readjustment of the weighting functions of decision space. This latter type of adjustment would be quite labile, in harmony with the idea of relatively rapid changes in decision space previously outlined, and would be consonant with the finding of transient nonvisual adaptations reported by Hay and Pick (1966). It would also form a natural basis for the two types of adjustment, in visual-motor coordination on the one hand, in phenomenal or "pictorial" adaptation on the other, discussed earlier in Chapter 8. In this way, the model for adaptation to visual distortions can be fitted into the general, multistage, theoretical framework for visual perception.

The speculative nature of these suggestions is once again emphasized, in that they go well beyond our stage of exact empirical knowledge about the workings of the visual system. It is maintained, however, that the various models can be put together reasonably coherently, and without insult to the known facts, and that some explicit properties of visual pattern perception and of perceptual learning are implied thereby, a number of which lend themselves to experimental investigation.

THE PROBLEM OF SERIAL ORDER

In a now classical paper, Lashley discussed the general problem of serial order in behavior (Lashley, 1951). More recently the specific interests of psychologists have been directed toward questions about visual search, scanning, and serial vs. parallel-processing models. This line of research is discussed by Neisser (1967) and suggestions for modeling some features have been made by Sperling (1963), Sternberg (1967), and Bryden (1967), among others. While the questions one can ask about serial order and the control of sequential behavior are clearly relevant to any comprehensive theoretical treatment of pattern recognition, they must inevitably raise questions about memory and language which go beyond the scope of the present discussion. I shall therefore not attempt any analysis of the problems there to be solved, while acknowledging that this limits the generality of the ideas here presented. Eventually an attempt at theoretical rapprochement between models for sequential behavior and the more "static" classificatory sorts of process I have discussed must be made.

THE LOGICAL STATUS OF STRUCTURAL MODELS AND STATEMENTS ABOUT PERCEPTION

On several occasions in earlier chapters I have referred to a very important question which has to do with the nature of psychological explanation. This is the philosophical, or epistemological, question of how scientific models of behavior are related to our ordinary, everyday use of psychological words like "perceive," "think," and "remember." It may be posed sharply as what I previously called the phenomenological question: Why does the world look the way it does, and what, if anything, can a psychological theory about perception contribute to our understanding of seeing *as a personal experience,* that is, the normal everyday connotation of "seeing."

Let us start by noticing that there is a characteristic difference between the layman's use of psychological words like "see" and "remember," and their use within a psychological model or theory. Usually when one says "I see a house" or "I remember his name," one is implicitly making a claim to the *correctness* of one's observations or memory. Although there are obviously many instances when some qualification of the claim is necessary (for example, "I think it must be a house") it is nevertheless true that the paradigm use of such words is normative. Now there are generally accepted procedures for verifying such claims, but they all make appeal, in the final analysis, to just that *type* of observational operation that they are called upon to verify. Thus the sort of move which is made to establish whether or not John Doe did see a house is to establish by further careful observation whether the object named really is a house, whether there is any object to be seen (perhaps he suffered from an hallucination?), or whether there are special circumstances which can explain a misperception. The point is that these procedures all have the same epistemological status as the original observation and the claim that is based on it. If this point is denied, the whole basis for making a scientific study of perception is undermined. There are philosophers who are willing to make the denial and to construct various metaphysical theories of perception on some other basis (many are discussed by Armstrong, 1964), but so far as the psychology of perception as an empirical, experimental discipline is concerned, they are fairly irrelevant.

Statements about perceiving, then, are usually validated by making further observations and further perceptual statements of the same sort. Does that mean that this is the *only* means of validation? One can think of numerous examples where visual observations are supplemented with special optical instruments, and of cases where observation can only be made by elaborate optical and electronic gear, as in astronomy or particle physics. But the meaning and interpretation of such observations always stem from a more immediate field of empirical observation. So observational statements are normally verified—or otherwise—by further observations, even though they may be of a very specialized type.

The peculiarity of the phenomenological question as we have posed it is that one tends to feel quite strongly that there must be more to it than simply a request for ordinary verification of an observation or a perception. One is tempted to see in it a request for an explanation that goes beyond the normal processes of observation or even of the specialized sorts of information-gathering which are typical of the natural sciences. The question, then, is: Can a psychological theory of perception provide the required explanation? To bring the matter down to brass tacks: Can structural modeling of the sort here advocated provide such an explanation?

The typical moves of the theorist in perception are concerned with mapping a highly variable stimulus input into a relatively small number of outputs or response categories—of correlating stimulus features with the ability of an organism to make discriminative responses to them. The uses of the words "recognize," "discriminate," or "see" in this context are not the same as the normative uses which they have in common parlance. In what sense, if any, are these scientific uses more precise, or more profound, than the everyday uses? Is there truly a way in which they *explain* perception by going beyond the processes of normal observation and verification? The arguments are involved, and of a sort perhaps not usual among psychologists, so before presenting them I shall state my conclusion and then attempt to explain it. My conclusion is that neither structural modeling nor any other of the systems of ideas that are called scientific theories of behavior can give a complete explanation of perception; but they *can* contribute to our understanding of perception in important ways by analysis and formulation of some of the *empirically necessary conditions* of perception. They cannot completely explain perception, because they can never specify the *logically sufficient conditions* for perception to occur. That is, from such a model or theory it is logically impossible to *deduce* a statement about perception, in the sense in which that word is normally used.

Those are strong claims, and they go against a whole tradition in scientific psychology. In attempting to justify them I hope to be able to establish a general thesis about the role of models and theories in psychology and to characterize some limitations on the field of valid scientific explanations of behavior—especially of human behavior.

MODELING, ENTAILMENT, AND EXPLANATION

The aim of a scientific model is to explain some set of phenomena, and to do so by showing that the facts can be deduced from, or in some weaker sense "follow from" the model. The structural models for pattern recognition with which we have been concerned attempt to explain stimulus categorization in terms of the operation of modules, or other quasi-physiological units, which are specified in terms of their input-output relations. The only sorts of statement one can *deduce* from such a model are statements about switching on, switching off, patterns of outputs, categorization, and the like. This is so because the relation of entailment requires that the statement which is entailed be of the same logical type as the statements from which it is deduced. The principle is a familiar one to philosophers, a particular instance having been put by Hume in the form: A statement about what *ought* to be the case is never entailed by a statement about what *is* the case. The one can never entail the other because the two sorts of statement have different logical features, different uses; a statement about what *ought* to be is not a simple factual statement, for one thing. Confusion over this point was labeled the "naturalistic fallacy" by G. E. Moore, and the label is now used to cover similar confusions in other fields of argument (see Toulmin, 1958, Ch. II, especially p. 68). What has all this to do with explanations about perception?

If only statements about input-output are deducible from our structural models, as the relation of entailment requires, then it follows that no statement about "perceiving" or "seeing"—as we ordinarily use those words—can be deduced. This is so because our ordinary use of the words is normative, in the sense of an implicit claim about the correctness of our perception, and also carries the clear commitment to an actual experience. To say "I see a house" and simultaneously to deny having any conscious visual experience is clearly paradoxical and a misuse of language. This is not to deny that there are some exceptional circumstances in which a person can make a visual discrimination without being fully aware of the nature of the visual stimulation; the point is to establish the paradigm use of the words "I see" and "perceive." The matter can be further elucidated by pointing out, as several philosophers have done, that the categories of description and evaluation that are relevant to perception are different from those which are appropriate to physiological, physical, chemical, or mechanical events. Thus a perception can be "vivid," "pleasurable," or "ambiguous," for instance, but these are not appropriate descriptions of brain states; more precisely, they are not appropriate to the description of brain states which may be found as concomitants of visual experience.[2]

Thus the view that a quasi-physiological or mechanistic model, such as those I have discussed, cannot *explain* perception seems to be established. At least, it cannot explain perception in the sense that a statement such as "the observer will see x under such-and-such conditions" could be deduced from it. This is the same as claiming that the sufficient conditions for perception to occur cannot be specified solely in terms of such a model.

A hard-headed psychologist might nevertheless maintain that "the observer sees x" can be *defined* as "the output from the model is x," and if he *is* hard-headed and consistent we cannot deny the point. What we can do is to point out that this is to prescribe a *new use* for the word "see." For the reasons just given, the phrase cannot, however, have the normal meaning of these words. Alternatively, one might argue that "the observer sees x" follows from a statement about the model's output in some weaker sense than that required by entailment. That formulation is acceptable, if it merely amounts to a claim that there is a one-to-one correspondence between a given output from the model and perception of a specified pattern. But the finding of such a correlation, while it allows one to *predict* the occurrence of a perception, is *not* necessarily an adequate ground for its explanation.

The sufficient conditions for an explanation and for a prediction are not equivalent, as I have argued in detail elsewhere (Dodwell, 1960). This is easy enough to see by considering a simple example: One might be surprised to find that a certain type of beetle always moves towards a light (assumed present) when placed on a flat horizontal surface, but

[2] It is not at all clear to me what the appropriate analysis of the relations between the "normative" aspect of perceptual statements and the "consciousness claim" may be. In the logical grammar of their everyday use they are clearly not independent, because claims to veridical perception are *based on* claims of conscious seeing, hearing, touching, and so forth.

that if the surface is tipped, the direction of locomotion changes. One might be able to work out some regularities, so that one could always *predict,* given starting position *x,* tilt *y,* and position of light *z,* in which direction the beetle would go. But this ability to predict obviously does *not* itself constitute an explanation. Perhaps an explanation suggests itself quite immediately in this case—the insect's locomotion is controlled by a heliotropic and a geotropic factor which interact in a certain way. Given this hypothesis (model?) the observed patterns of movement can be deduced from it, other consequences follow, and a whole variety of other tests of its adequacy are likely to come to mind. The grounds for an explanation here are clearly very different from the grounds for a prediction, which may be, after all, theoretically quite neutral. Explanations, on the other hand, are never so innocuous: They commit one to a theoretical stance, however general and vague it may be. Thus, to say that certain brain-states are correlated with particular perceptions (can be predicted from or can predict them) is certainly not equivalent to *explaining* one in terms of the other.

To return to the main question: If a statement about perception can never be entailed by quasi-physiological or similar statements, and perception (in the normal sense) therefore cannot be explained in such terms, in what ways can we claim that structural modeling in perception is useful as a theoretical tool? How, if at all, can it "go beyond" the everyday, commonsense level of discourse and clarification which are normally used when we talk about seeing, hearing, recognizing and observing? The answer is straightforward. Structural models, as well as direct investigation of the neurophysiology of the visual system and behavioral studies of discriminatory behavior, can contribute to our understanding of perception in this sense: They all can describe and analyze some of the *empirically necessary conditions* of perception. These may very well go beyond— "deeper than"—our everyday talk or thinking about perception, as most of the evidence described in earlier chapters shows. But despite this, despite the fact that in some senses these theoretical and experimental analyses are more basic than our everyday talk, and despite the fact that in this way our *understanding* of perception may be enormously increased, it is still true that in a strict sense we cannot fully *explain* perception on these conceptual premises alone.

THE INCOMPLETENESS OF MODELS

This assertion is, I am certain, far less damaging to psychology as a science than it appears to be. In the first place, no scientific principle, model, or theory ever really purports to account for *everything* in the field to which it is applied. This is not the place to argue the point in detail, but I think it is clear that scientific theorizing is selective and abstractive, however difficult it may be to characterize properly what it is about some features of a phenomenon that "call for" explanation, while other features do not. The basis for selecting "relevant" features is probably related, at least for the physical sciences, to the considerations which led the early empirical philosophers to distinguish between "primary" and "secondary" qualities. Anyway, it is always possible to find properties and attributes which a given theory does not "explain" in our strict sense. A physical scientist is not worried by these considerations, because he already has a good idea—or at least a strong tradition—about what needs explanation and the sorts of conceptual tools that can accomplish his aim. This is certainly not so true for psychologists, or behavioral scientists in general. Indeed a strong case can be made for the argument that experimental psychologists, at least in the rat-running tradition, have embraced the *wrong* traditions (Louch, 1966; C. Taylor, 1963). This argument rests on the assertion that explanations of human (and perhaps infrahuman) actions are *essentially* purposive, and do not explain unless they refer to goals and intentions, whereas the very strong bias among psychologists has been to attempt "neutral" description and explanation in terms of physiological and/or paramechanical models. The argument is very closely related to mine about explanations of perception.[3] So, if one asserts that structural models are relevant and can increase our understanding of perception, one has to face the objection that the essential job of a theory in psychology is to explain something which goes beyond the conceptual limitations of our models. That "something" in our case is the normative character of perception and the conscious experience that is perceiving. The only counter to this argument, in my view, is a blank denial that the psychologist's job *is* to explain perception in that sense. In fact I will assert dogmatically that we do not even know along what sorts of line such an explanation could be found. Yet, is it not true that consciousness, experience, is of the essence of perception, so that this assertion is tantamount to denying that we can grapple with the "core" characteristic of our subject? I do not think so. I do *not* deny that at some future time a comprehensive theoretical account of the perceiving organism may be possible in which "both sides of the coin," are explained within one

[3] The arguments are important, but too complex to go into here. Louch's and Taylor's books are recommended, particularly the latter for its explanation of the philosophical antecedents to the "positivistic" attitude of experimental psychologists. It is perhaps fair to add that Taylor attacks views which were current among psychologists about 20 years ago, although their *residua* are still evident in many ways in contemporary theoretical work.

system.[4] But on the other hand I think it is a mistake to worry too much about attempting to "reduce" consciousness to physiological processes, to attempt to define one in terms of the other, or to argue the niceties of various attempts to do this. Most attempts to date have anyway amounted to little more than circumlocutions, or inadequate prescriptive redefinitions of consciousness (for example, "higher stage of neural integration," whatever that means). For the present, we can say plenty about perception and the perceiving organism that is scientifically valid and furthers our understanding of perception without resolving that particular issue. To attempt to be omniscient, complete, irrefutable in one's claims, would be absurd. To accept the limitation is not as severe, at least in perception, as it may seem.[5]

Even if we cannot explain perception (consciousness, intention, and so forth) by structural modeling, we *can* explain—or attempt to explain— some *features* of perception, like the role of certain brain structures, of early experience, of special types of adaptation, and so on. The explication of these matters is fundamental to our understanding of perception as a process, and in this sense "goes beyond" the commonsense level of discourse. As a matter of fact one may well turn the argument around, and say that it is only (or mainly) insofar as our models are divorced from the conceptual apparatus of everyday description and explanation that they do provide the basis for scientific understanding. Generally one of the troubles with discourse in some areas of behavioral science (see Louch, 1966) is that it dresses up commonsense in a pseudoscientific garb that is misleading simply because it *can* be retranslated into the vernacular without loss. In attempting to specify some of the underlying conditions for visual perception, particularly in the physiological substrata of the visual system, one may claim to be going a few steps beyond the level of everyday talk, of commonsense. Delving into these matters may alter the focus of our interest, the specific sorts of question we may ask *about* perception, but—I say again, at the risk of being tedious—the sorts of question we can ask, or answer in this way, will not include questions such as: What is perception? How do you explain why a tree looks like a tree?

Our arguments apply a fortiori to other areas of psychology. It is questionable whether many learning theorists still cherish the goal of being able to deduce statements about human action from postulates about

---

[4] The outlook may not be good, but it is not logically impossible. (See Taylor, 1964, especially Ch. V.)

[5] It may be pointed out that other sciences, particularly the life sciences of biology and physiology, have managed well for decades without the sorts of logical worry and dispute we have been talking of, although the philosophers' considerations would be as apposite to those disciplines—or nearly so—as to psychology.

"colorless movement" and physiological states (Hull, 1952), or whether they ever think about the problem. To the extent that such reductionism is still a largely unexpressed article of faith, it is wrong. In this the arguments of Peters (1959), Taylor (1964), and Louch (1966) are, I think, quite correct. But instead of arguing the question of reductionism further, it would be more fruitful to characterize the scientific activities of psychologists more adequately. In studying questions of judgment, choice, learning, and so forth, psychologists are not (or should not be) attempting to *displace* the normative, rule-following, or purposive models of human action, but rather are attempting to investigate the external factors which affect actions, the nature of the individual decision processes which guide choice, and the most accurate description of their modes of interplay. (See also Dodwell, in press.)

It is instructive to compare this situation with some which occur in other sciences. It is not at all unusual for a structural model to be proposed, to be accepted as reasonable, and for it literally to "structure" thinking about a field of inquiry, without its in any way being able to *explain* everything about that field. The kinetic theory of gases, the wave-propagation model for light, and the molecular-coding model for genetic information come to mind as three very different examples. The kinetic theory did not account for *all* the properties of a gas (the foul odor of hydrogen sulphide, for example) nor did the wave model account for all we know about light, but this did not detract from their scientific usefulness. Similarly, it is quite certain that everything about inheritance cannot be explained in terms of molecular coding. As a matter of fact the parallel with our situation is here very close; molecular coding may be shown to be a necessary feature of genetic processes, but does not itself explain the features of a particular inheritance. *That* a particular heritable feature is dependent on a particular code is not in itself an *explanation* of how that code "carries" that feature. Similarly, that a particular discrimination is dependent on a particular physiological function is not in itself an *explanation* of the perceived difference between two patterns. Thus, it can reasonably be maintained that selectivity, abstractness, and incompleteness, are common—if not universal—features of all scientific models and theories.

A MORE POSITIVE NOTE ON WHICH TO END

I need scarcely add that I do not claim even vaguely comparable status for the models I have presented with the examples from other sciences discussed in the previous section. At the same time it is true that periods in a science's development when conceptually quite simple structural models seem to fit the state of current understanding, and hence provide the appropriate level of analysis, are often periods of very fruitful advance.

It would be too much to hope that the ideas in this book have hit upon completely correct solutions to the problems addressed; nevertheless, they may give psychological theorizing a nudge in the right direction. At least that is my hope, in proffering this essay on theoretical psychology.

REFERENCES

Adrian, E. D., & Matthews, R. The action of light on the eye. I. Impulses in optic nerve. *Journal of Physiology,* 1927, **63,** 378–414.

Andersen, E. E., & Weymouth, F. W. Visual perception and the retinal mosaic. I. Retinal mean local sign. *American Journal of Physiology,* 1923, **64,** 561–594.

Andrews, D. P. Error-correcting perceptual mechanisms. *Quarterly Journal of Experimental Psychology,* 1964, **16,** 104–115.

Andrews, D. P. Perception of contour orientation in the central fovea. Part I: Short lines. *Vision Research,* 1967, **7,** 975–997. (a)

Andrews, D. P. Perception of contour orientation in the central fovea. Part II: Spatial integration. *Vision Research,* 1967, **7,** 999–1013. (b)

Arbib, M. A. *Brains, machines, and mathematics.* New York: McGraw-Hill, 1964.

Armstrong, D. M. *Perception and the physical world.* New York: Humanities Press, 1964.

Arnoult, M. D. Shape discrimination as a function of the angular orientation of the stimuli. *Journal of Experimental Psychology,* 1954, **47,** 323–328.

Ashby, W. R. *Design for a brain: The origin of adaptive behavior.* New York: Wiley, 1952.

Asher, H. Suppression theory of binocular vision. *British Journal of Ophthalmology,* 1953, **37,** 37–49. (a)

Asher, H. The suppression theory. *British Orthoptic Journal,* 1953, **10,** 1–9. (b)

Attneave, F. Some informational aspects of visual perception. *Psychological Review,* 1954, **61,** 183–193.

Averbach, E., & Coriell, A. S. Short term memory in vision. *Bell System Technical Journal,* 1961, **40,** 309–328.

Barlow, H. B. Summation and inhibition in the frog's retina. *Journal of Physiology,* 1953, **119,** 69–88.

Barlow, H. B. Slippage of contact lenses and other artifacts in relation to fading and regeneration of supposedly stable retinal images. *Quarterly Journal of Experimental Psychology,* 1963, **15,** 36–51.

Barlow, H. B., Blakemore, C., & Pettigrew, J. D. The neural mechanism of binocular depth discrimination. *Journal of Physiology,* 1967, **193,** 327–342.

Barlow, H. B., Fitzhugh, R., & Kuffler, S. Dark adaptation, absolute threshold, and Purkinje shift in single units of the cat's retina. *Journal of Physiology,* 1957, **137,** 327–337. (a)

Barlow, H. B., Fitzhugh, R., & Kuffler, S. Change of organization in the receptive fields of the cat's retina during dark adaptation. *Journal of Physiology,* 1957, **137,** 338–354. (b)

Barlow, H. B., Hill, R. M., & Levick, W. R. Retinal ganglion cells responding selectively to direction and speed of image motions in the rabbit. *Journal of Physiology,* 1964, **173,** 377–407.

Barlow, H. B., Levick, W. R., & Westheimer, G. Computer-plotted receptive fields. *Science,* 1966, **154,** 920.

Bartlett, F. C. *Remembering—A study in experimental and social psychology.* Cambridge, England: Cambridge University Press, 1932.

Baumgartner, G., Brown, J. L., & Schulz, A. Responses of single units of the cat visual system to rectangular stimulus patterns. *Journal of Neurophysiology,* 1965, **28,** 1–18.

Bennet-Clark, H. C., & Evans, C. R. Fragmentation of patterned targets when viewed as prolonged after-images. *Nature,* 1963, **199,** 1215–1216.

Berlyne, D. E. *Conflict, arousal and curiosity.* New York: McGraw-Hill, 1960.

Bishop, P. O., Burke, W., & Davis, R. The identification of single units in the central visual pathways. *Journal of Physiology,* 1962, **162,** 409–431. (a)

Bishop, P. O., Burke, W., & Davis, R. Single unit recording from antidromically activated optic radiation neurons. *Journal of Physiology,* 1962, **162,** 433–450. (b)

Bishop, P. O., Burke, W., & Davis, R. The interpretation of the extracellular response of single lateral geniculate cells. *Journal of Physiology,* 1962, **162,** 452–472. (c)

Bledsoe, W. W., & Browning, I. Pattern recognition and reading by machine. *Proceedings of the Eastern Joint Computer Conference,* 1959, 225–232. (Reprinted in Uhr, 1966.)

Boring, E. G. *Sensation and perception in the history of experimental psychology.* New York: Appleton-Century, 1942.

Bouma, H., and Andriessen, J. J. Perceived orientation of isolated line segments. *Vision Research,* 1968, **8,** 493–507.

Brindley, G. S. *Physiology of the retina and the visual pathway.* London: Arnold, 1960.

Broadbent, D. E. Word-frequency effect and response bias. *Psychological Review,* 1967, **74,** 1–15.

Brown, J. E. Dendritic fields of retinal ganglion cells of the rat. *Journal of Neurophysiology,* 1965, **28,** 1091–1100.

Brown, J. E., & Rojas, J. A. Rat retinal ganglion cells: Receptive field organisation and maintained activity. *Journal of Neurophysiology,* 1965, **28,** 1073–1090.

Bruner, J. S. On perceptual readiness. *Psychological Review,* 1957, **64,** 123–152.

Bryden, M. P. Tachistoscopic recognition of non-alphabetical material. *Canadian Journal of Psychology,* 1960, **14,** 78–86.

Bryden, M. P. Accuracy and order of report in tachitoscopic recognition. *Canadian Journal of Psychology,* 1966, **20,** 262–272.

Bryden, M. P. A model for the sequential organization of behavior. *Canadian Journal of Psychology,* 1967, **21,** 37–56.

Cajal, S. R. Contribución al conocimiento de la retina y centros ópticos de los cefalópods. *Trabajos del Laboratorio de investigaciones biologicas de la Universidad de Madrid,* 1917, **15,** 1–82.

Campbell, F. W., & Kulikowski, J. J. Orientational selectivity of the human visual system. *Journal of Physiology,* 1966, **187,** 437–445.

Charnwood, J. R. B. *Essay on binocular vision.* London: Hutton, 1951.

Clowes, M. B. An hierarchical model of form perception. In W. Wathen-Dunn (Ed.), *Models for the perception of speech and visual form.* Cambridge, Mass.: M.I.T. Press, 1967.

Cornsweet, T. N. Determination of the stimuli for involuntary drifts and saccadic eye movements. *Journal of the Optical Society of America,* 1956, **46,** 987–993.

Coxeter, H. S. M. *Introduction to geometry.* New York: Wiley, 1961.

Davson, H. (Ed.), *The eye.* Vol. 2, *Visual process.* Vol. 4, *Visual optics and the optical sense.* New York: Academic Press, 1962.

Daw, N. W. Why after-images are not seen in normal circumstances. *Nature,* 1962, **196,** 1143–1145.

Daw, N. W. Goldfish retina: Organization for simultaneous color contrast. *Science,* 1967, **158,** 942–944.

Daw, N. W. Colour-coded ganglion cells in the goldfish retina: Extension of their receptive fields by means of new stimuli. *Journal of Physiology,* 1968, **197,** 567–592.

Deutsch, J. A. A theory of shape recognition. *British Journal of Psychology,* 1955, **46,** 30–37.

Deutsch, J. A. The plexiform zone and shape recognition in the octopus. *Nature,* 1960, **185,** 443–446. (a)

Deutsch, J. A. *The structural basis of behaviour.* Chicago: Chicago University Press, 1960. (b)

Deutsch, J. A. A system for shape recognition. *Psychological Review,* 1962, **69,** 492–500.

Deutsch, J. A. Neurophysiological contrast phenomena and figural after-effects. *Psychological Review,* 1964, **71,** 19–26.

De Valois, R. L. Color vision mechanisms in the monkey. *Journal of General Physiology,* 1960, **43,** 115–128.

Ditchburn, R. W., & Ginsborg, B. L. Vision with a stabilized retinal image. *Nature,* 1952, **170,** 36–37.

Ditchburn, R. W., & Pritchard, R. M. Stabilized interference fringes on the retina. *Nature,* 1956, **177,** 434.

Dixon, N. F. The effect of subliminal stimulation upon autonomic and verbal behavior. *Journal of Abnormal & Social Psychology,* 1958, **57,** 29–36.

Doan, H. M. Conditional discrimination and the effective cues in children's discrimination learning. Unpublished doctoral dissertation, Queen's University at Kingston, Ontario, 1966.

Dodwell, P. C. Shape recognition in rats. *British Journal of Psychology,* 1957, **48,** 221–229.

Dodwell, P. C. Shape recognition: A reply to Deutsch. *British Journal of Psychology,* 1958, **49,** 158.

Dodwell, P. C. Causes, and explanation in psychology. *Mind,* 1960, **69,** N.S., 1–13.

Dodwell, P. C. Coding and learning in shape discrimination. *Psychological Review,* 1961, **68,** 373–382.

Dodwell, P. C. Facts, and theories of shape discrimination. *Nature,* 1961, **191,** 578–581.

Dodwell, P. C. A test of two theories of shape discrimination. *Quarterly Journal of Experimental Psychology,* 1962, **14,** 65–70.

Dodwell, P. C. A coupled system for coding and learning in shape discrimination. *Psychological Review,* 1964, **71,** 148–159.

Dodwell, P. C. Anomalous transfer effects after shape discrimination training in the rat. *Psychonomic Science,* 1965, **3,** 97–98.

Dodwell, P. C. *Perceptual learning and adaptation.* London: Penguin Books, 1970. (a)

Dodwell, P. C. Anomalous transfer effects after pattern discrimination training in rats and squirrels. *Journal of Comparative and Physiological Psychology,* 1970. (b)

Dodwell, P. C. Is a theory of conceptual development necessary? In T. Mischel (Ed.), *Genetic psychology and epistemology.* New York: Academic Press, in press.

Dodwell, P. C., & Engel, G. R. A theory of binocular fusion. *Nature,* 1963, **198,** 39–40, 73–74.

Dodwell, P. C., & Gendreau, L. Figural after-effects, sensory coding, expectation and experience. *British Journal of Psychology,* 1969, **60,** 149–167.

Dodwell, P. C., & Niemi, R. R. Contour orientation and separation in shape discrimination by rats. *Psychonomic Science,* 1967, **9,** 519–520.

Dodwell, P. C., & Standing, L. G. Studies of visual backward masking and a model for the Crawford effect. *Acta Psychologica,* 1970, **32,** 31–47.

Edwards, E. *Information transmission.* London: Chapman & Hall, 1964.

Efron, R. Stereoscopic vision: 1. Effect of binocular temporal summation. *British Journal of Ophthalmology,* 1957, **61,** 709–730.

Efstathiou, A., Bauer, J., Greene, M., & Held, R. Altered reaching following adaptation to optical displacement of the hand. *Journal of Experimental Psychology,* 1967, **73,** 113–120.

Egeth, H. Selective attention. *Psychological Bulletin,* 1967, **67,** 41–57.

Engel, G. R. *Temporal summation and binocular vision.* Unpublished M.A. thesis, Queen's University at Kingston, Ontario, 1962.

Engel, G. R. *A mechanism for binocular vision.* Unpublished doctoral dissertation, Queen's University at Kingston, Ontario, 1964.

Engel, G. R. The autocorrelation function and binocular brightness mixing. *Vision Research,* 1969, **9,** 1111–1130.

Eriksen, C. W. Discrimination and learning without awareness–A methodological survey and evaluation. *Psychological Review,* 1960, **67,** 279–300.

Eriksen, C. W., & Collins, J. F. Backward masking in vision, *Psychonomic Science,* 1964, **1,** 101–102. (a)

Eriksen, C. W., & Collins, J. F. Investigating the effect of a priming stimulus on backward masking. *Psychonomic Science,* 1964, **1,** 249–250. (b)

Eriksen, C. W., & Collins, J. F. Some temporal characteristics of visual pattern perception. *Journal of Experimental Psychology,* 1967, **74,** 476–484.

Eriksen, C. W., & Hoffman, M. Form recognition at brief durations as a function of adapting field and interval between stimulations. *Journal of Experimental Psychology,* 1963, **66,** 485–499.

Eriksen, C. W., & Lappin, J. S. Luminance summation-contrast reduction as a basis for certain forward and backward masking effects. *Psychonomic Science,* 1964, **1,** 313–314.

Estes, W. K. Toward a statistical theory of learning. *Psychological Review,* 1950, **57,** 94–107.

Evans, C. R. Some studies of pattern perception using a stabilized retinal image. *British Journal of Psychology,* 1965, **56,** 121–133.

Ewert, P. H. A study of the effect of inverted retinal stimulation upon spatially co-ordinated behaviour. *Genetic Psychology Monographs,* 1930, **7,** Nos. 3 & 4.

Fantz, R. L. Visual perception and experience in early infancy: a look at the hidden side of behavior development. In Stevenson, H. W., Hess, E. H., & Rheingold, H. G. (Eds.), *Early behavior: Comparative and developmental approaches.* New York: Wiley, 1967.

Festinger, L., Burnham, C. A., Ono, H., & Bamber, D. Efference and the conscious experience of perception. *Journal of Experimental Psychology,* 1967, **74,** 1–36.

Fields, P. E. Studies in concept formation, I. The development of the concept of triangularity by the white rat. *Comparative Psychology Monographs,* 1932, **9,** No. 2.

Fisher, G. H. An experimental and theoretical appraisal of the inappropriate size-depth theories of illusions. *British Journal of Psychology,* 1968, **58,** 373–383.

Fox, R. Analysis of the suppression mechanism in binocular rivalry. Unpublished doctoral dissertation, University of Cincinnati, 1963.

Ganz, L. Mechanism of the figural after-effects. *Psychological Review,* 1966, **73,** 128–150. (a)

Ganz, L. Is the figural after-effect an after-effect? A review of its intensity, onset, decay and transfer characteristics. *Psychological Bulletin,* 1966, **66,** 157–165. (b)

Gardner, R. A. On box score methodology as illustrated by three reviews of overtraining reversal effects. *Psychological Bulletin,* 1966, **66,** 416–418.

Garner, W. R. *Uncertainty and structure as psychological concepts.* New York: Wiley, 1962.

Gaze, L., & Dodwell, P. C. The role of induced set in figural after-effects. *Psychonomic Science,* 1965, **2,** 275–276.

Gibson, E. J. *Principles of perceptual learning and development.* New York: Appleton-Century-Crofts, 1969.

Gibson, E. J., Gibson, J. J., Pick, A. D., & Osser, H. A developmental study of the discriminability of letter-like forms. *Journal of Comparative and Physiological Psychology,* 1962, **55,** 897–906.

Gibson, J. J. Adaptation with negative after-effect. *Psychological Review,* 1937, **42,** 222–243.

Gibson, J. J. *The perception of the visual world.* Boston: Houghton-Mifflin, 1950.

Gibson, J. J. *The senses considered as perceptual systems.* Boston: Houghton-Mifflin, 1966. (a)

Gibson, J. J. The problem of temporal order in stimulation and perception. *Journal of Psychology,* 1966, **62,** 141–149. (b)

Gibson, J. J., & Gibson, E. J. Perceptual learning: Differentiation or enrichment? *Psychological Review,* 1955, **62,** 1–32.

Granit, R. The development of retinal neurophysiology. *Science,* 1968, **160,** 1192–1196.

Granit, R., & Svaetichin, G. Principles and technique of the electrophysiological analysis of colour reception with the aid of microelectrodes. *Uppsala Läkareförenings Förhandlingar,* 1939, **65,** 161–177.

Green, D. M., & Swets, J. A. *Signal detection theory and psychophysics.* New York: Wiley, 1966.

Gregory, R. L. *Eye and brain.* London: Weidenfeld & Nicolson, 1966.

Gregory, R. L., & Zangwill, O. L. The origin of the autokinetic effect. *Quarterly Journal of Experimental Psychology,* 1963, **15,** 252–261.

Grimsdale, R. L., Sumner, F. H., Tunis, C. J., & Kilburn, T. A System for the automatic recognition of patterns. *Proceedings of the Institute of Electrical Engineers,* 1959, **106,** 210–221. (Reprinted in Uhr, 1966.)

Grindley, G. C., & Townsend, V. Further experiments on movement masking. *Quarterly Journal of Experimental Psychology.* 1966, **18,** 319–326.

Haber, R. N. The nature of the effect of set on perception. *Psychological Review,* 1966, **73,** 335–351.

Haber, R. N. *Informing processing approaches to visual perception.* New York: Holt, Rinehart and Winston, 1969.

Hamilton, C. R. Intermanual transfer of adaptation to prisms. *American Journal of Psychology,* 1964, **77,** 457–462.

Hamlyn, D. *The psychology of perception.* London: Routledge & Kegan Paul, 1957.

Hamlyn, D. W. *Sensation and perception: A history of the philosophy of perception.* New York: Humanities Press, 1961.

Harlow, H. F. The formation of learning sets. *Psychological Review,* 1949, **56,** 51–65.

Harris, C. S. Adaptation to displaced vision: Visual, motor or proprioceptive change? *Science,* 1963, **140,** 812–813.

Harris, C. S. Perceptual adaptation to inverted, reversed and displaced vision. *Psychological Review,* 1965, **72,** 419–444.

Hartline, H. K. The response of single optic nerve fibers in the vertebrate eye to illumination of the retina. *American Journal of Physiology,* 1938, **121,** 400–415.

Hartline, H. K. The nerve messages in the fibers of the visual pathway. *Journal of the Optical Society of America,* 1940, **30,** 239–247. (a)

Hartline, H. K. The receptive fields of optic nerve fibers. *American Journal of Physiology,* 1940, **130,** 690–699. (b)

Hartline, H. K. Inhibition of activity of visual receptors by illuminating nearby retinal areas in limulus. *Federation Proceedings,* 1949, **8,** 69.

Hartline, H. K., & Graham, C. H. Nerve impulses from single receptors in the eye. *Journal of Cellular & Comparative Physiology,* 1932, **1,** 277–295.

Hartline, H. K., Wagner, H. G., & MacNichol, E. F., Jr. The peripheral origins of nervous activity in the visual system. *Cold Spring Harbor Symposia on Quantitative Biology,* 1952, **17,** 125–141.

Hartline, H. K., Wagner, H. G., & Ratliff, F. Inhibition in the eye of limulus. *Journal of General Physiology,* 1956, **39,** 651–673.

Hay, J. C., & Pick, H. L. Visual and proprioceptive adaptation to optical displacement of the visual stimulus. *Journal of Experimental Psychology,* 1966, **71,** 150–158.

Hayek, F. A. *The sensory order.* London: Routledge & Kegan Paul, 1952.

Hebb, D. O. *The organization of behavior.* New York: Wiley, 1949.

Heckenmueller, E. G. Stabilization of the retinal image: A review of method, effects and theory. *Psychological Bulletin,* 1965, **63,** 157–169.

Held, R. Exposure-history as a factor in maintaining stability of perception and coordination. *Journal of Nervous and Mental Diseases,* 1961, **132,** 26–32.

Held, R. Plasticity in sensori-motor systems. *Scientific American,* 1965, **213,** 84–94.

Held, R. Dissociation of visual functions by deprivation and rearrangement. *Psychologische Forschung,* 1967, **31,** 338–348.

Held, R., & Bauer, J. A. Visually guided reaching in infant monkeys after restricted rearing. *Science,* 1966, **155,** 718–720.

Held, R., Efstathiou, A., & Greene, M. Adaptation to displaced and delayed visual feedback from the hand. *Journal of Experimental Psychology,* 1966, **72,** 887–891.

Held, R., & Hein, A. Movement-produced stimulation in the development of visually guided behavior. *Journal of Comparative and Physiological Psychology,* 1963, **56,** 872–876.

Held, R., & Hein, A. On the modifiability of form perception. In W. Wathen-Dunn (Ed.), *Models for the perception of speech and visual form.* Cambridge, Mass.: MIT Press, 1967.

Hilali, S., & Whitfield, I. C. Responses of the trapezoid body to acoustic stimulation with pure tones. *Journal of Physiology,* 1953, **122,** 158–171.

Hilgard, E. R., & Bower, G. H. *Theories of learning.* (3rd ed.) New York: Appleton-Century-Crofts, 1966.

Hochberg, J. Effects of the Gestalt revolution. *Psychological Review,* 1957, **64,** 73–84.

Hochberg, J. Depth perception loss with local monocular suppression: A problem in the explanation of stereopsis. *Science,* 1964, **145,** 1334–1335.

Hochberg, J. In the mind's eye. In R. N. Haber (Ed.), *Contemporary theory and research in visual perception.* New York: Holt, Rinehart and Winston, 1968.

Hochberg, J., & Brooks, V. "Edges" as fundamental components in the visual field. Paper read at the meeting of the Psychonomic Society, New York, 1962.

Hof, M. W. van. Discrimination between striated patterns of different orientation in the rabbit. *Vision Research,* 1966, **6,** 89–94.

Holst, E. von. Relations between the central nervous system and the peripheral organs. *British Journal of Animal Behaviour,* 1954, **2,** 89–94.

Hotopf, W. H. The size-constancy theory of visual illusions. *British Journal of Psychology,* 1966, **57,** 307–318.

House, B. J., & Zeaman, D. Transfer of a discrimination from objects to patterns. *Journal of Experimental Psychology,* 1960, **59,** 298–302.

Howard, I. P., & Templeton, W. B. *Human spatial orientation.* New York: Wiley, 1966.

Hubel, D. H., & Wiesel, T. N. Receptive fields of single neurones in the cat's striate cortex. *Journal of Physiology,* 1959, **148,** 574–591.

Hubel, D. H., & Wiesel, T. N. Receptive fields of optic nerve fibers in the spider monkey. *Journal of Physiology,* 1960, **154,** 572–580.

Hubel, D. H., & Wiesel, T. N. Integrative action in the cat's lateral geniculate body. *Journal of Physiology,* 1961, **155,** 385–398.

Hubel, D. H., & Wiesel, T. N. Receptive fields, binocular interaction and functional architecture in the cat's visual cortex. *Journal of Physiology,* 1962, **160,** 106–154.

Hubel, D. H., & Wiesel, T. N. Shape and arrangement of columns in cat's striate cortex. *Journal of Physiology,* 1963, **165,** 559–568. (a)

Hubel, D. H., & Wiesel, T. N. Receptive fields of cells in striate cortex of very young visually inexperienced kittens. *Journal of Neurophysiology,* 1963, **26,** 994–1002. (b)

Hubel, D. H., & Wiesel, T. N. Receptive fields and functional architecture in two non-striate visual areas (18 and 19) of the cat. *Journal of Neurophysiology,* 1965, **28,** 229–289. (a)

Hubel, D. H., & Wiesel, T. N. Binocular interaction in striate cortex of kittens reared with artificial squint. *Journal of Neurophysiology,* 1965, **28,** 1040–1059. (b)

Hubel, D. H., & Wiesel, T. N. Receptive fields and functional architecture of monkey striate cortex. *Journal of Physiology,* 1968, **195,** 215–243.

Hull, C. L. *A behavior system*. New Haven: Yale University Press, 1952.

Jastrow, J. On the judgment of horizontal, vertical and oblique positions of lines. *American Journal of Psychology*, 1893, **5**, 220–223.

Julesz, B. Binocular depth perception of computer-generated patterns. *Bell System Technical Journal*, 1960, **39**, 1125–1162.

Julesz, B. Binocular depth perception without familiarity cues. *Science*, 1964, **145**, 356–362.

Julesz, B., & Spivack, G. J. Stereopsis based on vernier cues alone. *Science*, 1967, **157**, 563–565.

Jung, R. Neuronal integration in the visual cortex and its significance for visual information. In W. Rosenblith (Ed.), *Sensory communication*. Cambridge, Mass.: MIT Press; New York: Wiley, 1961.

Jung, R., & Baumgartner, G. Hemmungsmechanismen und bremsende Stabilisierung an einzelnen Neuronen des optischen Cortex. *Pflügers Archiv für die gesamte Physiologie des Menschen und der Tiere*, 1955, **261**, 434–456.

Kahneman, D. Exposure duration and effective figure-ground contrast. *Quarterly Journal of Experimental Psychology*, 1965, **17**, 308–314.

Kahneman, D. Temporal effects in the perception of light and form. In W. Wathen-Dunn (Ed.), *Models for the perception of speech and visual form*. Cambridge, Mass.: MIT Press, 1967.

Kahneman, D. Method, findings, and theory in studies of visual masking. *Psychological Bulletin*, 1968, **69**, 408–425.

Kaufman, L. On the spread of suppression and binocular rivalry. *Vision Research*, 1963, **3**, 401–415.

Kaufman, L. Suppression and fusion in viewing complex stereograms. *American Journal of Psychology*, 1964, **77**, 193–205. (a)

Kaufman, L. On the nature of binocular disparity. *American Journal of Psychology*, 1964, **77**, 393–402. (b)

Keesey, V. K. Effects of involuntary eye movements on visual acuity. *Journal of the Optical Society of America*, 1960, **50**, 769–774.

Kendler, H. H., & Kendler, T. S. Some comments on Mackintosh's analysis of two-stage models of discrimination learning. *Psychological Bulletin*, 1966, **66**, 282–288.

Kilpatrick, F. P. *Explorations in transactional psychology*. New York: New York University Press, 1961.

Kober, H. *Dictionary of conformal representations*. (2d Ed.) New York: Dover, 1957.

Kohler, I. The formation and transformation of the perceptual world. Trans. by H. Fiss. *Psychological Issues*, 1964, **3** (4), 1–173.

Köhler, W. *Gestalt psychology*. New York: Liveright, 1929.

Köhler, W., & Wallach, H. Figural after-effects: An investigation of visual processes. *Proceedings of the American Philosophical Society,* 1944, **88,** 269–357.

Kolers, P. A. Intensity and contour effects in visual masking. *Vision Research,* 1962, **2,** 277–294.

Kolers, P. A. The recognition of geometrically transformed text. *Perception and Psychophysics,* 1968, **3,** 57–64.

Koppenfels, W. von, & Stallman, F. *Praxis der Konformen Abbildung.* Berlin: Springer, 1959.

Kozak, W., Rodieck, R. W., & Bishop, P. O. Responses of single units in lateral geniculate nucleus of cat to moving visual patterns. *Journal of Neurophysiology,* 1965, **28,** 19–47.

Krauskopf, J., Cornsweet, T. N., & Riggs, L. A. Analysis of eye movements during monocular and binocular fixation. *Journal of the Optical Society of America,* 1960, **50,** 572–578.

Krechevsky, I. An experimental investigation of the principle of proximity in the visual perception of the rat. *Journal of Experimental Psychology,* 1938, **22,** 497–523.

Kuffler, S. Discharge patterns and functional organization of mammalian retina. *Journal of Neurophysiology,* 1953, **16,** 37–68.

Lang, A. Perceptual behavior of 8- to 10-week old human infants. *Psychonomic Science,* 1965, **4,** 203–204.

Lashley, K. S. The mechanism of vision XV: Preliminary studies of the rat's capacity for detail vision. *Journal of General Psychology,* 1938, **18,** 123–193.

Lashley, K. S. The problem of cerebral organization in vision. *Biological Symposia,* 1942, **7,** 301–322.

Lashley, K. S. The problem of serial order in behaviour. In L. A. Jefress (Ed.), *Cerebral mechanisms in behavior* (The Hixon Symposium). New York: Wiley, 1951.

Lashley, K. S. Functional interpretation of anatomic patterns. In *Patterns of organization in the central nervous system.* Proceedings of the Association for Research in Nervous and Mental Diseases, 1952.

Lashley, K. S., Chow, K. L., & Semmes, J. An examination of the electrical field theory of cerebral integration. *Psychological Review,* 1951, **58,** 123–136.

Levick, W. R., Oyster, C. W., & Davis, D. C. Evidence that McIlwain's periphery effect is not a strong light artifact. *Journal of Neurophysiology,* 1965, **28,** 555–559.

Licklider, J. C. R. *Libraries of the future.* Cambridge, Mass.: MIT Press, 1965.

Licklider, J. C. R. Dynamic modelling. In W. Wathen-Dunn (Ed.), *Models for the perception of speech and visual form.* Cambridge, Mass.: MIT Press, 1967.

Linksz, A. *Physiology of the eye*. New York: Grune & Stratton, 1950.

Linschoten, J. *Strukturanalyse der binokularen Tiefenwahrnehmung*. Groningen (Holland): J. B. Wolters, 1956.

Logan, J. A. A. A general approach to the study of visual illusions and figural after-effects. *Australian Journal of Psychology*, 1960, **12**, 235–236.

Louch, A. R. *Explanation and human action*. Berkeley: University of California Press, 1966.

Lovejoy, E. P. An attention theory of discrimination learning. *Journal of Mathematical Psychology*, 1965, **2**, 342–362.

Lovejoy, E. P. Analysis of the overlearning reversal effect. *Psychological Review*, 1966, **73**, 87–103.

Mackintosh, N. J. Selective attention in animal discrimination learning. *Psychological Bulletin*, 1965, **64**, 124–150.

MacNichol, E. F., Jr. Three-pigment color vision. *Scientific American*, 1964, **221**, 48–56.

Matthews, W. A. Sutherland's two-stage theory of discrimination learning and its experimental support. *British Journal of Psychology*, 1966, **57**, 25–33.

Maturana, H. R., & Frenk, S. Directional movement and horizontal edge detectors in the pigeon retina. *Science*, 1963, **142**, 977–979.

Maturana, R. H., Lettvin, J. Y., McCulloch, W. S., & Pitts, W. H. Anatomy & physiology of vision in the frog (Rana Pipiens). *Journal of General Physiology*, 1960, **43**, 129–175.

McCulloch, W. S., & Pitts, W. A logical calculus of the ideas immanent in nervous activity. *Bulletin of Mathematical Biophysics*, 1943, **5**, 115–123.

McCullough, C. Color adaptation of edge-detectors in the human visual system. *Science*, 1965, **149**, 1115–1116.

McIlwain, J. T. Receptive fields of optic tract axons and lateral geniculate cells: Peripheral extent and barbiturate sensitivity. *Journal of Neurophysiology*, 1964, **27**, 1154–1172.

McKinney, J. P. Verbal meaning and perceptual stability. *Canadian Journal of Psychology*, 1966, **20**, 237–242.

McKinnon, G. E., Forde, J., & Piggins, D. J. Stabilized images, steadily fixated figures and prolonged after-images. *Canadian Journal of Psychology*, 1969, **23**, 184–195.

McLachlan, D., Jr. The role of optics in applying correlation functions to pattern recognition. *Journal of the Optical Society of America*, 1962, **52**, 454–459.

Mewhort, D. J. K. Familiarity of letter sequences, response uncertainty, and the tachistoscopic recognition experiment. *Canadian Journal of Psychology*, 1967, **21**, 309–321.

Mewhort, D. J. K., Merikle, P. M., & Bryden, M. P. On the transfer from iconic to short-term memory. *Journal of Experimental Psychology,* 1969, **81,** 89–94.

Michael, C. R. Receptive fields of opponent color units in the optic nerve of ground squirrel. *Science,* 1966, **152,** 1094–1097.

Mikaelian, H., & Held, R. Two types of adaptation to an optically rotated visual field. *American Journal of Psychology,* 1964, **77,** 257–263.

Miller, W. H. Morphology of the ommatidia of the compound eye of *limulus. Journal of Biophysical and Biochemcal Cytology,* 1957, **3,** 421–428.

Milner, P. M. The cell assembly: Mark II. *Psychological Review,* 1957, **64,** 242–252.

Minsky, M. *Semantic information processing.* Cambridge, Mass.: MIT Press, 1969.

Neisser, U. *Cognitive psychology.* New York: Appleton-Century-Crofts, 1967.

Nikara, T., Bishop, P. O., & Pettigrew, J. D. Analysis of retinal correspondence by studying receptive fields of binocular single units in cat striate cortex. *Experimental Brain Research,* 1968, **6,** 353–372.

Nilsson, N. J. *Learning machines: Foundations of trainable pattern classifying systems.* New York: McGraw-Hill, 1965.

Ogilvie, J. C., & Taylor, M. M. Effect of orientation on the visibility of fine wires. *Journal of the Optical Society of America,* 1958, **48,** 628–629.

Ogle, K. N. *Researches in binocular vision.* Philadelphia: Saunders, 1950.

Osgood, C. E., & Heyer, A. W. A new interpretation of the figural after-effect. *Psychological Review,* 1952, **59,** 98–118.

Peters, R. S. *The concept of motivation.* London: Routledge & Kegan Paul, 1958.

Pettigrew, J. D., Nikara, T., & Bishop, P. O. Responses to moving slits by single units in cat striate cortex. *Experimental Brain Research,* 1968, **6,** 373–390.

Pettigrew, J. D., Nikara, T., & Bishop, P. O. Binocular interaction of single units in cat striate cortex: Simultaneous stimulation by single moving slit with receptive fields in correspondence. *Experimental Brain Research,* 1968, **6,** 391–410.

Pevsner, N. *An outline of European architecture.* London: Penguin, 1942.

Phillips, E. G. *Functions of a complex variable with applications.* (5th Ed.) Edinburgh: Oliver and Boyd, 1947.

Piaget, J. *The child's construction of reality.* New York: Basic Books, 1954.

Pick, H. L., Jr., Hay, J. C., & Pabst, J. Kinesthetic adaptation to visual distortion. Paper presented at the meeting of the Midwestern Psychological Association, Chicago, May, 1963.

Pitts, W. H., & McCulloch, W. S. How we know Universals: The perception of auditory and visual forms. *Bulletin of Mathematical Biophysics,* 1947, **9**, 127–147.

Polyak, S. L. *The retina.* Chicago: Chicago University Press, 1941.

Postman, L. Association theory and perceptual learning. *Psychological Review,* 1955, **62**, 438–446.

Pritchard, R. M., Heron, W., & Hebb, D. O. Visual perception approached by the method of stabilised images. *Canadian Journal of Psychology,* 1960, **14**, 67–77.

Raab, D. H. Backward masking. *Psychological Bulletin,* 1963, **60**, 118–129.

Ratliff, F. Inhibitory interaction and the detection and enhancement of contours. In W. Rosenblith (Ed.), *Sensory Communication.* Cambridge, Mass.: MIT Press; New York: Wiley, 1961.

Ratliff, F., & Hartline, H. K. The response of *limulus* optic nerve fibers to patterns of illumination on the receptor mosaic. *Journal of General Physiology,* 1959, **42**, 1241.

Ratliff, F., Hartline, H. K., & Miller, W. H. Spatial and temporal aspects of retinal inhibitory interaction. *Journal of the Optical Society of America,* 1963, **53**, 110–120.

Ratliff, F., & Riggs, L. A. Involuntary motions of the eye during monocular fixation. *Journal of Experimental Psychology,* 1950, **40**, 687–700.

Reitman, W. R. *Computers and thought: An information-processing approach.* New York: Wiley, 1965.

Restle, F. A theory of discrimination learning. *Psychological Review,* 1955, **62**, 11–19.

Riggs, L. A., & Niehl, E. W. Eye movements recorded during convergence and divergence. *Journal of the Optical Society of America,* 1960, **50**, 913–920.

Riggs, L. A., Ratliff, F., Cornsweet, J. C., & Cornsweet, T. N. The disappearance of steadily fixated visual test objects. *Journal of the Optical Society of America,* 1953, **43**, 495–501.

Rock, I. The orientation of forms on the retina and in the environment. *American Journal of Psychology,* 1956, **69**, 513–528.

Rock, I. *The nature of perceptual adaptation.* New York: Basic Books, 1966.

Rock, I., & Heimer, W. The effect of retinal and phenomenal orientation on the perception of form. *American Journal of Psychology,* 1957, **70**, 493–511.

Rodieck, R. W., & Stone, J. Response of cat retinal ganglion cells to moving visual patterns. *Journal of Neurophysiology,* 1965, **28,** 819–832. (a)

Rodieck, R. W., & Stone, J. Analysis of receptive fields of cat retinal ganglion cells. *Journal of Neurophysiology,* 1965, **28,** 833-849. (b)

Rønne, G. The physiological basis of sensory fusion. *Acta ophthalmologica,* 1956, **34,** 1–26.

Ryle, G. *The concept of mind.* London: Hutchinson's University Library, 1949.

Salapatek, P., & Kessen, W. Visual scanning of triangles by the human newborn. *Journal of Experimental Child Psychology,* 1966, **3,** 155–167.

Segall, M. H., Campbell, D. T., & Herskovits, M. J. Cultural differences in the perception of illusions. *Science,* 1963, **139,** 769–771.

Selfridge, O. G. The organization of organization. In M. C. Yovits, G. T. Jacobi, & G. D. Goldstein (Eds.), *Self-organizing systems: 1962.* Washington, D.C.: Spartan, 1962.

Shortess, G. K., & Krauskopf, J. Role of involuntary eye movements in stereoscopic acuity. *Journal of the Optical Society of America,* 1961, **51,** 555–559.

Smith, K. U., & Smith, W. K. *Perception and motion.* Philadelphia: Saunders, 1962.

Spears, W. C. Assessment of visual preference and discrimination in the four-month old infant. *Journal of Comparative and Physiological Psychology,* 1964, **57,** 381–386.

Spence, K. W. The nature of discrimination learning in animals. *Psychological Review,* 1936, **43,** 427–449.

Sperling, G. The information available in brief visual presentations. *Psychological Monographs,* 1960, **74** (Whole No. 498).

Sperling, G. A model for visual memory tasks. *Human Factors,* 1963, **5,** 19–31.

Sperry, R. W., Miner, N., & Myers, R. E. Visual pattern perception following subpial slicing and tantalum wire implantations in the visual cortex. *Journal of Comparative and Physiological Psychology,* 1955, **48,** 50–58.

Spinelli, D. N. Visual receptive fields in the cat's retina: complications. *Science,* 1966, **152,** 1768–1769.

Spinelli, D. N., & Weingarten, M. Afferent & efferent activity in single units of the cat's optic nerve. *Experimental Neurology,* 1966, **15,** 347–362.

Spitz, R. A. The smiling response: A contribution to the ontogenesis of social relations. *Genetic Psychology Monographs,* 1946, **34,** 57–125.

Sternberg, S. Two operations in character recognition: Some evidence from reaction-time experiments. In W. Wathen-Dunn (Ed.), *Models for the Perception of Speech and Visual Form.* Cambridge, Mass.: MIT Press, 1967.

Stratton, G. M. Some preliminary experiments on vision without inversion of the retinal image. *Psychological Review,* 1896, **3,** 611–617.

Stratton, G. M. Vision without inversion of the retinal image. *Psychological Review,* 1897, **4,** 341–360; 463–481.

Sutherland, N. S. Visual discrimination of orientation and shape by the octopus. *Nature,* 1957, **179,** 11–13.

Sutherland, N. S. Stimulus analysing mechanisms. In *The mechanisation of thought processes.* London: H.M.S.O., 1959.

Sutherland, N. S. Visual discrimination of shape by octopus: Circles and squares, and circles and triangles. *Quarterly Journal of Experimental Psychology,* 1959, **11,** 24–32.

Sutherland, N. S. Theories of shape discrimination in octopus. *Nature,* 1960, **186,** 840–844.

Sutherland, N. S. The methods and findings of experiments on the visual discrimination of shape by animals. *Experimental Psychology Monographs,* 1962, **I.**

Sutherland, N. S. Cat's ability to discriminate oblique rectangles. *Science,* 1963, **139,** 209–210. (a)

Sutherland, N. S. Shape discrimination and receptive fields. *Nature,* 1963, **197,** 118–122. (b)

Sutherland, N. S. Visual discrimination in animals. *British Medical Bulletin,* 1964, **20** (1), 54–59. (a)

Sutherland, N. S. The learning of discrimination by animals. *Endeavour,* 1964, **23,** 140–152. (b)

Sutherland, N. S. Outlines of a theory of visual pattern recognition in animals and man. *Proceedings of the Royal Society,* B, 1968, **171,** 297–317.

Sutherland, N. S., & Carr, A. E. Visual discrimination of open and closed shapes by rats: II. Transfer tests. *Quarterly Journal of Experimental Psychology,* 1962, **14,** 140–156.

Sutherland, N. S., Carr, A. E., & Mackintosh, J. A. Visual discrimination of open and closed shapes by rats: I. Training. *Quarterly Journal of Experimental Psychology,* 1962, **14,** 129–139.

Sutherland, N. S., Mackintosh, N. J., & Mackintosh, J. A. The visual discrimination of reduplicated patterns by *Octopus. Animal Behavior,* 1963, **11,** 106–110.

Suzuki, H., & Kato, E. Binocular interaction at cat's lateral geniculate body. *Journal of Neurophysiology,* 1966, **29,** 909–920.

Taylor, C. *The explanation of behavior.* New York: The Humanities Press. London: Routledge & Kegan Paul, 1963.

Taylor, J. G. *The behavioral basis of perception.* New Haven: Yale University Press, 1962.

Taylor, J. G., & Papert, S. A theory of perceptual constancy. *British Journal of Psychology,* 1956, **47**, 216–224.

Taylor, M. M. Figural after-effects: A psychophysical theory of the displacement effect. *Canadian Journal of Psychology,* 1962, **16**, 267–275.

Taylor, M. M. Visual discrimination and orientation. *Journal of the Optical Society of America,* 1963, **53**, 763–765.

Taylor, W. K. The structure and functioning of the nervous system. *Nature,* 1957, **180**, 1388–1390.

Taylor, W. K. Pattern recognition by means of automatic analogue apparatus. *Proceedings of the Institute of Electrical Engineers,* 1959, **106**, 198–209.

Trabasso, T., & Bower, G. H. *Attention in learning.* New York: Wiley, 1968.

Treisman, A. Binocular rivalry and stereoscopic depth perception. *Quarterly Journal of Experimental Psychology,* 1962, **14**, 23–37.

Toulmin, S. *The uses of argument.* Cambridge, England: Cambridge Universtiy Press, 1958.

Uhr, L. *Pattern recognition.* New York: Wiley, 1966.

Uhr, L., & Vossler, C. A pattern-recognition program that generates, evaluates and adjusts its own operators. In E. A. Feigenbaum & J. Feldman (Eds.), *Computers and thought.* New York: McGraw-Hill, 1963. (Reprinted in Uhr, 1966.)

Uttley, A. M. The classification of signals in the nervous system. *EEG and Clinical Neurophysiology,* 1954, **6**, 479–494.

Uttley, A. M. Conditional probability computing in a nervous system. In *The mechanisation of thought processes.* London: H.M.S.O., 1958. (a)

Uttley, A. M. A theory of the mechanism of learning based on the computation of conditional probabilities. *Proceedings of the First International Congress on Cybernetics.* Paris: Gauthier-Villars, 1958. (b)

Uttley, A. M. The design of conditional probability computers. *Information and Control,* 1959, **2**, 1–24.

Vallentine, H. R. *Applied hydrodynamics.* London: Butterworth, 1959.

Wagner, H. G., MacNichol, E. F., and Wolbarsht, M. L. Functional basis for "on"-center and "off"-center receptive fields in the retina. *Journal of the Optical Society of America,* 1963, **53**, 66–70.

Wallace, G. K. The effect of background on the Zöllner illusion. *Acta Psychologica,* 1966, **25**, 373–380. (a)

Wallace, G. K. Optical illusions. *Nature,* 1966, **209**, 327–328. (b)

Wallace, G. K., & Crampin, D. J. The effect of background density on the Zöllner illusion. *Vision Research,* 1969, **9**, 167–177.

Walls, G. The problem of visual direction. Part I: The history to 1900. *American Journal of Optometry and Archives of the American Academy of Optometry,* 1951, **28**, 55–83.

Walls, G. The problem of visual direction. Part II: The tangible basis for nativism. *American Journal of Optometry and Archives of the American Academy of Optometry,* 1951, **28**, 115–146.

Walls, G. The problem of visual direction. Part III: Experimental attacks and their results. *American Journal of Optometry and Archives of the American Academy of Optometry,* 1951, **28**, 173–212.

Walter, W. G. *The living brain.* London: Duckworth, 1953.

Weingarten, M., & Spinelli, D. N. Retinal receptive field changes produced by auditory and somatic stimulation. *Experimental Neurology,* 1966, **15**, 363–376.

Weisstein, N., & Haber, R. N. A U-shaped backward masking function in vision. *Psychonomic Science,* 1965, **2**, 75–76.

Werner, H. Dynamics in binocular depth perception. *Psychological Monographs,* 1937, **49**, No. 2.

Westheimer, G. Spatial interaction in human cone vision. *Journal of Physiology,* 1967, **190**, 139–154.

Wheatstone, C. On some remarkable, and hitherto unobserved, phenomena of binocular vision. Royal Society of London, *Philosophical Transactions,* 1838, 371–394.

White, B. W. Stimulus-conditions affecting a recently discovered stereoscopic effect. *American Journal of Psychology,* 1962, **75**, 411–420.

White, B. W. The use of statistically defined dot matrices in studies of stereoscopic depth and contour formation. Paper presented at the meeting of the Psychonomic Society, New York, 1962.

Wiesel, T. N. Receptive fields of ganglion cells in the cat's retina. *Journal of Physiology,* 1960, **153**, 583–594.

Wiesel, T. N., & Hubel, D. H. Comparison of the effects of unilateral and bilateral eye closure on cortical unit responses in kittens. *Journal of Neurophysiology,* 1965, **28**, 1029–1040. (a)

Wiesel, T. N., & Hubel, D. H. Extent of recovery from the effects of visual deprivation in kittens. *Journal of Neurophysiology,* 1965, **28**, 1060–1072. (b)

Wiesel, T. N., & Hubel, D. H. Spatial and chromatic interactions in the lateral geniculate body of the rhesus monkey. *Journal of Neurophysiology,* 1966, **29**, 1115–1156.

Wittgenstein, L. *Philosophical investigations.* Oxford: Blackwell, 1953.

Worthington, A. G. Differential rates of dark adaptation to "taboo" and neutral words. *Canadian Journal of Psychology,* 1964, **19**, 823–826.

Worthington, A. G. Generalization phenomena associated with previous pairings of U.C.S. (shock) and subliminal visual stimuli. *Journal of Personality and Social Psychology,* 1966, **3,** 634–640.

Yarbus, A. L. A new method of studying the activity of various parts of the retina. *Biophysics,* 1957, **2,** 165–167. (a)

Yarbus, A. L. The perception of an image fixed with respect to the retina. *Biophysics,* 1957, **2,** 683–690. (b)

Young, J. Z. Regularities in the retina and optic lobes of *Octopus* in relation to form discrimination. *Nature,* 1960, **186,** 836–839.

Young, J. Z. Learning and discrimination in the *Octopus. Biological Review,* 1961, **36,** 32–96.

Young, J. Z. *A model of the brain.* Oxford: Clarendon Press, 1964.

Zanforlin, M. Some observations on Gregory's theory of perceptual illusions. *Quarterly Journal of Experimental Psychology,* 1967, **19,** 193–194.

Zeaman, D., & House, B. J. The role of attention in learning. In N. R. Ellis (Ed.), *Handbook of Mental Deficiency.* New York: McGraw-Hill, 1963.

Name Index

Subject Index

DATE DUE

MAY 15 '79			
MAY 2 7 '80			
MAY 1 5 80			
GAYLORD			PRINTED IN U S.A